By the Grace of God

The True Life Journey of 100 Years

BY: Dr. Marie L. Greenwood

ACKNOWLEDGMENTS

There are no adequate words to express my deep, sincere appreciation to Patricia Raybon for the amazing Foreward she has written for my book. I am honored to have this spiritual leader and noted author take time from her busy schedule to read my manuscript and write these complimentary words. Thank you, Patricia!

Valerie Thomas is my most valuable Author's Assistant. She typed the chapters of my book from handwritten manuscripts. At various events, she takes charge of book sales and keeps an account of all expenses. She has spent hours with me, going over my vast collection of pictures we chose to include in my autobiography. She kept a complete record of those chosen. It was only with Valerie's efficient help that I am able to complete writing my life's history.

Thanks to my son, Bill Greenwood, who takes care of the business end of getting my books published. He is my Publicity Agent. Bill takes care of all my book orders.

I thank my family and friends who have enthusiastically encouraged me to document my life's history to be passed on to my children, grandchildren and descendents!

DEDICATION

I dedicate this book to the unforgettable memory of my amazing husband, William Rivers Greenwood, Sr., with whom I spent forty wonderful years of caring, sharing and most loving companionship.

PREFACE

I have included some traumatic and near- death experiences that happened to me when I was too young to understand the significance of these occurrences. I now realize that, for some reason, the Lord was not ready for me. I believe I am still alive and active only by the Grace of God.

This quote from the *Daily Word®* expresses how I feel:

"Through grace, I live a God-centered life.

Grace not only continually blesses me, it guides me in living a God-centered life.

Each day I actively engage in life using the qualities of Spirit that are inherent in me.

Through God's grace I receive unconditional love at the core of my being, and from this love I think, speak and act in loving ways.

Through God's grace, I am wise. I understand that circumstances are not all they seem to be on the surface. I use my divine wisdom, and I discern the spirit of God in every experience.

Through the grace of God I have eternal life. My spirit is made in the image and likeness of God. I am eternally at one with and blessed by God's grace."[1]

---

[1] Reprinted with permission of Unity®, publisher of Daily Word®

FOREWARD

When Dr. Marie Greenwood called me on the telephone on a sunny fall morning in 2011, I stopped everything to answer. I learn something remarkable whenever I talk to this extraordinary educator. She is wisdom itself, of course. Just as important, she is generous with her knowledge. So I was all ears when she phoned, eager to hear a precious piece of "Marie Greenwood insight" about life, work, family, health, friendship and spiritual toughness—or how to survive life's twists and turns and come through the crucible still smiling and thriving.

As we spoke that morning, however, it became clear she wanted to ask a favor. To my surprise and great honor, she invited me to write the foreword for her autobiography—this story of the first 99 years of her life—called *By the Grace of God*.

Once I sat down to read her manuscript, however, I quickly realized that the honor would be more than mine. It will be yours also as you savor the life story of this beloved Colorado educator and author, loving wife, mother and grandmother, community advocate, life-long learner, loyal church member, faithful friend and treasured citizen. Yet her book's greatest asset is its certainty that all she has accomplished, enjoyed and overcome is due most and first to God.

 "That is what I want people to know," Dr. Greenwood said recently with her characteristic humility. "It's *by the Grace of God* that I have lived this life and that I'm still here to write about it." She laughed her sparkling laugh which, on that day—as she neared her 99th birthday—was strong, lively, inspiring and hopeful.

All that bright Greenwood hope is what comes through most in her remarkable story. It is the compelling chronicle of how a spitfire of a little girl—born to a poor, young, hard-working and loving African American couple—managed to survive her early illnesses (before penicillin and vaccinations), plus childhood misadventures, teenage challenges and adult obstacles, yet still stay alive and thrive. Along the way, she overcame the sting of racial discrimination, Jim Crow segregation, institutional bias, family losses and life's trials and tests by fighting back with optimism, a spirit of adventure, a determination to help others, a strong sense of integrity and a faith in God that still sustains her.

Nothing in life, it seems, has managed to drag down Marie Anderson

Greenwood and break her spirit. Thus, you will read here the inside story of her many "firsts"—including her appointment in 1935 by the Denver Board of Education to be Denver Public School's first African American contract teacher, among other professional achievements.

Yet this book conveys the whole of her life, including wonderful stories of her years as a student athlete, camp counselor, youth church leader, civil rights worker and active club member—and the life-long friend-ships and community improvements that resulted. A highlight is also the joyful and heart-warming account of her loving, 40-year marriage to her "best friend" William "Bill" Greenwood and their fulfilling experiences raising four talented and wonderful children.

Thankfully, her astounding memory allowed Dr. Greenwood to take us along on this journey. On page after entertaining page, this pioneering educator recalls with impressive detail the astonishing twists and turns, dates and places, names and milestones, travels and experiences, secrets and successes of her long and remarkable life.

Patricia Raybon

Denver, Colorado

Table of Contents

INTRODUCTION

It was a bright, sunny day in Los Angeles, California, on November 24, 1912 when I interrupted my mother's day by arriving at four o'clock that Sunday afternoon. My father named this bouncing baby girl, Marie Louise, after two of his favorite sisters.

My parents were Joseph August Anderson and Sarah Lee Anderson. My father was a cook on the railroad. My mother was a domestic worker. My mother's grandmother took care of me while my parents worked.

Joseph Anderson was a French speaking *Creole* from Louisiana who had lived in Mexico for five years before returning to the United States by way of Texas. He also spoke fluent Spanish; his English was minimal – only what he had been taught by the nuns when he was in school. He had a heavy accent, but being an intelligent man, he was learning his native language, English. He loved horses and would tell many exciting stories of riding with Pancho Villa while living in Mexico. My father was a feisty, little man no more than 5 feet 5 inches tall with a quick temper and a positive outlook on life.

My mother was a native of Texas, the only surviving child of my grandfather's first family. She had been reared on a farm with her maternal grandparents' family. She was only seventeen years old when she met this nomadic stranger who was twelve years older than she. After a short courtship, they were married in November 1908 and soon moved to California.

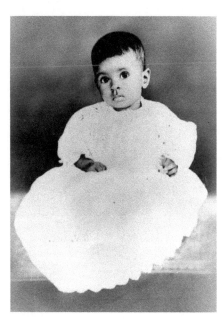

Marie Louise Anderson, age 6 months

CHAPTER 1
Childhood Memories

My earliest memory was when I asked my mother how old I would be. I knew I was to have a birthday soon. She told me I would be three years old. This was in Los Angeles, California.

"Am I going to have a party?" I wanted to know.

"Yes, you are going to have a party," she answered me.

I was so excited that each day I asked when would my party be, and the day finally came! I do not remember if there were any children. I had ice cream and cake and I was thrilled to be three years old!

Sarah Johnson and Joseph Johnson - great-grandparents

My next recollection was that we had moved across the street or somewhere near. We were living in a little green house with white trim which was in the rear of another large house. There was a fence with a gate between, but to get to our house we had to come through the big front yard. There was a large fig tree in the big yard.

My grandma, who was really my great-grandma (Sarah Johnson), looked after me while my parents were at work. My mother's mother died when my

mother was three years old, so her maternal grandmother took her and her five-year-old brother to her home and reared them with her other children. My mother called her "Mama."

Since the owners of the big house did nothing with the figs, they told my folks they could have them. I loved figs, so my grandma would take me out and hold me up under the fig tree so I could pull the fruit off and I would eat figs until my mouth was so sore I could eat no more. However, it did not stop me from eating more figs another day. I was grown before I learned that the fig skin has a stinging affect, although the fruit is delicious. I would eat the whole fig, skin and all.

My Uncle J.C., who was my father's youngest brother, would come to visit and he always played with me. One trick he performed that always made me laugh was really dangerous; although no one ever stopped him. He would hook together several matches, place them over the open globe of gas light (no electricity); they would flair up and go sailing around. It's a wonder that he didn't set the house on fire! I loved it!

My grandma would always put me to bed for a nap, after a snack, about 2:00pm. One day, while I was sleeping, I thought I woke up, but I seemed to be hovering over my crib and I could see myself lying there asleep. I didn't like it up there, and after struggling for some time I finally returned to my body. I seemed to relax.

I remember nothing else until I found myself being tossed in the air outdoors. It was my father tossing me up and catching me. Since he was always doing something to make me laugh, I thought he was playing, so I started to laugh. He stopped and hugged me. Standing nearby were mother and grandma. They were in tears. I was told that when my parents came home about five o'clock, I was still asleep. I was usually awake about four o'clock and was up busy playing. When they tried to wake me I was limp, and seemed not to be breathing. Where my father had heard about tossing in the air to get me breathing again, I do not know; but that is what he was doing, and it worked! I guess I died, but BY THE GRACE OF GOD the Lord was not ready for me yet!

My next recollection was when I was four-years-old. (I do not remember when I turned four). We had moved to a bigger house, which was back from the street with a sidewalk leading to a few steps that went up to a small porch. There were buildings on each side of us built out to the street. Our steps had two banisters of wood that were shaped to points on the ends.

Since I was an only child with a very active imagination, I was constantly devising ways to amuse myself. This time I made up a game of walking down the sidewalk from our steps to the street and walking back again to see if my steps would be the same each way. I could not count my steps, but I could feel the "sameness" as I walked. I began going faster and then running. I would stop just as I got to the street, and I would stop just as I reached the steps of the porch. Then I closed my eyes to see if I could stop at the steps just from the "feel" of the distance covered. (I did not close my eyes going to the street, since I was forbidden to cross that sidewalk). After many trials, and sometimes peeking a bit to be sure of where I was, I managed to succeed in stopping just as I reached the step without opening my eyes. This was a real "for fun" game and I felt that I had actually figured something out for myself.

About the middle of the afternoon, every day the tinkling of the ice cream vendor's bell could be heard. He sold ice cream bars called "Dainty's" wrapped in waxed paper – my favorite treat. We called him the "Dainty Man." Occasionally, my grandmother would give me a nickel to buy a "Dainty." On this particular day, I cheerfully bought my ice cream and slowly ate it as I walked up my sidewalk to the steps and sat down to finish it. As I licked off the last of the ice cream, I didn't want to go into the house to throw away the wrapper so I thought, "What can I do with this waxed paper?"

I went back to playing my sidewalk game and since I had the sticky wrapper in my hand, I thought it might be fun to see if I could walk to the steps with it plastered over my eyes. I made it just as I had done before with my eyes closed. After walking faster a few times and reaching the steps successfully, I decided to run with my eyes covered with the sticky wrapping.

That was my big mistake! I was running as fast as I could, but I had veered just a little bit to the left. Suddenly I banged full force into the pointed end of the banister. It hit me just above the right eye in my eyebrow. If I had been a half an inch taller, I would have put out my eye! I screamed, tore off the blindfold and ran up the steps. As I held my hand over my eye, blood was pouring through my fingers.

My grandmother came running to the door and met me as I entered. I am sure she thought my eye was gone when she saw the blood covering it. I was scared to death, because I was sure that the banister had rammed into my eye.

After my grandmother washed my face, she could see that the gash was in my eyebrow and assured me that my eye was all right. She did not take me to a doctor. She used some of her many old fashioned remedies that she knew how to use to cure almost anything. The injury healed and my vision was fine. For many years I had a scar, but only one small spot was noticeable because over the years my heavy eyebrow grew out and eventually covered it up.

Needless to say, I never played my sidewalk game again with my eyes closed!

One day, my mother told me that we were going to leave Los Angeles. It dawned on me that grandma had not been around for a while.

"Is Grandma going to go with us?" I asked.

"No, Grandma is not here," was mother's answer.

"Where is Grandma?" I wanted to know. "I want Grandma to go with us."

My mother looked sad as she said, "Grandma went away and she will not be back."

I assumed that she had gone back to Texas to be with her other children, as she had done once before for a short time. It wasn't until I was much older that my mother told me that grandma got sick, was taken to the hospital and died.

I had my first train ride when we moved to Phoenix, Arizona. My only memory of Phoenix was that it was hot! Hot!! HOT!!! I could not play outdoors but a few minutes during the day; most activity was after sunset. The sidewalk was so hot I could not go barefoot. I could even feel the heat through the soles of my sandals!

My mother was Baptist and she would take me to a little Missionary Baptist Church that was unbearably hot. I hated it! There was no such thing as air conditioning – only fans that moved the hot air around!

We finally moved to cool, comfortable Prescott, Arizona (over 6,000 feet up in the mountains). This was a small, resort type of community. You could walk from one side of Prescott to the other in half an hour or less. The railroad station was on one edge of downtown, which covered only a few square blocks where one could find a grocery market, a shoe store, a dry goods shop, a library, a movie theater, a few other kinds of small business and a park in the center of which were the Court House and a band stand.

Just south of downtown was a small community of "colored" people, many of whom had nice homes with indoor plumbing (outhouses were still all over Prescott). There was a nice A.M.E. Zion Church which most of these residents attended, but my mother found the small, struggling Missionary Baptist Church which she joined and took me. My father was Catholic and did not attend any church. Lincoln Elementary School was also in that area.

We lived just north of downtown and our next door neighbors were a Mexican family with whom my dad could communicate. One of the young men played the violin beautifully and sang songs in Spanish. One of the songs he sang was "La Golondrina." It was the beginning of my love of music and especially the violin. I was only four or five years old, but I can remember standing outside their window, day after day, just listening to that beautiful music and being completely carried away. I finally told my dad about how much I loved the music and asked him if he knew the name of that beautiful song. I had heard him singing it, occasionally. He told me "La Golondrina" meant "The Dove."

The only other brown face in our neighborhood was an old lady who lived in the next block. She was known as "Grandma Coopwood." She was highly respected, was a midwife and seemed to know everything that was going on in Prescott. She and my mother became very good friends, and Grandma Coopwood often looked after me.

Across the street from Grandma Coopwood was a white family with a pair of pretty, blond identical twins. It was the first time I had ever seen two people who looked and dressed exactly alike. I was fascinated every time I saw them. It was a quiet area and on the east end of our block was Washington Elementary School. A few blocks away was the only high school.

World War I was raging in Europe and my father wanted to join the Army when the United States entered the war in 1917. He was 38 years old and too old for the draft. He was disappointed. My mother was glad. However, there was some kind of a government project in operation in West Virginia, so in late 1917 or early 1918 he was sent there to work. He would send money back to my mother to take care of us. I don't know how long he was gone, but it seemed like a longtime to me. When my father returned, he was ill. This was at the outbreak of the disastrous world-wide Influenza epidemic of 1918-1919.

My mother contracted a mild case of the Flu; so she was up and around. My father was in bed recovering; then, the Flu caught me in the spring of 1918 and I almost died! I was five years old, but I was so small that I was still sleeping in my crib. For days I was burning up with a fever of 104 degrees. Most of the time I was unconscious. On rare times that I would awaken, I could see my mother sitting beside my bed, often crying. With the high fever, I was soaking wet from profuse sweating, but too weak to move or talk. The doctor finally told my mother that he could do no more for me unless he could find some whiskey. That seemed to be the basic medication for the Flu at that time since there were no vaccinations (except for Small Pox), no inoculations, serums or drugs for fighting many diseases. Doctors depended on many old fashioned remedies. Of course, my mother was devastated at the thought of possibly losing her one and only child.

For the second time I had that same out of body experience that I had when I was three years old. I rose up over my bed and, as a spirit, I looked down and I could see my body as I lay motionless in my crib. I seemed suspended in midair for sometime before I returned to that body lying below me. It was as though the Lord was saying once again, "I am not ready for you!"

My mother told me that soon after the doctor had given up on me, he came pounding on the door one night after midnight. He had found some whiskey! He mixed it with something that my mother had and somehow got me to swallow some of it. In those days you did not go to the doctor, the doctor came to your home. He then left instructions with my mother for continuing to give me this improvised medication. My fever broke. I woke up and actually said, "Mama." My mother shed tears of relief. Within a few days I wanted to get out of bed, but I had been ill for so long and with the intense sweating from the high fever, I was very weak. My mother changed my gown, lifted me out of my bed and put me on the floor. I tried to stand up, but my legs were like rubber; they would not hold me. I couldn't even crawl because my arms were also weak. I was scared to death! After days of my mother giving me nourishment, I was finally able to crawl. I was still frightened because I was afraid that I would never be able to walk and run again. However, as time went on, I began pulling myself up onto my feet and taking a few steps at a time as I held on to furniture. When my legs got stronger I learned to walk once more, and "By the Grace of God," at last, I became my little active self again!

I do not know how or when my mother found an old _Beacon Primer_, but she began to read stories to me from this book. This was actually a simple reader composed of mostly condensed Aesop's Fables written in language that children could read and understand. There were even morals at the end of the stories, like "The Fox and the Grapes." I loved listening to these stories and would have my mother read many of them over and over. I liked the pictures because, in my imagination, I could visualize what was happening in the story.

After hearing the stories so many times, I finally could repeat the first three verbatim as my mother read them to me. One day when I had the book all by myself, I started repeating the first story out loud just as my mother had read it to me. I was so proud of myself! As I looked at the printed words, it dawned on me that what I was saying must be the same as what was printed there, so I began pointing to those symbols as I spoke and they matched what I was saying. Although I could not identify the printed words, I learned what reading was about, and I was excited!

When school started that September I wanted to go to kindergarten, but my mother was so protective of me that she said I could go to school when I turned six years old. I was tiny, but I was really ready for school!

*So, after I had my sixth birthday she put me in kindergarten, but that big Flu epidemic was still raging. I was only in school for a short time when all the schools were closed. They didn't open again until spring. It was about May. Well, my mother decided that it was only going to be a month or so of school, so I stayed at home. Come September, here I was almost seven years old and she put me back in kindergarten, which was a big mistake!

I was not any bigger than the kindergarteners, but I was one pest. I'm sure the teacher didn't know what to do with me because I really could raise a lot of confusion. I had a little neighbor friend; we'd been going to school together. She was in first grade, so I asked her one day,

"How do you get in the first grade?"

She said, "I don't know. I just get in line."

So I got to thinking, "Is that all it takes?" I thought about it day after day and finally one day I just got in the first grade line and marched on in. When I got inside I asked my little friend, Eliza,

"Where shall I sit?" She said she didn't know. So I just kept sitting in the seats until somebody would claim it as theirs. Finally, I found one nobody claimed, so I just scrunched into it.

I do not know how I never thought that that teacher wouldn't know there was another child in the room, particularly since my little friend was the only brown face in the class and now there were two little brown faces. On top of everything else, I will always remember that teacher's name, Miss Griswold, who had been teaching for years. Miss Griswold came in. She started looking around and when she began taking attendance, she spotted me. I was trying to hide somehow and she called me up to her desk. She asked me my name. Of course, at that age, if you asked me my name you might as well wait until I gave you all the information that my folks had told me. When asked my name, my answer would be I was Marie Louise Anderson I was born in Los Angeles, California. My birth date was November 24, 1912. My mother and dad were Joseph and Sarah Anderson and I would give my address. We didn't have a telephone.

She just looked at me because that was it. She said, "We'll go to the principal's office." I thought, "Ooh, I'm in deep trouble now!"

She had me sit on the bench when we got in the office. She then went into the principal's office. When she came back out, she went back to her room. The principal came out and asked me why I was in the first grade. I told him that the kindergarten teacher told me to go to the first grade. Then he asked me my name and I gave him the whole spiel. He asked who the kindergarten teacher was and I told him her name. He disappeared out the door of the office. Back he came with the kindergarten teacher and they went into his office. I knew I was in deep trouble then. The kindergarten teacher never said a word as she went by. She just looked at me as she came out of the office and away she went. The principal came out and he said,

"We're going to let you stay in first grade. We will give you six weeks…" (that was the grading period I think), "…and if you get along all right you can stay."

I got along all right. I didn't tell my mother how I put myself in first grade. I told her the kindergarten teacher sent me to first grade.

The _Beacon Primer_ was the basic reader, and since I knew the first three stories verbatim, you would think I was reading but I couldn't read a word. When they got past those stories, the teacher found out I needed help. I wanted so desperately to learn. I loved school, I really did. Miss Griswold was teaching Phonics and I learned to sound out words. I really began to read. I buckled down to work and within a few weeks I was doing everything. I was, however, beginning to get into mischief again. Fortunately, the teacher didn't tell my mother because my mother was a disciplinarian and there would have been trouble for me at home!

At the end of the six weeks, I was called back into the principal's office and I thought maybe I had done something wrong.

He said, "You are doing so well. Wouldn't you like to go into second grade?"

I had seen the second grade teacher and she was a delightful, blond, blue-eyed, very pleasant little teacher, but I said, "No. I don't want to go to second grade."

"Well, why?" he asked.

"I want to find out what every grade is like," I answered. So they let me stay in first grade. I really didn't want to leave my little friend, Eliza. I went through school about a year older than everybody else which was really quite good because it gave me a little extra maturity.[1]

When I did get to second grade, though, that little teacher was as sweet as she could be and I was such a little devil. I would get my work done and nobody could disturb me, but when I finished I would pester everyone around me. Since I became a teacher, I realized just how she had handled me. She gave me the "honor" of being in charge of the supply room when I finished my work. That got me completely out of the class and I thought I was doing something very, very special. I'll always remember that. Every day when I finished my work I would go to the supply room. Anyone who needed anything could come to the supply room and I would see that they got it. Unfortunately, very few needed anything, but the classroom was much more peaceful!*

Eliza and I were in second and third grade together. (There really was only one room for each grade – kindergarten through eighth grade). Our third grade teacher was positive and let us know that there would be no foolishness tolerated; we were there to learn! I got away with nothing in her class because she seemed to always know what everyone was doing. I was convinced that she had eyes in the back of her head!

¹* excerpt taken from Trail Blazers Oral History Series transcript, courtesy of Denver Public Library, Blair-Caldwell

My father had been teaching me how to fight to protect myself. He was a short, feisty little man who could take care of himself with anybody, and since I was so small, he wanted me to be prepared. My mother did not approve of his treating me like a boy, but I loved it!

In my third grade there was a boy who quietly made fun of me and called me names because of my color. This really frustrated me since I did not know what to do about it. Now, with my new knowledge of self-defense, I figured I needed to try it out on someone and this boy was the logical one on whom I could retaliate. So, one day I told him that I was going to beat him up after school. Fortunately for him, he lived next door to the school, so when he took off running I was right behind him and as he ran up on his porch and into his house, I ran up on his porch just as the door opened. In he went and out came his **BIG** brother who said something to me. I did not wait to listen, but took off on the run with **BIG** brother behind me!

My little, short legs were pounding the sidewalk like pistons; I was running faster than I had ever run and I was normally a speedy runner. After several blocks of going non-stop, I looked back and saw that **BIG** brother was no longer behind me. That was a blessing because I had been pushing so hard I was gasping for air. I could hardly breathe and my chest hurt so I went on home; but, I did not tell my mother what I did. Needless to say, that little boy never said another word to me and we gave each other a wide space.

At the end of third grade I was passed to fourth grade, but Eliza was sent to a small building that was known as "Special." I felt left out and wondered why I was not going to a class that was so very "Special." It took some time before I found out that that was not the kind of "Special" class I thought it was. I learned that Eliza was falling behind in school and needed extra help so that was why she was in "Special" and I was not.

*I did run into my first *real* discriminatory problem in fourth grade. Eliza's brother had had this teacher and he told me that she was prejudiced. Of course, I hadn't run into anything like that up to that point. However, I got the same teacher for fourth grade and sure enough that teacher would not call on me if I raised my hand and looked like I knew the answer. The minute I wasn't sure or didn't know the answer,

Marie, age 8, with Sarah (mother)
& Joseph (father) Anderson

she would call on me and when my answer was wrong she would then make some disparaging remark. That went on for weeks. Even when I would take a test, I could never get a decent grade. I reported it to the assistant principal, but I don't think anything was done about it. So I decided to do something about it. I figured that when I *did* know I would look a little dumb and confused. If I *didn't* know the answer, my hand would wave. I think she got a little confused because if my hand was waving and she ignored me, fine. If I knew the answer, but looked unsure, she would call on me as usual. I passed the class!*[1]

I was quite a tomboy. I shot marbles and spun tops with the boys. My father taught me how and I was pretty good at both. I climbed the old oak tree that was on a hill near our house and I could climb higher and faster than most of the neighborhood boys.

One day Eliza's brother, Harvey, dared me to beat him climbing and said he could climb higher than I could. Of course, I took the challenge and since I was smaller and lighter than he, I really was faster. I kept going higher, even after he stopped; the branches were getting smaller and when I grabbed for one it broke! As I fell, in my imagination, I could see myself splattered on the ground below and I knew I would be badly injured or die. Fortunately, on the way down I caught a lower limb, swung there and dropped to the ground. I am sure

[1]* excerpt taken from Trail Blazers Oral History Series transcript, courtesy of Denver Public Library, Blair-Caldwell

my guardian angel was with me that day!

We had a picket fence with the sharp, pointed boards nailed to two-by-fours, top and bottom. I decided to try walking the top two-by-four; it was an exciting idea. So one day I climbed up on the fence to try it. It took some skill to balance on that narrow four inches. After losing my balance a number of times and successfully jumping off without impaling myself on the pickets, I finally managed to get balanced and slowly walk that fence. It took several days of practice.

Most of the time my mother was at work and had no ideas of what I was doing, but one day when she was at home, she looked out the kitchen window and saw her only child walking high upon the picket fence! She could not call to me because it might startle me, making me lose my balance. I was cheerfully, slowly, walking the fence, carefully pivoted around and reversed my direction. When I finally jumped to the ground my mother ran out the door and blew up all over me. She was scared to death and I could not figure out why. I felt perfectly safe!

My father was a "jack-of-all-trades" and let me help him with small jobs of fixing electrical items, doing a bit of plumbing or carpentry work. He taught me how to use tools, so I learned to fix almost anything if I had a screw driver, a hammer and a pair of pliers. He even took me hunting for quail. The first time he had me shoot the 16-gauge shotgun, it kicked back and knocked me flat! He forgot to tell me to hold it firmly against my shoulder. I eventually became a pretty good marksman.

I bless my mother for never giving up on teaching me the attributes of being a little girl, and a graceful young lady. In spite of the fact that I did not like being dressed up, my mother would dress me in pretty ruffles and ribbons for church, or to go visiting her friends. She would remind me of the rules of conduct and I knew I had to obey them. My mother loved her one and only little child. However, she was a disciplinarian and if I got out of line, she would remove me immediately, take me out, make sure that I was taken care of and understood what she meant, then bring me back…and I behaved.

Eliza was my little neighborhood friend and schoolmate. I had another very close friend, Amanda, whose parents were good friends of my mother and father. They lived across town in the colored community. Amanda was a typical little girl who loved being dressed up, liked to play house with her dolls, play jacks, read books and all the other "little girl" activities. I really enjoyed those times with her and sometimes, when I was alone I would play with my dolls, play jacks, read a book and make believe. I guess I had a kind of dual personality; I liked being a tomboy, but I also enjoyed being a girl. I just preferred being dressed in my coveralls!

The little Baptist Church that my mother attended had very few children and as I grew older and made friends with other children who attended the A.M.E. Zion Church, I wanted to go to that church, too. Soon the little Missionary Baptist Church dwindled down to almost no membership and closed. So my mother let me go to Sunday School at the A.M.E. Zion Church and finally joined herself, since there was no

Marie with her church group, circa 1921; second row, second from left

other place for us to worship.

My mother had a strong faith in God, so she accepted this Methodist Church as a place where she could serve the Lord. Her friends were there. She joined the choir and sang with her melodious soprano voice. She became an active member.

Of course, I attended Sunday School every Sunday and looked forward to being with the children since I was alone so much. However, after church I was to wait for the Sunday paper to arrive from Los Angeles. The _Los Angeles Examiner_ was our big newspaper that came by train about noon every Sunday. Sometimes it was late and I would play in the park while I waited. My friend Amanda would stay with me sometimes, but if it took too long she would go home. I could always figure out some game to play, or just read my Sunday School papers or book.

One day in autumn, when the dry leaves in the park had been raked up into big piles, my imagination turned on! I told Amanda what fun it would be to jump in those leaves, but she would have no part of it dressed in her pretty dress. So she went on home. I was dressed in my one and only dress-up ruffles and ribbons, but those leaves drew me to them like a magnet! I ran full force, jumped in those crunchy leaves and the dust covered me from head to toe, but I was having the time of my life! By the time I heard the train whistle blow, I was one dusty mess with lose ribbons, dusty hair and scuffed patent-leather pumps, but as happy as a little lark!

When I got home with the paper, my mother took one look at me and asked me what on earth had I been doing? I happily told her of the fun I had jumping in the leaves in the park. I think she was dumb-founded because all she said was, "Oh, Louise…," (my mother called me Louise most of the time), "…in your pretty Sunday dress!" She had me change into my play clothes. She brushed as much dust out of my hair as she could and let me go without saying anything.

One hot summer day, my mother had dressed me up in a white, ruffled party dress. My hair was in curls and I had a big, ribbon bow in my hair. We were going to something special. Usually, I had to sit in my little chair after she dressed me, so that nothing would go wrong while she finished getting dressed. On this particular day, the house was miserably hot! I begged my mother to please let me go out on the porch where there was a bit of a hot breeze. I promised to stay on the porch and be very careful not to get dirty. By then, both of us were sweating. My mother finally said, "All right, but stay on the porch and keep still. I will be ready in a few minutes."

I went outside with every intention of being careful and following my mother's request. However, after a few minutes, I thought it would be all right to move around as long as I stayed "on the porch," so I began playing a little game. How many steps would it take to walk across the porch to the edge? As I walked, I counted and stopped at the edge of the porch. It took the same number of steps back. After a few tries, I decided to count my steps as I ran to the edge. It worked, and I was having fun. Then, I closed my eyes and walked as I counted, and I stopped right at the edge of the porch. Then, I decided to run, and see if I could stop just right. When I ran, I peeked and stopped just at the edge. The next time I ran, I did not peek and my steps must have been a bit longer, because my count sent me right off the porch into the hot dust on the ground!   I was scared, and I felt terrible that I had not kept my promise to my mother when I really meant to stay on the porch.

My mother came to the door just as I was coming up on the porch, all dusty and dirty. "Oh, Louise!" my mother exclaimed. "You said you would stay on the porch. What will I do?

"I didn't mean to," I cried. "I was just playing a game and I fell off."

Both of us began to cry, and it hurt me terribly to realize that I had made my mother cry. My mother dusted me off, and put one of my school dresses on me, since there was no way to clean the party dress.

We were late getting to the affair. I was miserable the whole time because I had made my mother so unhappy!!!

I was really excited about going to fifth grade because I would go upstairs to class. The BIG boys and girls went UPSTAIRS! That did not last very long because my mother took me to Flagstaff. There we attended a small Black Baptist church. I remembered only two things that happened to me in Flagstaff.

At school I loved to swing and I decided to make my swing go as high as possible. What would it be like to make the swing go way up parallel with the top bar? It would be like flying!!! Standing up in the swing was forbidden, but that was the only way I could pump up as high as I wanted to go, so one day I stood up in the swing. I pumped until I was close to swinging out parallel to the ground. As the swing went forward, I started to sit down, but lost my hold. I went flying over the playground fence! I landed partly on the sidewalk and partly on the ground. Thank goodness my head hit the ground instead of the sidewalk! When I gained consciousness, a teacher was holding me and children were around me. I did not know where I was. I really thought I had died. I had a terrific headache and my right shoulder and hip ached. I must have landed on my right side. I was taken to the school nurse who had me lie down. She gave me something for my headache and put a band-aid on a badly skinned spot on my right elbow and one on my right knee. I managed to limp home. I don't remember what my story was this time for my mother. Again, By the Grace of God I was alive! It took several days for my head to stop aching. It took even longer for the pain to ease at my elbow and on my knee. I still have those very faint scars.

The other incident I remember was having my eleventh birthday with a few of the girls from the church. I do not know who they were because I did not make any particular friends in Flagstaff. I really missed my two best friends in Prescott, Eliza and Amanda. I was very happy when we went back home.

Above:- Fourth Grade Group
Flagstaff, Ariz.-1923

Marie – first row, first from right

27

Prescott was really home to me. My parents bought a comfortable little house on the far north side of town. We were one of the few families of color in the neighborhood. My little friend, Eliza Lowe, was next to the youngest of a large family who lived a half a block from us.

Next door was a pretty, light-skinned elderly lady who lived in a beautiful brick house. It was a long time before I found out Mrs. Moker was not white. She was always pleasant, kind and friendly with my parents and me although she stayed mostly to herself.

The Taylor family moved into a big house just northeast of us. There were two teenage boys, an older sister (Valerie) and a very young child (Madaline) about four years old. Valerie was very protective of her little sister, more so than their mother. My parents wondered, why? Madaline could not come over to play with me, but I could go over to play with her always under the protective eye of big sister, Valerie! I didn't go very often. It was really no fun. The one thing I enjoyed over there, however, was listening to the beautiful music played on their Victrola record player. It was the first time I had seen or heard a record. I was fascinated!

Mr. Taylor dug a big barbeque pit over which he barbequed whole hogs and quarters of beef. The aroma was unbelievable. The meat was absolutely delicious. His barbeque sold as fast as he could cook it. Sometimes it took days and he usually had standing orders!

There was no interaction with our white neighbors. Since my father was so foreign looking, he would talk with one or two occasionally.

Next door were two little girls. Norma, who was about three or four years old, and Isabell, who was school age. Isabell had been taught prejudice, so I saw very little of her. Norma, however, was so young she had not yet learned about discrimination so she would climb over the fence and come to play with me. I would read stories to her. We would play house and with my vivid imagination I would make up all kinds of stories that she loved to hear.

My mother and father worked hard to keep our home. My mother did day work in some of the wealthy homes – cooking, cleaning, caring for children and bringing baskets of laundry home which she washed in a tub on a washboard, then hung out to dry, then ironed it with a cast iron (no electric iron) heated on the kitchen stove. She folded the laundry neatly in the basket which she carried back the next day – walking! The only transportation we had were our feet!

My father raised chickens and rabbits so we always had meat. He sold them as well as eggs. My father always had a job of some kind and he finally was hired at Fort Whipple working in the laundry. This was a military hospital near Prescott (like Fitzsimons was in Denver and Aurora). Soon after, my mother went to work at Fort Whipple working in the kitchen. It was on the north side of Prescott not far from where we lived, so it was easy for my parents to get there.

A ditch ran across our back yard. We had a large front yard on which our house was built. There was always a vegetable garden which my mother and father planted every year. My mother would can vegetables from the garden so we always had nourishing food. However, whenever they worked in the garden I would disappear because I have never enjoyed working in the yard. A little bridge spanned the ditch to the part of our back yard where my father raised the chickens and rabbits; and, that was where our outhouse was located also. One of the happiest days of my life was when we finally could afford to have a toilet installed inside our house! We still bathed in the wash tub and washed up in the metal wash pan, but we did not have to go out to that cold outhouse!

I heard my folks talk about those who were poor, and our friends had far more than we had, but I never thought of **US** as being **<u>poor</u>**!

One Christmas Eliza got a little red bicycle, and she was having a hard time learning to ride it. I saw boys riding bicycles and it looked so easy that I asked Eliza to let me try. I was about ten years old. I found out that riding a bike was not as simple as it appeared; I was falling off just like my friend. Her brother, Harvey, came along while I was trying to stay balanced. He looked at me as though I was stupid and said, "Stop looking at the front wheel and look where you're going!" I raised my head, looked ahead at the sidewalk, and before I knew it was actually pedaling along on the bike. Even though Eliza followed her brother's advice, it took her a little longer to learn to ride her own bicycle.

I told my parents that I had learned to ride a bike and I wanted one of my own. As soon as my father had enough money, he ordered a full sized bike for me from the Montgomery Ward catalogue. It was a pretty big, blue bicycle. I was so small that the seat and the handle bars were much too high. My father sawed off a couple inches of the seat bar and the handle bar so that they were all the way down and my feet could reach the pedals. I rode my bike everywhere – usually very fast!

Montgomery Ward's catalog had just about everything in it and was the way my folks could order cheaply almost anything they needed. When my mother decided I was to take piano lessons, they ordered a player piano from Montgomery Ward. It was a beautiful solid mahogany instrument which we still have.

Years later my father removed the player mechanism because the piano was so heavy. I really wanted to play the violin, but my mother insisted that I learn to play the piano. I had eight years of piano lessons during which time I learned to read music, enjoy hearing music and, appreciate all kinds of music; but, my performance was limited to playing for my own amusement and often to my own amazement, when alone. Most of the time I played the player rolls and sang along with them. I practiced only when necessary. I froze if expected to play in a program or for other people. I still wanted a violin!

My father eventually got a puppy for me. He was only about a month old, so I had to take care of him like a baby. I fed him with an eye-dropper, kept him warm and I loved him. He was white with black ears and a black spot on his back, so I named him Spot. As he grew, his hair became long. His ears were floppy and his legs were short, so he ran close to the ground. When I asked my dad what kind of dog he was, he told me Spot was a "Water Spaniel." Spot became my buddy. He met me when I came home from school. He followed me around the neighborhood. He loved to ride in the basket on my bicycle. We played games with a ball or a stick. I taught him to sit up and beg, waving his front paws. This friendly little dog was very special to me!

Marie's little dog, Spot

I was in sixth grade when I turned twelve. It was sometime thereafter that my mother told me that we were going to Hondo, Texas, to visit her relatives that she had not seen in many years. Aunt Nancy, Uncle George Elam and their family lived on the farm in the old house in which my mother grew up. My mother's father, Henry Garrett, was still living on his farm across the creek.

This was a new adventure for me. There were horses to ride, cows to be milked, hogs and chickens to be fed. Aunt Nancy was like my mother's sister since they grew up together. Uncle George was a pleasant, quiet man. There were two grown daughters, Nathalee and Josie, and a fifteen-year-old son Frank, still at home. Everyone had chores so I eventually learned to milk a cow, after she kicked me over the first time. I was proud of myself when I learned to ride a horse after Uncle George unearthed a little saddle that Frank had used as a small boy. I was only a little over four feet tall, but I was interested in doing everything.

My greatest experience was going to school with three long-legged boys! They were Cousin Frank, my fourteen-year-old Uncle Frank (mother's half-brother), and another fifteen-year-old cousin, Joe Boy. We had to walk a long country mile on a dusty country road to a one room building on the edge of town. This was the school for the few "colored" children in the area. The teacher was an attractive young woman who had to teach kindergarten through fifth grade. There were a few children in kindergarten, first and second grades – no third grade – a couple of fourth graders and five in fifth grade. Then here I came in sixth grade, and she had to figure out what to do with me!

By the time I got to school, I was exhausted trying to keep up with those three boys whose one step was equal to three of my short steps. I was trotting to keep up. Eventually, I learned to take long strides with my short legs and walk that country mile comfortably with the boys.

I already knew most of what the teacher gave me, but she was wise enough to increase the difficulty of the material. Since I got my work done so quickly, she had me help with the younger children when I had nothing more to do. The fifth grade boys and one girl needed help – especially the boys. They also needed discipline to keep them in line. My three "buddies" were among them. I made some suggestions while watching them so the teacher put me in charge of helping the fifth grade with reading and math. It took a while for these big boys to adjust to little me telling them what to do, but they had to conform because the teacher was agreeing with me. I set up a bit of competition by complimenting whoever came up with the correct answers. Since the girl usually had the answers, the boys began to compete for compliments. If someone made a dumb mistake, we laughed about it and moved on. The boys began working so hard at getting assignments done that there was little disturbance and they began to enjoy learning. We actually had fun!

On the farm, I enjoyed riding with Frank or one of his sisters to herd the cows in from the field to be milked. A sow had a litter of piglets and I took one as a pet until it grew too big. I learned so much living on this big farm. Almost everything we ate was grown on the farm. One kind of corn was grown for eating and another corn was for feeding the livestock, and for grinding into corn meal. There was a vegetable garden and a smoke house for curing bacon, ham and sausage, or any other kind of meat. A few things like sugar and flour were bought in town.

The boys would take me down to the creek and we would fish for perch, sunfish and catfish. One day my mother took me over to meet my grandfather. He was a jolly little, short, rusty, Black man. I was afraid of him because he was so dark. My mother was light brown. As time went on and I would go to visit him, I gradually began to enjoy being with him. I was his oldest grandchild and he would do all kinds of fun things with me. He had an old T-model Ford and he let me steer it as he drove around the farm. I felt as though I was really driving!

There were seven children in my grandfather's second family. All of the older children were gone from home except Frank and Sam, the two younger sons. The youngest daughter, Esther, had been adopted by her mother's sister and lived in Uvalde. She was eleven years old, one year younger than I. I went to visit this young aunt and had a new experience in discrimination.

Her "mother," who was her aunt, worked for some wealthy white people, and was well respected. One day she took Esther and me to the house with her. It was beautifully furnished, but we had to be careful where we went and what we did there. We were sent to the store for something and when we went in there were a few white people being served. They left as some others came in. Although Esther and I had been there waiting, we were ignored and the new arrivals were taken care of. This was not fair so I spoke up with, "We were here first!" The clerk could tell from my voice that I was not from the South and before he could speak, Esther had me out of the store and back at the big house. I was mad at being ignored and confused by Esther's reaction. I later found out that I had spoken "out of turn" and it was for my safety that she had taken me out of the store immediately. She went back later and got what was needed, but she and her aunt kept me well protected after that episode.

I enjoyed going to the Baptist Church where Esther played the piano and sang with the choir. She was very talented and was always dressed pretty. We played together at home and I enjoyed our activity, but I was glad to get back to the freedom of the farm.

Although Texas had laws of segregation, it was not as obvious in Hondo; however, Frank had to rescue me from retaliating when some white kids in town called us names.

One day I wanted to ride my horse. I had no idea where everyone was, but little independent me decided that I would get my horse and go. The only horse in the barn was Uncle George's favorite animal that he did not let anyone ride. He wasn't home, so I figured I could go for a ride and be back before he came, since my gentle mare was not around. I could not find the little saddle, so I put a regular saddle on the horse.

(I had learned how to do this properly). Since my legs were too short to reach the stirrups, I put my feet in the leather loops that held the stirrups, and away I went. My big mistake was, instead of going down the road, I decided to ride across the plowed field! This was a spirited horse, unlike my gentle mare. Given slack reign he took off on a full gallop and I was thrilled to be riding like this. I felt like I was flying! As I was riding back, Frank was frantically waving his arms and yelling at me. He was furious and told me that was the dumbest thing to ride a running horse across a plowed field because it could have stumbled and broke a leg as well as possibly have injured me. Worst of all, I was riding his father's favorite horse that nobody but Uncle George rode. I was in deep trouble. Fortunately Uncle George was not at home and he was never told about this episode!!!

I was told that there were rattle snakes in the area and what to do if one was encountered. One day I was walking along a narrow path when I heard a suspicious rattle. I did as I had been told. I stopped and looked to see where the sound was coming from. In the shadow of the trees along the path, I saw a rattler coiled and shaking its rattle. I was petrified, but I remembered the warning to make no quick movement. I looked at the snake and it looked at me as I began to very slowly move away. It seemed like forever before I was far enough away to be safe; then I ran for my life!!

Apparently my father had the nomadic urge again, because he wrote to us and said he was going to Denver. He wanted to see it since he had heard so much about the city. It was to be a temporary trip. Friends would look after the house in Prescott and a neighbor would take care of Spot.

My father liked Denver and he wanted us to come to see the city before going back to Arizona. So, another new chapter opened up in my life…

Marie and mother, Sarah

Surprise 10th birthday party – 1922; second
row, second from left

CHAPTER 2

Coming to Denver

It was spring of 1925 when my mother and I came by train from Texas to Denver. My father met us at the Union Station, which overwhelmed me with its massive size. As we came out of the huge building, there was the famous "Arch" welcoming arriving visitors and awesome 17th Street stretching as far as one could see with its clanging trolley cars on which I had my first ride!

As usual, my father had found a job. He was a janitor at the Manor Apartments on the corner of East 13th Avenue and Pennsylvania Street. We had a small apartment in the basement with an outside entrance. There was a living room, a bedroom, a kitchen and the one room that was a true luxury for me – a complete bathroom – toilet, washbasin and tub!!! I still remember the thrill of actually having running hot and cold water!! My parents slept in the bedroom and I slept on the living room couch. It was a new experience, but it was warm and comfortable.

One tenant, Claude Pendelton, and his wife took an interest in me. He was the boys' advisor at Morey Junior High School, which was only three blocks up 13th Avenue at Clarkson Street. I told Mr. Pendelton that I was in sixth grade and wanted to know where I would go to school. There were only a few weeks of school days left. He said, "There are so few days before the end of the school year, why not wait until next Fall and enter seventh grade at Morey Junior High School?" this was a surprise for me in many ways. I had never heard of Junior High School; I thought I would be going to elementary school through eighth grade and then to High School. (Denver had changed from the "eight-four system" to the "six-three-three system" only two years before.

When I told Mr. Pendelton that I expected to go to elementary school, he realized how confused I was. He assured me that in September he would take me to Morey and see that I was properly enrolled and to let him know if I had any questions or problems. That calmed my fears!

In the meantime, my father took us to the Five Points area, the center of the African-American activities. He knew about the Y.M.C.A. and the Phyllis Wheatley Branch Y.W.C.A.

My mother was anxious to find a church to attend and somehow she found little New Hope Baptist Church (now Pipkin Mortuary), and took me there. I attended Sunday School, but never made any friends. I tried Zion Baptist Sunday School a few times, but I wasn't comfortable, so I went back to New Hope where, at least, I knew the people. My mother made some wonderful friends there, sang in the choir and New Hope Baptist Church became her church.

I was curious to find out what was in my neighborhood so I would frequently go exploring. Next door to us on the corner of 13th and Logan Street was an art museum. The Capital was only a few blocks away so I walked around the grounds and finally one day I had the nerve to enter the Capital building. I was awed as I looked up into the dome.

I liked to prowl around Civic Center. For a long time I wondered what was that one building there. I finally found out that it was the Denver Public Library. I wanted to go in, but I was afraid I would be turned away, as I had been in Prescott. There were steps that went up to the main part of the library. There was also another entrance at one side that went under those steps and into the lower part of the building. Out of curiosity, one day I went down to find out where those steps went and there was the Children's Library!

It took me a while to get up the nerve to enter the building, but one day I went down the steps and into the Children's Library. The many books, magazines, tables, chairs and the quiet room was amazing. I found _Boy's Life_ and _Boy Scout Magazine_, and sat down to read. No one asked me to leave!!! From that day on, I was in the library as often as possible. If I found a book to read and could not finish it, I would get that book the next time I was in and continue reading it.

One day the librarian came over to me when I was at the book shelf and asked if she could help me. She had noticed that I was in so often, but never checked out a book. I told her I didn't know I could check out books. "If you have a library card you may take home books for two weeks," she said. I was amazed! She gave me an application for my mother to sign. When I brought it back, I was issued a card and I could check out books to read at home – the greatest experience of my life!

The _Bobbsie Twins_ series was my favorite, but I was introduced to Louisa May Alcott's _Little Women_ and many other famous authors. When I was at home, I was constantly reading. My mother finally forbade me to bring my book to the table at mealtime. After going to bed at night with the light turned off, I used a flashlight to read under the covers.

In my excursions around the area, I found St. Mary's Academy, at that time it was on the corner of 14th Avenue and Pennsylvania. Across the street from our apartment building on Pennsylvania St. was a house with two carved granite lions in front. Those stone lions always fascinated me. (I was in high school before I found out that this was the famous "Molly Brown House"!)

I finally found a little friend. Her parents were janitors in an apartment building in the next block from us. Bernice was eleven (an only child like me) and her mother was very protective of her; but since her parents knew my parents and liked me, we had a good time together. I took her on neighborhood adventures with me, which was new to her, and she loved it. However, we spent most of our time together in her apartment kitchen. Cooking was not my bag, but Bernice loved to make goodies. We baked cookies, and made candy – fudge, taffy, brownies and peanut brittle. For me, the best part was eating it! One time I pulled taffy until I had blisters on my hands; that was not fun! When school started, she was in sixth grade and went to Emerson Elementary School and I was in seventh grade so I went to Morey Junior High School. We didn't see much of

Marie, 1926 – soon after arriving in Denver

each other after that, and soon thereafter, they moved away.

Mr. Pendelton kept his word and told me exactly what to do to

Gym Suit worn for Morey
Junior High School

get enrolled at Morey. I was to let him know if I had any questions or problems, which eased my anxiety of going into an unknown situation. Periodically, at home he would check with me to see if I was getting along all right.

It took me a while to get used to going from room to room, and adjusting to a different teacher for every subject.

*I was plunked, very green, into a situation where I had to go from class to class. I was getting adjusted, but I had this one teacher in a class called Social Science. I had never heard of that subject before. It seemed to be a combination of geography and history and many other topics. So here I was making another adjustment, but this teacher was prejudiced. She was the only one of all the teachers I had that showed prejudice. She did the same thing my fourth grade teacher did. If she thought I didn't know it, she would call on me. If she thought I knew it, forget it!

The other thing that happened one day was she announced that there were so many children having problems that if we stayed after school she would answer our questions. So one day I stayed after school. There were quite a few children, and she answered all their questions. I was the last one. She said it was time to go home. She didn't have any more time. She never even asked me what my question was. After that I would stay and I would listen to the questions; I'd listen to the answers. I'd find the answers in my book. I pulled the same technique on this teacher that I used in fourth grade in Prescott – wave my hand if I did not know, and look dumb if I knew. I came up from the first "D" I'd ever had in my life to a "B" as my last grade. [1]

---

[1]* excerpt taken from Trail Blazers Oral History Series transcript, courtesy of Denver Public Library, Blair-Caldwell

I have fond memories of my math teacher at Morey. I found out that mathematics was really another name for arithmetic, but it was more advanced than I had been taught, and I was having trouble understanding it. He had me stay after class, made simple explanations of the problems and showed me how to solve them. I caught on so quickly that he finally told me I had a mathematical mind. That was a real compliment!

We moved to an apartment one block from the Manor Apartments at 13th and Pearl Street, two blocks from Morey. My dad began to talk about going to the Northwest since he had never been to Oregon or Washington. However, my mother was a homebody who liked to stay put and I was old enough to say I did not want to move because I liked the school here in Denver.

Since my father was out voted, we were going to stay here, so my parents decided to sell our house in Arizona. Our furniture was shipped to us and my little dog, Spot, was sent to me. I was happy!

We moved again to 17th and Sherman Street, which was approximately ten blocks from Morey – a long walk. My parents were still janitors, but my father was also working as a custodian at the exclusive Daniels and Fisher Department Store, which left most of the work at the apartment for my mother.

It was in physical education that I finally found my REAL place, where my color did not matter. At first I was just another student and I was neither accepted nor rejected. As I continued to excel with enthusiasm in all the activities, I felt free! I could climb the ropes faster and higher than anyone else; my reflexes were quick. I could run faster and jump higher than most. The crowning glory was when I was asked to play on teams! After school sports became the joy of my existence.

My mother was not happy with me and sports. One morning before I left for school she told me not to stay for a soccer game but to come home immediately after school. She was really upset and told me that I was going to get hurt if I played. She wanted me at home. My mother must have had premonitions, because that was the day that I did get hurt.

I stayed for my soccer game and was having a great time when I had a chance to kick the ball into the goal. However, I missed the ball as my foot hit the ground full force just in front of the ball. My foot hurt so bad that I blacked out, and when I regained consciousness the teacher and the girls were around me. I had a long ten blocks to walk home, and the big toe of my right foot was so painful I had to walk on my heel.

As I slowly made my way home I concocted a story to tell my mother that had nothing to do with my soccer game. For days I limped back and forth to school as the pain eased and finally went away. I still have a bent and knotted big toe on my right foot and have always had to fit my right foot comfortably when buying shoes.

My favorite classroom was sewing. I had already started some basic sewing at home and here I began learning some of the finer techniques of the art. However, in this beginner class, while the other students were working on simple projects, I would have my part done and would be waiting for the teacher to check it. Finally, one day, I told her what I should do next so I would not have to wait. She told me I was doing so well to go on working on my own. I was happily surprised and continued sewing on my own. I had to undo a couple of mistakes, but otherwise my work was perfect.

The next semester I was assigned to cooking class. I was not interested in cooking, but there were so many in the class (many of them boys) that the teacher asked if anyone would be willing to go to sewing class. I was one of the first to volunteer. It was advanced sewing and I loved it!

This time we were taught various kinds of seams in making clothes – flat seam, French seam and false French seam. We learned how to lay out patterns to get maximum use of material. I actually made my first dress with French seams in this class. This was the beginning of my designing and making my own clothes which I continued to do through high school. I even thought of becoming a costume designer!

Since I was so small (a little over 4 ½ feet) I could make a dress with less material than called for in a pattern. Joslin Department Store had a remnant table where I could usually find silk crepe leftovers for one or two dollars with just enough material to make a dress. I could visualize the dress I wanted to make, and would sketch it out on paper. I would buy a pattern that was a close fit to the picture I had drawn, or I would use parts from previous patterns that would work. Parts for which I had no pattern I would draw and cut out of newspaper. My clothes had no raw seams; they were either French or false French finished. I was proud of my sewing. My clothes always fit perfectly. I continued designing and making my own dresses on into high school until I became so active with athletics and academics that I did not have time to sew.

In the fall of 1926 when I entered eighth grade, I noticed a girl of color who had a locker near me. I wanted to speak to her but I was shy about approaching people – believe it or not! That's why I had made no friends at New Hope. One day this girl came over to me, and with a bubbly smile said, "I have been watching you and I came over to say 'hello.' My name is Constance Nelson, but everyone calls me Connie. I'm in seventh grade and I'm new here. What grade are you in?"

"I'm in eighth grade," I replied. "I've seen you and wondered when you came to Morey. I haven't seen any other colored girls."

"Oh, there are some more girls and we sit together in assembly. Would you like to come and sit with us?" said Connie.

I was delighted to have been invited to meet some other girls, since Connie was so friendly. I had always been by myself through seventh grade and had not remembered seeing any other brown faces except Roberta DeFrantz from New Hope who was in ninth grade. I would see her occasionally in the lunchroom, but we did not communicate.

I liked Connie and we had happy times meeting at our lockers. She told me where they sat in the auditorium. At the next assembly she was watching for me and I went over to meet the girls. I was not too sure what to expect and hoped they would accept me as Connie had. There were three more: Eleanor Hawkins, Katherine Norton and Vivian Rose. They seemed to be glad to have me join them and were interested in learning as much about me as possible. Eleanor said they had seen me before, but they thought I was a Mexican until Roberta told them I had

43

attended Sunday School at New Hope. Roberta was now in high school.

All of these girls attended Shorter A. M. E. Church which had a devastating fire just a few months before we came to Denver in 1925. They were in the process of building a new church which was completed in 1926. I had heard so much about that great church I attended the wonderful Easter Service of dedication and was awed by the big, magnificent sanctuary. The service was one like I had never experienced before – quiet, dignified and highlighted by a sermon by Rev. A. Wayman Ward that was an educational religious lecture. The congregation quietly absorbed every word, and I enjoyed it.

I told the girls about my one time experience at their church and they invited me to come to Shorter for Sunday School; they were all in the same class for teenage girls. That was the beginning of my attending Shorter A.M.E. Church. Beulah Tee Fant, the church secretary, was the teacher and she made the class so interesting that I was anxious to get there on Sunday mornings. She had rules to abide by, but she also knew how to make our Biblical learning fun!

Eleanor, Connie, Katherine and I became a foursome that had fun doing things together: going to City Park, visiting the museum and zoo, enjoying YPD (Young People's Department) activities at church and going to the movies. (I was so small that I got into the movies for half-fare until I was in high school!)

They told me about Girl Reserves at the Phyllis Wheatley branch YWCA, located at 25th and Welton Street. My father had told me to go to the YWCA before to meet other girls, but I was shy about going since I did not know anyone. So I decided to go with my friends and a whole new world gradually opened up to me! There were crafts, games, companions, parties and the white uniform which I felt so proud to wear. I loved every minute there and actively participated in all the activities. Then I heard about Camp Nizhoni which became a brand new way of life for me!

Since we were not permitted to attend the main YWCA camp,

Phyllis Wheatley Branch ran Camp Nizhoni for us girls of color each summer in Lincoln Hills, a small, busy African-American resort in Gilpin County. Families owned homes or rented cabins; there were picnics and recreation outings by churches and individuals. Winks Lodge was a popular meeting place (now on the National Register of Historic Places).

The summer of 1928 I had the privilege of attending Camp Nizhoni for the first time. I had never been to a camp or to the mountains. I was so excited I could not sleep the night before. At 8:00 a.m. we were to meet at the Moffet Station, a little train station somewhere near the Union Station; I had never heard of it before, but it had this name because this was the only train that went through the famous Moffet Tunnel!

Eleanor had told me we would go through tunnels, but I never expected going through so many before we reached the little mountain town of Pinecliffe. I was amazed and thrilled! A couple of miles farther and the train stopped at our Lincoln Hills platform. We disembarked from the train and followed a narrow trail through the growth of bushes, crossed over Beaver Creek on a little wooden bridge and there on a slight uprising was Camp Nizhoni – one big building backed against the trees and facing a spreading meadow.

To me it was awesome! I loved my two weeks at camp: hiking, crafts, singing around the camp fire, toasting marshmallows and making "smores," enjoying good food and the companionship of the other girls. But, I missed Eleanor. She was in summer school and didn't get to camp. (We had developed a life time friendship.) The Girl Reserve Secretary was our camp director and she was a very caring young woman who made camping a happy experience.

At Camp Nizhoni – 1928

45

In early 1930 a new Girl Reserve Secretary was sent to us, Mary E. Wood. She was one of the most dynamic leaders our Phyllis Wheatley Branch YWCA ever had! We girls always felt that we were the important part of her exciting plans for us, and she respected our opinions. Most of all, she made Nizhoni come alive! She did not want to be called Miss Wood. Her nickname was "Woody," and all of the counselors had camp names. "Woody" inspired us girls to build a rustic chapel among the pines where we had a quiet, simple devotion each morning for fifteen minutes to half an hour (depending on plans for the day). We were assigned duties usually in small groups, to learn assuming responsibility and working together.

Y.W.C.A. Camp Nizhoni building

Phyllis Wheatley Y.W.C.A. Camp Nizhoni, (L-R) Mary Wood (Woody), unknown, Marie Louise Anderson (Andy), Ruby Hawkins, Ethel Wood, unknown, Eleanor Hawkins (Hawky)

"Woody"

There were nature hikes to learn about the flora and fauna of the area. We had fun times. One of our campers, Charlotte Moseley, was a talented musician, and we would sing happy songs as she played the piano. We played active outdoor games, and for fun, indoor games. I anticipated going to Camp Nizhoni <u>every</u> summer for many years.

I loved the mountains and the great out-of-doors. As the years went by, I became a junior counselor, then a nature and arts counselor. I was called "Andy." I had some craft classes, but my greatest interest was taking the girls on hikes, showing them the variety of plants, flowers, trees, small animals, even insects that surround us in our majestic mountains. I wanted them to learn to appreciate the natural beauty of the great outdoors. We slept out under the stars on beds of pine boughs. We cooked breakfast, eggs and bacon, on hot rocks over a camp fire, making biscuits on thin green willow sticks held over the hot coals. It was quite an exciting adventure that most campers enjoyed while a few just tolerated it.

One of the most fascinating activities all of us enjoyed was visiting what we called "Echo Mountain." Woody had found a hill where, from a certain spot, we could call out and our voices would echo back from a far away mountain that we could see. We had a song that we sang over and over as we sat on the hill and listened for Echo's voice. Our song was called, "Little Sir Echo."

For me, living and learning in God's majestic mountains made me realize how small and insignificant we humans really are! I spent most of my summers at Camp Nizhoni until I married in 1943.

The summer of 1936, shortly after camp season opened, Woody fell and broke her ankle. She had gone to see a neighbor, but she had been gone so unusually long that I went to find her because we needed her for whatever activity was scheduled. I was shocked when I saw Woody lying on the ground a short way up the path. She was trying to get up. I rushed over to help her, then I could see that her left foot was unnaturally bent. I knew it was broken. I called for help but I was too far away to be heard, so I told Woody to just lie there while I went back for assistance.

Counselors and campers came back with me. We brought the little red wagon with us that we used to haul wood since we could not carry her safely down the hill. I do not remember what I used as a temporary splint, but I carefully straightened her foot and secured it. We got her on the wagon and slowly rolled her back to camp. There I got two boards, padded them and taped the splints securely to her leg and foot. (Thank goodness for a first aid class I had taken!)

I sent up my prayers of thanks for the telephone which had recently been installed at Nizhoni. Boulder was the nearest town out of the mountains, so I arbitrarily chose a doctor's name and dialed. Fortunately, I got a young doctor in Boulder who seemed familiar with mountain accidents. He told me what to do and where to meet him. He said he would be waiting for me. I told him it would take me an hour or more to get Woody to Boulder in the old camp (a panel) truck; he understood. All I could say to myself was, "Thank you Lord for leading me to this doctor!"

We "bedded" Woody in the enclosed truck as comfortably as possible, and I took off. Woody and I were the only camp staff who could drive the truck on those mountain roads. I had to go over to Nederland and down Boulder Canyon – a LONG drive!!!

In 1936, most of those mountain roads were not paved and could be quite bumpy and rough. I drove as carefully as possible as not to jar Woody too much. We had given her aspirin for her pain, but she was still hurting.

Thanks to the Good Lord we made it safely to Boulder, and to my surprise, the doctor was waiting on the corner for us! He got Woody into his office, checked what I had done and complimented me on my good work. He had only one criticism: the splints were fine, but I should not have used heavy tape to hold them on her leg. I should have tied them with gauze or strips of cloth because it was difficult cutting through all that sticky tape to remove the splints. However, he re-splinted her leg and called her hospital in Denver, St. Joseph, to let them know we would be there soon. I got Woody to St. Joseph Hospital and stayed with her until she was comfortably bedded in her room.

She thanked me for "saving her life," and since I was the most experienced of the Nizhoni staff, she said for me to take over as director since she did not know when she would be able to return.

I lived near the hospital with my parents, so I rested over night. I went to see Woody the next morning, then drove the truck back to camp, and <u>by the Grace of God</u>, became the director at Camp Nizhoni for the rest of the camping weeks.

Woody had a cast on her foot, ankle and part of her leg, but it did not slow her down. She called her cast "Peggy." Friends would drive her any place she needed to go. I drove her many places just for fun. At the end of camp in August, we drove up to Nizhoni to spend the last day, "Peggy," crutches and all!

At the end of summer, we took a train trip to the little resort of Glenwood Springs. Nelsine Campbell, (an active member of Phyllis Wheatley Branch YWCA Committee of Management), Woody and I were three adventurous "gadabouts." We had to sleep three in one double bed, so we just slept cross ways! The food was great and the scenery was fantastic we had a ball!!! Woody and I were friends for the rest of her life.

August 1936 - Camp Staff
Breakfast at Mother Gross'

Marie with Camp
Counselors

These are only a few highlights of the years at Camp Nizhoni. The wonderful stories of this early camp for African-American girls would fill another book!

At church Mrs. Fant had organized us teenage girls into a little service club called "The Sunshine Makers," to spread sunshine and happiness to others. We delivered baskets to the needy at Thanksgiving and Easter. We sang carols throughout neighborhoods during Christmas holidays. We went out to Fitzsimmons Military Hospital and sang hymns, and for fun, songs to the patients. We met regularly at each other's homes or at church to plan our activities and have fun.

Rev. and Mrs. John M. Brown who came to Shorter after Rev. A. Wayman Ward was transferred to Chicago, had no children, but were dedicated to the activities and welfare of children and youth. Rev. Brown was an elderly, old fashioned, spiritual preacher that the quiet congregation had to get used to hearing!

Mrs. Brown had hot cocoa and smores at the parsonage for us girls on New Year's Eve so we could all go together to the meeting at church to watch the New Year come in. We had fun playing games to stay awake until 11:30p.m., then over to the church a half block away. After the service we went back to the parsonage and slept for a few hours. Mrs. Brown had breakfast for us and we went happily on our ways home.

One time before Easter, Mrs. Brown had the Sunshine Makers over night and bedded us down so we could attend the sunrise service at church. There were ten or twelve girls in our club; Eleanor and I were two active members. We also participated in YPD and sang in the Youth choir.

At one time Rev. Brown spent several weeks encouraging the young people in Sunday School to be baptized; many had not. Since my mother had kept me in Baptist churches as a child, I had not been baptized. When I told Eleanor that I was thinking about it, I was surprised to find out that she had not been baptized either. The Sunday that Rev. Brown performed the special Sunday School ritual; Eleanor and I were in the group. In the Community Room, where we gathered to open Sunday School before going to separate classes and come together to close our service, there was a Baptismal pool under the stage. Two of the teenagers chose to be immersed. The rest of us were baptized with Holy Water on our heads. Rev. Brown made it very clear that, in the name of the Lord, we were all baptized equally.

Rev. Brown was thinking of retiring, but we kept him at Shorter as long as possible. He and Mrs. Brown had become our beloved leaders. When they left for California, Rev. Brown's younger brother, Rev. Russell S. Brown, was assigned to our church. He and his wife had a teenage daughter and two younger sons.

In my senior year in high school, I took the Sunday School teacher training class at church, passed it and was assigned to help in the nursery class. I had already decided to be a teacher of physical education since I loved my sports, but the joy of working with these toddlers in Sunday School convinced me that my true profession would be teaching kindergarten!

Sunday School pals - Marie, Charlotte Mosley, Margaret Mackie

Marie, about age 16

CHAPTER 3
Education: Pro and Con

Hearing the word EDUCATION brings to mind schools, classrooms, books, teachers and high school graduation; colleges, universities, professors, lectures, term papers, tests, commencement and the joy of receiving a diploma with a degree.

These academic achievements are important but are merely necessary tools to be used in preparation for success in one's vocation or trade. The greatest education comes from life's experiences with people and worldly activities.

In ninth grade there were two classes that I remember so well because they opened new doors for me. I took metal craft and made a beautiful ring of German silver with a large, flawless blue turquoise stone. I learned that I had a talent for crafts. I was so proud of that ring that I wore it all the time.

The other class was Home Economics where we were assigned to list ten faults we would like to change. I have no idea which faults I listed, except for number one – learning to control my temper!

Unfortunately, I had inherited my father's hot temper and my mother was constantly reminding me that it was not "lady-like." My temper was not explosive like my father's; mine was a slow burn that gradually built up until I could actually see red, and then explode! I was not afraid of anybody or anything, and would say or do whatever came to mind in retaliation against whoever had offended me. I knew this was dangerous because I or the other person could get hurt, and I really wanted to change.

The teacher in this class was a great help to all of us. For me, she was my salvation. She taught me to count to ten when I felt my temper rising; stop, and think about the situation. If necessary, walk away and cool down. I still had quite a temper, but I followed her advice and learned to save myself from many unpleasant conflicts!

I wanted to learn how to swim, and the only place where we could go was the "Bath House" downtown on 20th and Larimer Streets (now the Twentieth Street Recreation Center). Women of color were permitted to swim on Friday and men on Saturday. The pool was drained over the weekend so there would be "fresh water" for white swimmers each week.

I went with Eleanor and Connie. There were several women who taught me to float, to splash around and to Dog Paddle, but they were not real swimmers. I had a problem keeping my eyes open in the water, and having bubbles in my face when I exhaled bothered me. I loved being in the water, but I was making no progress. So I went to the library and checked out a book on beginning swimming. To learn to keep my eyes open, and to inhale and exhale properly I would fill the wash basin with water in the bathroom, place my face in the water with my eyes open and exhale, then inhale over my shoulder, and then exhale in the water to get used to the bubbles in my face.

The book had instructions and illustrations of various strokes, so I started working at home on the "Australian Crawl" (Free Style, now), moving my arms to get the feel and coordinating my inhaling over my shoulder to get the rhythm.

In the pool, I tried to follow directions, but my kicking was not right. With the encouragement of some of the women, and many days of practice I finally learned to arch my back, coordinate my strokes with my kicking and I actually began to swim! I taught myself other strokes and began diving. I loved the water!!!

Near the Bath House there was a small hamburger stand where we could buy burgers for ten cents or three for a quarter. The three of us were always so hungry after swimming. Connie and Eleanor never really learned to swim, but they had fun. We would buy three burgers for eight cents apiece and take turns paying the extra penny.

In sports at Morey, when the girls found out that I could swim, they wanted me on their team. However, I was informed by the principal that I was not permitted to swim in the pool because of my race.

54

I "Continuated" from Morey Jr. High School in 1928 as an Honor Student, and entered East Denver High School as the only brown face in the sophomore class. There were only seven of us in East High - five girls and two boys. Eleanor and Roberta were seniors. They were the only students that I knew. Of Denver's five high schools, East was the elite school where most of the wealthy students attended.

*As far as going to school at East was concerned, we went to classes. That was it. We could not belong to a club. We could not belong to anything. Just go to school!

I had gotten into sports at Morey. The girls and everybody accepted me because I was good and I enjoyed it. I went out for sports at East. Nothing. The teacher ignored me. This was after school sports and I was not selected for a team. I was the last one left and I had to be put on a team where I was completely ignored by the girls, so I just dropped my athletics there. It was a terrible blow for me to have to give up the sports that I loved so dearly.

*I did have one teacher that I will always remember. I was taking French. I had started taking French in the 9th grade at Morey, so she let me join the French Club and she was just great. No prejudice whatsoever. She encouraged me. My math teacher also encouraged me. I loved math and I was getting into an advanced class. He was very helpful. I can't say that everybody was. [1]

I took a class in Public Speaking that helped me to overcome my fear and "freezing up" when faced with talking to a group. This was good, and I have been giving speeches ever since!!!

*One experience I will always remember was one day in early spring. I was in study hall and I was told that the Dean of Girls advisor wanted to see me. I wondered if I had done anything wrong. I went down and I entered her office. She was busy at her desk so she didn't look up. I stood quietly. Finally, she looked up and she wanted to know what she could do for me. I said, "I was told you wanted to see me."

She said, "Well, what is your name?"

---

[1]* excerpt taken from Trail Blazers Oral History Series transcript, courtesy of Denver Public Library, Blair-Caldwell

I answered, "I am Marie Louise Anderson and I wanted to know why I was called in."

She replied, "We're checking all of the students who are in the upper ten percent of the sophomore class to see if they are going to college. We want to be sure they are taking the right classes."

She looked through, and here was my record. She had never taken a look at that record to see that it had "Negro" on it because in those days race was recorded and I was definitely checked as Negro.

I said, "Yes, I plan to go to college."

She asked, "Why?"

My answer was, "My father and my mother told me that I am to get an education and I'm going to college because they don't want me to have to work as hard as they have to work."

"Well, there's no point in your wasting your father's money because all you can do is work in somebody's kitchen or clean somebody's house" was her answer.

That hit me because at that time I was JUST beginning to control my temper and I could almost see the red coming up! Then I thought no, this isn't the time to blow up Marie, so I just said, "I am going to college," and I walked out of the office. It hurt. Oh, did it hurt!

I went to the girl's lavatory. Fortunately, nobody was in there. I just pounded the walls and I cried, "I'm going to show them. I'm going to show them. I'm not only as good, I'm better."

I was just talking it out. Then I washed my face, dried my tears and went on back to study hall. And I did show them eventually!!! [1]

Denver Public Schools still had the old A and B semester system.

---

[1]* excerpt taken from Trail Blazers Oral History Series transcript, courtesy of Denver Public Library, Blair-Caldwell

Eleanor was scheduled to complete 12A in January of 1930. She did not want to graduate mid-year, so she went to summer school for two summers and completed a semester's credits. She then graduated at the end of summer school in 1929. She entered Denver University on a partial scholarship that fall. We kept in touch, but I did not see her as often and she was so busy studying that she could participate in our church activities only occasionally.

*Fortunately, the Lord takes care of so many things. In late summer of 1929 my folks moved to the west side of Denver. My parents decided to get out of the apartment work. My father had a better job. He was working for Daniels and Fisher and I think he was working at something else part time. My mother was doing day work and taking care of two small children. They rented a house just half a block from West High School so that I enrolled at West as a junior. It was a 180 from East High School. I couldn't believe it! The first day of school at our opening assembly, Mr. Kepner, (who was the principal) had everybody there, and he made it very clear that in his school there was to be NO discrimination, racially, religiously, gender or otherwise; that we were there to get an education and the education we would get was up to us. This went not only for the students, but for the faculty as well; and, he meant it.

I'll never forget the day a notice came around, "Assembly immediately!" (We didn't have intercoms then.) That was unusual. When he called an assembly it was usually at a break of some kind. I mean to tell you that everybody filed into that auditorium dead silent. Mr. Kepner was on the stage and as he looked around he noticed there were two teachers missing. He told one of the teachers to go get Miss So-and-so and Miss So-and-so, and I mean those teachers were in there in a hurry. Mr. Kepner was mad. His face was red and even his bald head was red! Two boys in the gym had had some kind of racial conflict, and the gym teacher had reported it. Mr. Kepner didn't wait. He chewed those boys out in that auditorium. He let everybody know he meant what he said. That at West High School no discrimination would be tolerated!

The Dean of Girls was another revelation I ran into that I couldn't believe. It took me days to get up enough courage to go in to see her after what I'd run into at East. I walked into her office. Hildegarde

Sweet looked up and smiled at me and said, "What can I do for you?" I told her that I wanted to go to college and I needed to have some help. I wondered where I stood in my rating.

She said, "Well, just a minute."

Then she asked my name and said, "I'll look it up."

She was just as nice as she could be. She checked my record and I was number 17. At that time the state gave honorary scholarships to the first five graduates in the classes of each of the five high schools every year. In those early years there were only East, West, South, North and Manual High Schools. The scholarships covered tuition to any state college or university.

*That was what I was aiming for but you had to be one, two, three, four or five. She said, "Don't worry about it. You have plenty of time. There are always shifts in grade levels."

She was so nice. I think I became a nuisance because she knew that when report cards came out I would be right there asking, "Where do I stand?"

She kept me going and kept encouraging me. Sure enough, by the time I was a senior, I remember going in when the grades came out. I think it was around the early part of 1931 and I had moved up to number 7. I was still two below scholarship qualification. She said don't worry about it, there still can be changes.

My mother and father decided to return to working in an apartment building, so they would be able to help me go to college. They became janitors, again, at the Putnam Apartments in the 12 hundred block of Pennsylvania Street, a half block from the Manor Apartments where we lived when we first came to Denver. It was quite a distance from West High.

In 1928, my father bought a 1924 Chevrolet touring car – open all around with isinglass curtains to hang to protect from rain or snow.

I learned about driving by watching and asking questions when I rode in other people's cars. They would patiently explain about the clutch and shifting gears, etc. By the time we got our car, I just had to learn to actually operate it and steer it. It was trial and error with my father coaching me, but I became a very good driver. After we moved I would drive to West High School sometimes, but most of the time I walked. Of course, I was happily back in my sports!

The last semester of my senior year at West High School, I decided to elect Auto Mechanics since my father had taught me so much about maintaining our little Chevrolet. When I told my advisor that I would like to learn more about automobiles, she was surprised and told me to check with the Mechanics teacher since no girl had ever asked to take the class.

I found the teacher and he looked at me as though he couldn't believe what he heard. I told him that I enjoyed helping my father with our car and since automobile engines were changing, I wanted to learn more about how to repair and maintain them. His reply was, "I've never had a girl in our mechanics class, so I'll ask the boys how they feel about it. I'll let you know."

My mother could never understand why I would spend hours with my father working on the car, as happy as could be, come in with hands and finger nails so covered with black grease that I would have to scrub my hands with a brush. But if I were in the kitchen with her, I didn't want my hands to have food or cooking oil sticking to them. I spent very little time in the kitchen with my mother who was a wonderful cook. I enjoyed eating, but I never liked to cook.

I did not hear from the Mechanics teacher for several days and I needed another elective to complete my schedule. I enrolled in Advanced Algebra, since I loved Mathematics. A few days later the teacher found me and said the boys wouldn't mind having a girl in the class. I was sorry, but it was too late since I was already in Algebra class.

After I graduated, I was told that the next year the class was open to girls!

I was still a teenager at Shorter A.M.E. Church where I made lifetime friends of four adult members who took me under their guidance – Josephine Price, Beula Tee Fant, Addie Lightner and Dr. Mary Ellison. They were a team of women who were dedicated to working for the good in Shorter, the Y.W.C.A. and the community. I learned how people of diverse personalities could resolve their differences amicably, maintain a strong friendship and continue to work together for years to achieve many goals.

When Mrs. Price brought her niece and nephew to Denver from Kentucky, Margaret and Herman Mackey, "Margie" and I became good friends. I learned about the kind of segregated life she experienced in the South. I helped Margie to adjust to her new life in Denver. Although, we still had discrimination in Denver, it was much freer than the life she had known.

We graduated from high school the same year, 1931. She and her brother from Manual, and I from West. They returned to Kentucky and I went on to college, but Mrs. Price became one of my best friends for the rest of her life.

Marie, West High School (stairs) - 1931

While I was still in high school, I developed an acrobatic act that I thoroughly enjoyed performing occasionally in programs at school, at church and in the community. I had excellent balance and was quite limber so I put together a short sequence of standing on my head, tumbling, back bending, walking on my hands and a few other stunts that I dreamed up. I continued to perform into my freshman year in college until I became so involved with my studies that I seldom came to Denver.

*It was approximately several weeks after I had talked to the Dean (at West) about my grades that there was a big assembly and all the National Honor Seniors were up on the stage. I was sitting on the stage with the National Honor Society and they were giving out all the honors. They started on the scholarships. Number One was Nora Bates, our Head Girl; Number Two was Sirion St. John, our Head Boy, and about that time I lost it because all I could see was "Number Seven". They said, "Number Three…" But I never heard

Marie, West High School (stairs) – 2009

West High School – 1931

Manny Martinez Middle School – 2009

Number Three. They must have said it again because the girl next to me punched me with her elbow and said, "Marie, they're calling your name." I was off in limbo some place because I was devastated at not making Number Five. Sure enough, here it was Number Three, Marie Loiuse Anderson. I couldn't believe what I heard. I had my scholarship all because I had changed to West High School. I had graduated Number Three in a class of 357 because of hard work, encouragement and unbiased recognition! Again, by the Grace of God!!!

I had decided long ago that I was going to be a primary teacher, a kindergarten teacher really, because I wanted to teach small children. I loved small children and so I chose going to Greeley which at that time was just plain old Colorado's Teacher's College (CTC) in 1931.

Since Denver University was so expensive, Eleanor transferred to CTC her sophomore year. So we were roommates. She was a junior, I was a freshman. Eleanor helped me adjust to my new way of life.

It was pretty much like anywhere else. We couldn't live on campus. We girls had a house of our own in the 600 block of 13th Street near the railroad tracks. We walked to school and it was a long, cold walk. We could not belong to clubs. We could just go to classes and get an education. The freshman class was divided into thirds from the entrance exams and I wound up in the top one-third, so I didn't have to take many of the regular courses.

I was placed in Dr. Ethan Allen Cross' advanced English class – only five of us were freshman. When Dr. Cross gave an assignment, he absolutely meant for us to be prepared! Most of the class were juniors and seniors. Only three of us freshmen completed the class. I learned a great lesson from this first college exposure. No reminding, no explaining, just get the job done!!!

I had seen a list of the Board of Trustees and there was a name, Dr. Harry V. Kepner which I thought that was unusual. It was the same name as Mr. Kepner at West. However, he did not use the title, so I figured it was just another Kepner until I saw his picture and *Dr*. Harry V. Kepner really *was* the principal at West High School!

Before I graduated they renamed the training school Kepner Hall. I often thought it was so unfortunate that the college wasn't run under the same rules that Mr. Kepner ran West High School, but they weren't.

Many years before I was ever in college, Alpha Kappa chapter of Alpha Kappa Alpha Sorority was organized. The sorors had a house that they had rented and that same house was being used all those years by African-American students. We would pay by the month. I think it was fifty dollars a month. But you must remember in 1931 the economy was in the middle of the Great Depression. My scholarship, believe it or not, covered fifteen dollars a quarter. That fifteen dollars could have been $1500 so far as we were concerned, because just to get a dollar meant an awful lot during the depression. In '31 that was just two years after the disastrous BIG crash. When my parents would drive up to see me, I was lucky and thankful if my father could give me fifty cents!

Our house, over the time that I was there, could house anywhere from eight to ten girls. One year we had fifteen and how we got them all in there I don't know. We had four or five bedrooms. We had a house mother who was our cook and took care of all the downstairs and our cooking. We divided everything else into chores with groups of two or three so that everybody was responsible for something. We did all of the shopping and everything. We'd pay our money to whichever committee was in charge of the money, and then it would be proportioned out as necessary. It was amazing what you could do with a nickel in those days. We had good food. We'd go shopping every week. In fact, the committee in charge of the food would make out menus for each day and then we'd break it down into what we had to buy and how much. Then the shopping committee would go and do the shopping. Our house mother was a cook out of this world. We had plenty. Our house mother was the aunt of Ruth Beck, one of the girls who came from Seattle. Her aunt was there with us until Ruth graduated, then we had another house mother who was just as good during my last two years.

Most of the girls had boyfriends, but they were from Denver. The fellows came up occasionally to visit or to bring girls back from weekends in Denver. For a long time there weren't any black boys on campus at all, period. My senior year, we had one or two. We had girls from Kansas. There was one named Marie Marshall from Kansas City. Gertrude Jett was another one. She was a little bitty shorty, but could play the piano like you wouldn't believe. She was from Kansas City, also. I don't remember the names of the others from Kansas. Ruth Beck played the piano, also. We had many happy times singing around the piano as Gertrude or Ruth played. Of course the Denver girls were, when I first went up there, Helen Adams and her friend Thelma Page. They were buddies who had grown up together. Thelma's folks had a restaurant down on the Points in Denver. Of course, Eleanor Hawkins was there. She and I were roommates. We'd been friends since junior high school. There was a girl from Cheyenne, Dorothy Forbush who was a delight to know. I had met Dorothy at church conferences. [1]

Living in this house with the variety of personalities during my four years in Greeley, I learned many valuable life lessons: living *peacefully* with varied personalities, taking criticism graciously, the joy of sharing, working cooperatively with others, being accepted for being myself, and many other attributes of value. These were lessons I could not have learned in the classroom!

In the early 1930's, we lived through the awful Dust Bowl era. For months there was no rain, and the wind across the prairies whipped the fine dry dust into the air in Greeley. It hung suspended, so thick that the sunshine filtering through cast an eerie glow over all. In our long walk to the campus, we had to cover our noses and mouths with handkerchiefs or scarves to avoid breathing in the dust. Keeping the house dust-free was impossible because it was so fine that it just seeped in. What a relief when the rains finally came and cleared the air!

*For me, what I was told I could not do on campus didn't matter, I got into the Physical Education Department and that's one place if you are good nobody cares what color you are. I just became a part of the Physical Ed Department even though my major was Kindergarten Primary. I took theory courses. I was on all the teams. I was back with my beloved sports.

They had a meeting of the Women's Athletic Association and I didn't go because I wasn't supposed to be in any clubs. Let me tell you, the next day after that meeting those girls wanted to know, "Where were you? We thought you would be at the meeting." I couldn't tell them that I didn't think I belonged. I had an excuse. I said I thought it was for majors and I was only a P.E. minor. I became vice-president of the Women's Athletic association my senior year. [1]

One year my teammates asked if I could swim. Of course, I was pleasantly surprised. However, when I signed up for the swim team I was told by the head of the department that I would not be permitted in the pool. She gave the same excuses that I had heard at Morey, even

---

[1]* excerpt taken from Trail Blazers Oral History Series transcript, courtesy of Denver Public Library, Blair-Caldwell

though we were now young adults.

*I had forty-two hours of physical education. Six more and I would have had another major. Even the head of the department, Jean Cave, thought that I was a major. She called me in spring quarter of my senior year to check my credits. I told her that I saw the notice on the bulletin board, but it said "majors" and I was just a "minor." She said, "You're not a major? You're in all the classes." I ran sports tournaments. I did everything. I was in assembly programs which was unheard of for us. Only through the Phys Ed Department could I have had this experience.

One of the highlights of the programs I was in was the final performance put on by my Interpretive Dance class winter quarter of my senior year. We worked hard on many dances, but the main production was dancing the story of _La Enfanta._ The two main characters were the Spanish princess and the deformed dwarf who fell in love with her. _The Enfanta,_ the princess, was Frances Blaur, whom I had known in sports at West High. She was a Phys. Ed. Major and we had renewed our friendship. To my surprise, I was asked to dance the dwarf! The rehearsals were a riot and the program was a success!

*That was my big one. My experience in college was a very pleasant one because of my Physical Education and sports.

When I checked my credits for graduation with my wonderful counselor, Annie McCowen, I was surprised to find that along with my Kindergarten Primary major, I had three minors – Phys. Ed., Art and Science! I always took "overload" so I could learn as much as possible while I had the opportunity, but I was amazed to find out what I had achieved. One of my prize art classes was Book Binding in which I was able to put a hard, leather embossed cover on my paperback high school _Westward Ho!_Annual! (I was on the West High Annual Board in 1930-31. We could not afford a hard cover during the Big Depression). I am still proud of that Annual.

June 8, 1935 was graduation day, and it was the thrill of my life to be able to don my cap and gown. I was so proud to receive my diploma that I wanted to cry – Bachelor of Arts in Kindergarten Primary Education!!! Most of all, I knew how proud my parents were.

While I was holding my diploma, I suddenly realized that all of the education I had acquired was only a "drop in the ocean" compared with what I would have to learn in the unknown world which I was about to face. It was scary! I have no idea why I had that thought, but <u>by the Grace of God</u>, I have never forgotten it. I have been learning all my life. I am still learning!!!

Marie (center) with college friends, Eleanor Hawkins (left) & Helen Adams (right)

Marie's college graduation, 1935; with best friend Eleanor Hawkins

Gunter Hall, Colorado State Teacher's College

Marie and mother, Sarah Anderson

CHAPTER 4

My Early Career and Other Activities

After many years of requests from the Black community to the Denver Public School board of Education to hire minority teachers, in 1934 Lila O'Boyle, principal of Whittier Elementary School announced that she would be happy to accept a "Colored" teacher on her faculty. Whittier School was in the center of the African-American Community. Miss O'Boyle had been a strong influence in the Denver Public Schools for so many years that School Board members listened to her and granted her request.

*In the spring of 1934, Mr. William Parks (who was a community leader and Sunday School Superintendent of Shorter), and Rev. Russell Brown (my minister) had approached me to take the test to apply for teaching. In those days, Denver Public Schools had two tests. You went in for an oral test and a written test. The applicants were divided into two groups, half would be doing the oral and half would be doing the written, in the morning. Then they would switch in the afternoon. They would be there all day. I qualified since I had earned my Life Certificate to teach in Colorado after I completed two years training at Colorado Teachers College.

I said, "No." It took me a long time to make the decision because my folks had worked so hard. My mother's health had gone downhill. It was hard for me to say, "No" in 1934. I had another year until graduation and I had worked so hard for that little scholarship, I was determined to get my degree. I figured, "well, that's that." Fortunately since Lila O'Boyle had said that she would be willing to have a "Colored" faculty member, they hired Dorothy Burdine who was a Denver woman and had been teaching for many, many years in Oklahoma and Texas.

I found out later that she was not hired on contract. She was hired as a permanent substitute in the beginning. However, that kept the door open.

In 1935, that early spring, Mr. Parks and Rev. Brown were trying to persuade me again to take the test. I went to the administration building and I took the written test that morning. I had a wonderful oral test in the afternoon with Mr. Palmer. Mr. Palmer was a little gray-haired, pleasant, elderly, pink-faced man, and as I walked into his office he greeted me very nicely. He wanted to know why I wanted to teach in elementary school. I gave him my reasons: because I always wanted to teach small children and laying the foundation at an early age was the important thing.

"Well, suppose you went to secondary school and taught in junior or senior high school," he said.

He knew we couldn't teach in those schools. Whittier was the only school open to us. Mr. Palmer was just testing me. In those days the salary in secondary schools was much more than that for elementary teachers. He said, "You'd make more money."

I just forgot everything. I said, "No. those teachers in junior and senior high school couldn't do anything with the children if we didn't lay a foundation in elementary school for them to work with. That is most important, right in the beginning!" I was wound up and I just went on telling my theories of education. He never said a word. I thought to myself, "Oh, Marie, you blew it again. You talk too much."

Then Mr. Palmer broke into the biggest grin and said, "You know, I'm with you." What a relief!!!

By and large I'm a very optimistic soul, and most of the time I'm happy, but I was depressed. My mother was worried about me. We had no money. Not even enough to buy stationary and three cent stamps (postage in 1930's) to send for applications for jobs. I did not expect to be hired in the Denver Public Schools since I had turned down the opportunity in 1934.

One day, approximately a week after taking the tests, I was sitting in the apartment at my wit's end. I just didn't know what I was going to do. I brought the mail in and here was this letter from the Denver Public Schools. I thought, "Oh, oh, this is it." I expected if they had ONE teacher of Color, they weren't going to hire me. In my devastated state of mind I could not face a letter of rejection. I don't know how long it took me to muster the courage to open this announcement. I finally, slowly opened it and this is what I read:

June 13, 1935

My Dear Miss Anderson,

At the regular meeting of the Board of Education on June 12, 1935, your

Probational appointment was approved, effective September 1, 1935.

Yours very truly,

R.A. Puffer

Enclosed was a pink probation appointment card appointing Miss Marie Louise Anderson to a position as a teacher in the Denver Public Schools for an annual salary of $1200.00 effective from September 1, 1935 to September 1, 1936.

They had selected me as a teacher at Whittier School!!!! I still have the letter and appointment notice. I let out a war whoop and my poor mother who was in the kitchen came out rushing. She knew how bad I had been feeling. "What's the matter?" she asked. She thought something had happened to me. I was crying and I showed her the mail. I was going to have a contract to teach for twelve hundred dollars a year; one hundred dollars a month. In 1935 that went a long way and when you don't have anything, it's a fortune! I just could hardly believe it!

The next thing I did when I hadn't even started the job yet, was to go looking for a house for my folks to get my mother out of that basement and get my parents out of that awful drudgery of being custodians in the apartment.

My friend Eleanor told me that the house next door to her family was vacant. I checked it out and we moved in before I started teaching. By the time I started school in September, I had them in that house. My dad and I shared the expenses.

I had been over to Whittier, of course, and talked with the principal, Lila O'Boyle. I found out I was to teach first grade. Kindergarten was what I expected to teach and that's what I thought I would have, but I was assigned to first grade which was all right with me because it was still the primary level that I wanted to teach.

I had not had a day of student teaching. I got an "A" in student teaching and had never taught a day. I'd made excellent lesson plans and then sat in the kindergarten and watched somebody else teach my plans. Because of my color, in Greeley I was not permitted to actually teach a class. All I had witnessed was a class limited to twenty-five little children whose IQ's were a hundred or more. In the campus training school they would not take a child whose IQ was under a hundred.

So where was all this ideal teaching environment that I expected? I had been taught in all my theory classes that you use a soft voice and gentle control. At Whittier, I received a class of almost thirty children. I had one little boy with an IQ of 65 and they went up to children with IQ's of 110. I had all this variety of youngsters who came from all types of homes. Some of them weren't used to being spoken to with that nice soft voice. I didn't know what to do with them.

My first few weeks were MURDER! On top of everything else, Miss O'Boyle had me in a room next to Dorothy Burdine. I knew why she did it. Dorothy had a third grade and I'm sure Miss O'Boyle thought Dorothy was going to help me. She was no help at all. I did not know what to do with those children. I tried every technique that I had been taught, but it didn't work. You would open the door and the noise would blow you right out into the hall.

Several times I went into Dorothy's room and asked her for help, but all I got was a look down her nose at little five-foot me and say, "Why, girl, don't you know?" If I knew what to do I would not have asked!

There were two teachers who did everything they could to be of help. Geraldine Tracewell, head teacher, went out of her way to keep me informed of school rules and activities. Mary Schurmann, first grade teacher and positive disciplinarian, gave me suggestions, but I still had problems. However, I appreciated knowing that someone cared! I felt I was a failure for the first time in my life!!!

One day Miss O'Boyle walked in and I didn't think she would get in the door it was so noisy. I was trying and I guess by that time my voice was up in "high C" or somewhere. She didn't say anything at first. She quietly came over to me and said, "Miss Anderson, I will see you after school in my office." I thought, "Here goes my job."

When I entered her office, she said, "You've got to get control. You can't teach anything until you get control." She was one stern, person.

I said, "I'm doing what I was taught."

She said, "You do whatever it takes! Forget the theory! You do whatever it takes to get control and don't worry about teaching, because when you get control you can teach."

I said, "You mean *do whatever it takes*?" I said it just like that.

"Whatever it takes!" was her answer. I was surprised!

That was on Friday. I spent the weekend thinking about what to do. I didn't sleep very much those nights but the wheels were going around in my mind. I remembered how my mother had disciplined me. By the time Monday rolled around those little kids didn't know what had happened to Miss Anderson. Miss Anderson hit that classroom with determination to get control. I made it very clear that work would be done quietly; I expected to have everyone's attention; and, there would be serious consequences for misbehavior! There was very little teaching that day. I got control of my class and from then on I began to teach – the joy of my life!!!

The little boy with the 65 IQ would walk up on the desk. Speaking to him didn't do any good. On this Monday I grabbed that little boy, sat him down and told him he was going to stay in his seat. In those days you could grab kids. You could "pop" them if you had to. I really felt sorry for some of the little children because I had some nice little children in my class. They were not a part of the discipline problem.

Little IQ 65 got so that, finally, he'd take one look at me and wouldn't move out of his seat. He learned to go ahead and color instead of scribbling all over the paper. He couldn't stay in the lines, but he was trying. I learned something from this little boy that has been my philosophy all through my teaching: **every child can learn something.** I don't care what. Now that little child may not have had the ability to really do much reading or writing, but he learned to control himself. He learned that when he was given something to do that he could do, to go on and try to do it. I lost little IQ 65 when they moved. To tell the truth, it was a kind of mixed blessing because he was beginning to show some learning ability.

It wasn't long after that when Miss O'Boyle came in. I had the door open. She smiled. She told the children how nice they were and she looked at me and smiled.

Many of the "light-skinned" parents did not want their children to attend Whittier. When I first started teaching, some of these people didn't want their children to have a black teacher, although Whittier students were practically all black. When they hired this black first grade teacher, they didn't want their children in my room. But it wasn't too many months after I began teaching that I had parents asking to have their children put in my class because I was doing so much for the community as I helped their children to learn. [1]

My last encounter with Dorothy Burdine happened after Miss O'Boyle announced her plan to have an evening faculty party. Apparently she had one every year or two at a hotel or restaurant. This would be my first. In those days all parties were dress up, but I was not sure whether it would be formal or not.

I had been thinking about asking, but I did not feel comfortable asking the white teachers. So when Dorothy and I happened to be in the office checking out one day after school, I very quietly said to her, "What is being worn at the party on Saturday."

She replied in a loud voice that everyone could hear, "Why, don't you know that you wear long dress after five?!" I knew that was usually the rule for our parties in the 30's, but I did not know about the faculty party of just women. I was so embarrassed that I never, ever asked

---

[1]* excerpt taken from Trail Blazers Oral History Series transcript, courtesy of Denver Public Library, Blair-Caldwell

Dorothy another question and I only spoke to her pleasantly when necessary.

The party was where Miss O'Boyle lived, the Argonaut Hotel and Apartments, across from the Capital on the corner of Colfax and Grant Street. The apartments had a private entrance (on Grant Street) away from the hotel entrance (on Colfax). Our faculty affair was in a nice little quiet party room.

I wore my long dress and felt at ease since the teachers were, also, dressed in evening wear. There was food and drinks – even wine! We sang around the piano as Dorothy, or the music teacher, played familiar songs. We played simple games, told humorous experiences and stories, relaxed and laughed. To my surprise, I found out that Lila O'Boyle actually had a great sense of humor – a complete, happy reversal from the positive principal that we knew at school! This was a wonderful bonding experience for me. I felt that I had been accepted as the youngest, inexperienced faculty member and I really belonged at Whittier!

One of the times that Miss O'Boyle decided to have a faculty luncheon, she had to check with restaurants down town. When she went to the Denver Dry Goods' lovely, well-known Tea Room she was greeted with open arms until she told them that she had two teachers of color on her faculty. The reception cooled down and she was told that they could only serve her faculty if we were not included.

Lila O'Boyle was furious! She walked out and said she would never set foot in the Denver Dry Goods Tea Room again!

She went to the expensive Daniels and Fisher Department Store where there was a special, exclusive dining room used mostly by the wealthy socialites. Again, she was welcomed warmly, but this time when she told them that two of her teachers were Colored, she was told there would be no problem. Since we were a part of the faculty we would be served with the group.

In the 30's, that was one of the biggest breaks in discrimination. However, no one knew anything about it, but us!

My father could hardly believe that I would be eating in Daniels and Fisher's beautiful diner up in the Tower while he was downstairs doing his job as a custodian. He was so proud of me!

From my experience with Dorothy I learned a valuable lesson. I vowed that I would always help those who needed help – especially beginning teachers!

Fortunately my second year Miss O'Boyle moved me to a larger room across from the office. I heard some of the teachers talking about being invited to Dorothy's home and seeing the wonderful appliances she had installed for her parents. She was always talking with the teachers and bragging about what she had acquired, and what she was doing.

I learned to keep my professional teaching experience separate from my personal activities. In those days there was still "Black Society" and "White Society," and they did not mix. It was expedient to be careful what you did, where you were seen and with whom you associated. I was determined to keep my record clear so there would be no question when there was a professional evaluation of my qualifications as a teacher.

In June of 1937, I assumed that Dorothy had received her tenure since she had been teaching for three years. I was surprised in the Fall, to hear rumors that Miss Burdine would not receive tenure in the Denver Public Schools in December. She had been hired as a permanent substitute in 1934 and only received a contract as a "probationary" teacher in December of that year. I was amazed because I had been hired directly on contract and was going into my third and last year of probation.

Lila O'Boyle knew everyone in the community and she knew everything that was happening. She was not pleased with some of the things Dorothy was saying and doing, or with her attitude of superiority. Therefore, Miss O'Boyle refused to sign her certificate of tenure. Dorothy was told she would have another semester to prove herself qualified; that would be spring of 1938.

Dorothy was furious! She went through the community talking about the unfairness of the Whittier principal and the D.P.S. School

Board. She even made the statement that Marie Anderson need not feel secure because she would not make it either!

After Miss O'Boyle heard about that statement, she called me out of my room one day to tell me not to worry about the rumors I was hearing about Miss Burdine because I was going to make it – just say nothing about it!! Coming from Lila O'Boyle, that was a great compliment!

In the Spring of 1938, just before school was out, I received my tenure contract as a permanent teacher in the Denver Public Schools. Dorothy Burdine went back to Texas to teach.

I had achieved my goal of keeping my job and holding the door open for others to come in. That Fall two more of "our" teachers were hired to teach at Whittier, Eleanor Hawkins was given a probationary contract to teach second grade; and, Elaine Brown (my minister's daughter) was placed in fifth grade as a permanent substitute. (D.P.S. would grant only ONE contract!) Elaine did receive her probationary contract in December.

In 1937, while I was still on probation, I heard about the Denver Teachers Chorus. I told Miss O'Boyle that I loved music, sang in my church choir and would like to join the Teachers Chorus. She told me to go ahead and sign up for it.

I arrived early on my first day of rehearsal at Morey Junior High School music room. There were two white-haired ladies there ahead of me. They ignored me and continued visiting. As other teachers came in, they looked at me but said nothing.

The highly respected director of the D.P.S. Music Department was John Roberts. When he came in, he greeted everyone with a flourish, and to my astonishment he welcomed me by name, introduced me to the group and said how glad he was to have me join the Teachers Chorus. The only way he could have known who I was would have been because Miss O'Boyle must have let him know that Miss Marie Anderson, a

Colored teacher, would be joining the Chorus. John Roberts made me feel free of discrimination and it eased the tension of my questionable acceptance by the members of the Chorus!

I found out that the white-haired members were really retirees who had been with the group since its original organization. It took them a while to warm up to me, but since they adored John Roberts they had no other choice but to accept me.

I am a first soprano and I thoroughly enjoyed singing the beautiful music which Mr. Roberts explained to us; and, he actually made rehearsals a lot of fun. We sang for radio broadcasts and each Spring we had a full concert for the Louise Sherret Welfare Fund.

Singing with the Denver Teachers Chorus was so stimulating and rewarding that I hated to see it disband after so many years of activity. John Roberts had assumed so much more responsibility with the growth in the Denver Public Schools that his time was limited and membership in the Chorus had decreased. We sang a last concert and ended the Denver Teachers Chorus.

Years later, when John Roberts was retiring, I received a call for a meeting of the Chorus! The members were to meet with him and I thought it was just a retirement farewell. We met at West High School, which seemed odd, until on arrival I was told that we were to plan for a final concert with Mr. Roberts and we would be performing in the West High auditorium.

It was amazing how many members showed up and how great it was to see each other, to learn what changes had occurred in our lives. We not only looked different and older, but we really hoped our voices would hold up.

The big surprise was when John Roberts told us we would be singing _The Mikado_!!! The rehearsals were hilarious with our mistakes and getting our harmony back together again. As usual, Mr. Roberts laughed with us and guided us through with his expert direction.

The night of the concert found us quite nervous, but thrilled. The production was a huge success and a great final tribute to the retiring John Roberts, one of Denver Public Schools' greatest Directors of

Music!

I remained active in the Denver Public Schools and in the community. I was secretary of Whittier P.T.A. As Denver Teachers Club representative, I collected money for Denver Teachers Club (which provides wheelchairs and other equipment on loan to D.P.S. employees and their families) and attended meetings.

In 1939, I was a Whittier representative at the Community Chest luncheon held at the Shirley Savoy Hotel. For the first time **I** was permitted to enter through the **front** door.

At the Progressive Education Conference, in 1940, I was a discussion group leader on the topic "Natural Resources of Colorado." Eventually, the School Board realized that Elementary School Teachers were an essential part of the school system and decided to equalize the pay schedule so that the rules were the same for **all** teachers! It meant that we Elementary teachers were allotted a raise that equaled the salary of Junior High and Senior High School teachers – at last!!!

The next good news was the removal of the ban on the marriage of women teachers. It was amazing how many D.P.S. teachers revealed that they were already secretly married. Two of our teachers at Whittier had been married for years!! This was the early 1940's. The biggest blow came soon after when the School Board set the definite retirement age at sixty-five. Until then, one could remain a teacher, principal, administrator or any worker in the Denver Public Schools indefinitely. This hit Lila O'Boyle and at least four of our teachers who had been at Whittier for many, many years and were far past sixty-five.

For Lila O'Boyle retirement was extremely traumatic. She had no family and lived alone. Her whole life was centered around being principal of Whittier and Gilpin Schools. Fortunately, the School Board allotted one or two years for these older retirees to make adjustments in their lives. Unfortunately, we lost track of Miss O'Boyle, but I will always remember Lila O'Boyle as the principal who opened the door for us minorities to teach in the Denver Public Schools.

Whittier School continued academically strong with another experienced principal who was a little more lenient.

Whittier Elementary School, circa1930's

Whittier Faculty, Marie (black dress) - 1st row, 2nd from right; Eleanor Hawkins – 1st row, 3rd from right; Lila O'Boyle, top row, 1st on left.

I remained active in my church: teaching Sunday School, working with young people in Christian Endeavor, serving meals at special activities, driving groups to varied activities and singing in the choir. <u>By the Grace of God</u>, I was truly blessed!

I was pleased when my mother joined Shorter during my teenage activities. She made friends and joined the Gospel Choir. This was a small group of friendly senior ladies who got together to sing beautiful old spirituals. My mother had a lovely soprano voice and thoroughly enjoyed this companionship. Once a month they would sing a number at church.

My mother, however, still kept in touch with her New Hope Baptist friends and participated in many of their activities. This taught me a valuable, basic lesson in philosophy: don't discard the old for the new, just add the new to the old! She did not drive, so I or my dad would be sure to take her to church, or wherever she wanted to go. I had bought another car. A little brown Ford sedan. It was a real luxury from the open air touring car that one of my college roommates had named "Pneumonia Wagon." My father joined Shorter, eventually, but he attended only on special occasions.

In 1937, Mrs. Price and Mrs. Fant asked me if I would be interested in joining Coterie. I had never heard of it and I was not interested in joining a social club. They explained that this was purely a study group that had been organized in 1915 by a few dedicated women to keep their minds active through study of the arts, drama, history, classic literature and ethnic writings. The membership was limited to only twenty ladies. There was an opening and I was invited to join this unique club. Of course, I accepted and became a fascinated member.

Coterie met once a month every third Saturday, September through May, at the Phyllis Wheatley branch Y.W.C.A. There was a closing luncheon in June to which guests were invited.

At every meeting we were dressed up as though going to church. Meetings started <u>on time</u>. If you were five minutes late, nothing was said, but the looks could freeze you, so being on time was a priority. Excuses for not attending were purely for emergencies, and must be given to the President or Secretary ahead of time, if possible.

I was an active member until 1949, when my family was growing. I resigned with the request that I be considered for membership again when my children were older.

Twenty years later, in 1969, I was accepted again as a Coterie member on the death of Mrs. Josephine Price. This was a special honor for me to return to Coterie to replace one of the most beloved, special friends I have ever known!

I continued volunteering at Phyllis Wheatley Branch Y.W.C.A. I became a Girl Reserve Advisor, a representative at Y.W.C.A. National Summer Conference, remained a counselor of the Phyllis Wheatley Camp Nizhoni, and became a member of the Phyllis Wheatley Committee of Management.

In the late 1940's, the Board of Directors of the main Y.W.C.A. realized that it was time to include a representative from Phyllis Wheatley. We had always been treated as a separate unit. Addie Lightner, from our Committee of Management was selected. To my amazement, a year later I was asked to join the Board along with Mrs. Lightner. My next surprise was being asked to assume the position of secretary! When I asked why, I was told that Mrs. Lightner recommended me since I had been secretary for the Committee of Management at Phyllis Wheatley. The secretary for the Board of Directors had resigned, so I accepted.

When I received the secretary's ledger I could not believe what I read – the most inadequate, poorly written minutes I had ever witnessed!!! My minutes were always complete.

After the first few meetings I took the ledger and my notes home with me to write the complete minutes, but I was so busy with my family that I had a problem finding time to get them written. I decided to try to write the minutes during the meeting. I would listen to the discussion, take notes on a pad and write the information in the ledger during logical breaks. Fortunately, I have always been able to do more than one thing at a time, but with this concentrated effort, I had little time to participate in the meeting vocally. At the end of the meeting, however, the minutes were complete.

The first time I gave the book to the president she said, "Oh, you can take it home and write it up."

I replied, "The minutes are all finished."

She looked at me in surprise, opened the book and saw the completely written information. "This is hard to believe!" she said. "How did you do it?!"

I was a member of the Cosmopolitan Club, an interracial group dedicated to breaking down segregation in Denver in the 1940's. We could enter a hotel only as an employee through the back door. A brown face would not be served in any restaurant, not even at the counter in Woolworth. Some theaters would not admit us. Those that did had a corner in the balcony section reserved for us, if there was enough room. We were banned from buying property or living in certain sections of Denver.

Members of the Cosmopolitan Club somehow unearthed an old, buried, forgotten, Colorado law that stated there would be no racist discrimination in public places or businesses in Colorado.

Based on this law, Cosmopolitan Club members would enter a restaurant as a group to be told that the white members would be served, but not the black members. The group would leave and file suit against the eatery. The law would be invoked and the Restaurant Association would be charged. After a time with charges being filed against one restaurant after another, the Association made it clear to its members that there would be no more discrimination or their membership would be cancelled.

The famous Blue Parrot Inn on Broadway across from the Brown

Palace Hotel was the last to give in when we entered there, and it was faced with losing its Restaurant Association membership.

Realtors reluctantly opened up houses for sale or rent in some of the all white areas. Many hotels opened their doors to us.

The theaters eliminated the seating ban, and we could sit where we wanted to. We were permitted to attend all theaters.

With all these avenues opening up to us, there was no "flood" of minorities pouring into the restaurants or moving into exclusive residential areas. The Cosmopolitan Club achieved its purpose of breaking down barriers of discrimination so that we had the **privilege of choosing** where to eat, where to go, or where to live, just like any other citizen. Most African-Americans preferred to be near their own. Many could not afford the expensive hotels, restaurants, and homes, but it was consoling to know that the doors were open.

In 1940, skiing was becoming quite a popular activity. Since I no longer had the opportunity to participate in sports, it sounded like a chance to do something I had never done before. I joined a ski class at the Y.W.C.A. where we were taught elementary safety basics of "snow plow" and "stem turn." The exercises were great and I discovered I had to tone up a few muscles I had not used for a while!

In those days, Berthoud Pass was the skiing mecca. If there was enough snow, we rented a bus, and the class was excited in anticipating actually getting on the slope. One time about half way up to Berthoud, our bus got stuck in the snow. By the time it was released, it was too late to continue on to the Pass. A very disappointed ski class returned to Denver.

Later, I decided to drive up to the ski area with my limited knowledge of dry land instruction. My father did not want me to go alone, so he went with me and visited with people in the warming house while I tried out my rented skis on the beginner's slope.

I finally learned how to hang on to the rope tow and get off without falling down. I spent most of the time picking myself up out of the snow as I came down the slope (until I managed to get control of the snow plow position with my skis). I drove up to Berthoud Pass several times during that winter and became a snow plow, stem turn expert on the beginner's slope!!

I don't know how I handled those six-foot long wooden skis with the leather boots securely fastened on with metal toe holds and ankle straps. I am only five feet tall! There was no safety release. If there were an accident, either you broke or the skis broke!

Several times I fell in such a manner that I could feel my ankle pull out of joint and then snap back in. It would hurt, but it did not break, as I had seen happen with other skiers. I would usually go to school with an aching, swollen ankle for a few days. Someone told me I must be double-jointed. Some of the teachers and some of my friends were concerned about my safety and my sanity, being the only black woman in Denver participating in this wild sport. I loved every minute of it!!!

When I told my friend, Bill Greenwood, about my love of skiing and how I wished I had someone to go with me, he said his cousin, Bryce Parks, was a skier and maybe I could go with him. Bryce was seventeen years old and in high school. Bill told him about me and Bryce called to tell me he would be glad to take me if it was all right with the other boys. I told him I would help pay for gas and I just wanted a ride so I would not have to drive again.

When Bryce called back, he said it was okay and they would pick me up at eight o'clock on Saturday morning. I was ready when they came, so away we went. There was only one other boy with Bryce that day; they rode up front and I rode in the back.

As we drove along, they were very quiet at first, then one said something in a whisper that made them laugh. I could tell they were holding back on their usual jokes and teenage laughter, so I spoke up, "Don't mind me; go on and have your fun. I am a teacher only at school in my classroom. Right now, I am just another person going up to Berthoud to ski." That eased things quite a bit. They occasionally became a bit loud, but they were once again their own relaxed selves.

When we arrived at Berthoud Pass, I told the fellows to go on and ski wherever they wanted because I would be on the beginner's slope. As time went on, I became a regular passenger with those high school boys. Sometimes there would be four of them. I decided to pay for half the gas and would make a box full of sandwiches. Of course, I took my sandwich out first because those guys would finish off every crumb. One fellow worked at a drug store and he would bring cans of pop. They would bury the pop in the snow bank by the car. We would agree to a time for me to meet them back at the car for lunch.

One day when I arrived for lunch the car was gone. I waited and waited, but no one showed up, so I went into the warming house. After nearly an hour, I saw the car return. I rushed out and told them how worried I had been. I even thought they might have left me!! The boys apologized, and assured me they would never leave me.

Bryce explained that three of them had gone down Hell's Half Acre, and then decided to continue down Seven Mile Trail. The fourth fellow drove down to pick them up, but it had taken much longer than they had expected. They were usually picked up at the end of Hell's Half Acre. I had never heard of either one, so Bryce explained that it was a run down the other side of Berthoud Pass that dropped another fifteen hundred feet, and that is where they were usually picked up. This was the first time they had continued on The Trail. We had our lunch, but by then it was so late in the afternoon we headed for home.

The boys were laughing and talking about how much fun they had, so I asked what was Hell's Half Acre like. If it wasn't too difficult, I would like to try it since I had only skied the beginner's slope and was doing very well. The boys looked at each other, then Bryce said, "I think you could make it."

On our next trip Bryce said to me, "We're going down Hell's Half Acre today. Do you want to go?"

"Sure," I said. "Just let me know when."

We spent some time on warm up runs, then headed for the adventure. As I looked down the narrow trail among the trees, there was a sharp turn where Bryce had skied down and was waiting for me. I made it and actually turned successfully. There were several zigzag turns half way down and with Bryce's help I got through them.

The rest was a straight run which I made with my snow plow control. The other boys had skied down and were waiting for Bryce and me. They even complimented me for my bravery. They didn't think I would make it! I was proud of my achievement.

The car was waiting to take us back up to the ski area at Berthoud, but I did not ski. I spent the rest of the time relaxing in the warming house. I was exhausted, but happy! The boys continued to ski.

After that experience, I skied down Hell's half Acre with the boys a number of times. I missed a turn once, plowed into the snow bank and pulled out only half of my right ski! I had to walk the rest of the way down.

Another time I planned to continue on down Seven Mile Trail with them. When we reached the bottom of Hell's Half Acre, one of the guys who had been behind us never showed up. After waiting a reasonable length of time, Bryce told the driver of the car to go back up and report an accident to the Ski Patrol. The other three boys and I went down Seven Mile Trail. That proved to be my biggest mistake. It was actually a snow covered hiker's trail so there were many stretches of walking. With my short legs and those six-foot long wooden skis, I had to stop often to rest. Bryce would wait for me and he sent the others on. I thanked Bryce for his thoughtfulness and I never took the Trail again. I would ride in the car after finishing Hell's Half Acre.

When we got back to Berthoud Pass, we found out that the Ski Patrol had brought our skier back with a broken leg. They had taken excellent care of him and splinted his leg, so we headed back to Denver.

I sent up my prayers of thanks to those high school boys who accepted me as a skiing partner. The ski areas were closed in the 1940's during World War II and thus ended my exciting skiing adventures!!! Twenty-five years later, I began skiing again.

Breckenridge
March 6, 1979

Skiing in Breckenridge

I continued using my vow to help those who needed help at school and in the community. When Jessie Maxwell came to Whittier as piano teacher, she would join Eleanor and me for lunch in my room on the days that she was there. She was a delightful, up-beat personality and we became good friends. She was working on her Education Degree at Denver University. She applied to the Denver Public Schools.

The kindergarten teacher, Vera Reichelt, became ill. She was one of the old teachers who was past sixty-five and would have to retire. (She had been Eleanor's kindergarten teacher!) Jessie Maxwell was called to substitute in this kindergarten. She came to me, frantically, saying, "Marie, I don't know what to do with little children and this is my first assignment!"

I said, "I have never been in Miss Reichelt's kindergarten, but we will go over and I will help you work out what to do with what we find in her room."

I explained how to work with young children using the equipment that we found. I helped her make out a possible schedule. I told her to feel free to ask me any questions at any time; I was just across the hall. We often laughed about this experience.

Jessie Maxwell did just fine. She became an excellent teacher and eventually was appointed as the first Black Principal in the Denver Public Schools at Whittier School!!

In the early 1940's, my mother received a letter from her baby sister, Esther Garrett, whom I had not seen since we were in Texas in 1925. She was planning to attend Denver University and asked to stay with us. In those days, schools in Texas were segregated, but the state would pay for students of color to attend a college or university outside of their state. Of course, my mother welcomed Esther to stay with us. I took her to social affairs and introduced her to my friends. I introduced her to Lester Nelson, which became a romance and they were married. Esther taught first grade at Whittier, became a coordinator and retired as principal of Barrett Elementary School.

CHAPTER 5
1939 Adventures

Mary E. Wood was such a great girl Reserve Secretary when she left Denver, she was assigned to Newark, New Jersey as the General Secretary over the Y.W.C.A.'s of that city – a first for minorities! "Woody" (our nickname for her) and I kept in touch with each other and told of our activities.

In the spring of 1939 Woody called me to tell me about their summer camp and wanted to know if I would be interested in being a counselor there. I told her to send me the information. This was the year of the World's Fair in New York and the prospects sounded exciting.

The camp was run by the Black branch of the Y.W.C.A.'s of New York City and Newark in the Catskill Mountains. This would be my first time back East, so Woody and I made plans for my big adventure of visiting New York, the Fair and spending the summer in a camp completely different from Nizhoni! The camp schedule was from the middle of June to the middle of August, so I left Denver soon after school was out about the first week of June. This gave Woody and me a week to renew our friendship and have fun before camp.

In 1939, travel was by train. I left Denver at 8:30 a.m. and changed trains in Chicago. My train for New York was late, so it was evening before I arrived at Pennsylvania Railroad Station where Woody was waiting to meet me. We then took a local train to Newark. By the time we reached Woody's apartment, I was exhausted. We talked and ate a bit, then I went to bed.

The next day we took it easy so I could get rested. She took me out to breakfast and introduced me to lox and bagels; I loved them. We drove through various communities and Woody told me bits of history of the areas.

When I asked, "All of this is Newark?" Woody laughed and said,

"No. We have been through several other towns." I couldn't believe it, because there was no space in between! Here in Colorado I always knew one town from another because they were always separated by a barren area.

I was really excited when Woody said we were going to New York City! We took the train to Penn Station and then the subway. I was amazed at the train system, the shopping areas and the vast number of people all underground!!! When we came above ground in Times Square, the traffic noise, the theaters, the hustling people and the immense skyscrapers were awesome!

Woody had told me earlier that she would not be able to go to camp with me, as we had originally planned. The day that I was to leave for camp she was leaving for Buffalo, New York. She had been asked to serve on the National Board of Directors of the Y.W.C.A., another first. Therefore, she was making sure that I knew how to get around on the complicated New York transportation system, the subway. She did not know where she would be when I returned from camp.

Almost every day during that week we went into New York City. We went to the fabulous Radio City Music Hall and witnessed the famous Rockettes. _The Wizard of Oz_ had recently premiered and we happened to attend on a day that Judy Garland and Mickey Rooney appeared in person.

Woody introduced me to the Automat where you bought your food from a wall of tiny compartments. Amazing!

The most exciting experience of all was the day we spent at the World's Fair. The huge Trylon and Perisphere were awe inspiring. I saw my first unbelievable black and white, grainy television on which we watched parts of a champion boxing fight; I think it was Max Schmeling and Joe Louis. We spent the day taking in everything that we could. We walked until we were so tired we could walk no more. By nighttime, we finally went happily home.

Woody was not pleased with the Camp Director who had been selected by the New York Y.W.C.A. branch. She was a young woman who had no camping experience and was planning to get married.

She had an uncle on the New York Board and he had influenced the committee to hire her. Woody clued me in to as much advance information as possible.

Woody gave me a key to her apartment so I would have a place to stay (if she were away when I returned from camp). She informed the manager so I would have no problem.

On the day that we were leaving, Woody took me to where I was to depart by bus and she left for Buffalo. There was quite a group of us. At my age, and with my years of experience, they all seemed so young. The Director was involved with her wedding plans and would not be at camp for the first few days!

The first night, after dinner, we gathered together in one of the cabins to get acquainted. There were several junior counselors from various areas of New York, seventeen and eighteen- year-old girls. Some of them had been to camp before. There were three of us Activity Counselors: Fannie Moten (from Washington, D.C.) who was a senior Physical Education major at Howard University and had been to this camp before in charge of the Waterfront and Swimming, Jeanne Critchlow (from Charleston, West Virginia), who was a sophomore at West Virginia State College. I don't remember what her expertise was, I was Nature Counselor. As the teenagers introduced themselves, there was a lot of giggling and telling funny stories about what they did.

Fannie told about experiences of her previous two years at this camp. She was twenty years old and looking forward to graduation from Howard, then eventually marrying her boyfriend, Emerson Williams, who was the son of her minister.

Jeanne did not have much to say, except that she would be entering her sophomore year at West Virginia State and this was her first camping experience. She was nineteen years old.

When I started to talk, everyone got dead silent. I couldn't figure out why. I told them that I had been teaching for four years. I was twenty-six years old and had been Nature Counselor at our Y.W.C.A. camp in Colorado for many years. I found out later why the meeting ended quietly and we all went to our cabins. They thought my speaking was "put on."

The second day went by and there was no Director. The cook was a nice elderly woman and she was getting concerned. She and the Director had rooms in the big building that served as a dining room and a recreation hall.

The young children were due to arrive the next day, so I decided to get my clothes washed beforehand. There was a separate laundry room with necessary equipment. I could see that I was going to be a "loner," because those young people avoided contact with me. While I was washing my clothes I was quietly singing songs of my state, "Dreaming of Colorado," "Oh, Colorado," "Beautiful Colorado" and "America, the Beautiful." I really was feeling a bit lonely.

I was surprised when Fannie came in. She noticed that I was all alone so she stopped in to say "Hi." She told me about her former experiences here at camp and I told her about Camp Nizhoni.

We laughed and Fannie, said, "You have an accent and the girls think you are just putting on."

"I don't have an accent," I said. "This is just the way I talk."

Fannie grinned and replied, "I can see that is the way you talk, but you sound different. The gals had said, 'Give her time and she will be talking like us!'"

Al I could say was, "I guess I do sound different because all of you have Southern accents, but I live out West so I guess I have a Western accent." I really had never thought of it before.

The children arrived and fortunately the girls had lists of those who would be their charges, and in which cabins. There was still no Director, no plans and no schedule of activities. It was one wild, disorganized confusion. I hesitated to do anything since I was not in charge.

One evening the children and the teenage counselors were so wild and noisy that the cook was upset. I had had enough, so I called out, but they could not hear my voice. That did it! I yelled, "QUIET!" Everybody stopped and looked at me. I told them they were acting like wild animals and we were going to have no more of it.

I told the young counselors to take their children quietly to their cabins and get them bedded down. I was to hear no sound out of any of them. When I heard loud talking in one of the cabins, I went in and chewed them out. I told the young counselors to return to the main hall within half an hour after settling the children.

I did not know what the staff thought of me and I didn't care. I let them know that since the Director was not there, we were going to delegate responsibility and follow a schedule of activities under strict supervision. Together we worked out a program schedule and I set down rules of discipline and responsibilities.

I was not sure how to go about my assignment as Nature Counselor. I knew all about nature in Colorado from my years at Nizhoni, but I discovered that I knew very little about birds, plants, trees, animals and insects found in East Coast nature. I did the best I could with my limited knowledge for a few days until I found some books on Nature in the main building. I learned that there are several kinds of oak and maple trees and how to identify them. There were evergreens I never heard of, and plants, insects and animals we never see in our high altitude. I was fascinated with what I was learning so that I would be the kind of Nature Counselor I had always been, and could pass on to the children correct information

When the Director finally arrived one afternoon after five days' absence, I could not believe what I saw. She was small, about my height, young, dressed in a pretty yellow sun dress and high heeled shoes! She was so wrapped up in her wedding plans that she really was not interested in camp. She immediately closed herself up in her room and did not come out until almost dinner time. When she finally appeared, I clued her in on what was going on. None of it really registered with her, but she thanked me for what I had done.

I had pulled a real "boner" after organizing and emphasizing "follow the rules." I neglected to check with Fannie as to the rules for swimming in the lake. The day I decided to swim was a warm, sunny afternoon after I had finished with my nature groups. I swam near the dock where Fannie had her class. I soon got bored with the splashing children, so I swam off into the lake alone. It was a long, narrow, calm body of water bordered by trees. I decided to find out what was at the far end of the lake, so I went leisurely swimming away.

After a few minutes, I heard someone yelling, but I kept on swimming until I heard a splashing sound. I looked over my shoulder to see Fannie coming toward me in a boat. She was furious!

"You have no business swimming out into this lake like this. It is dangerous," she yelled. "This lake flows over an embankment and into the river below, and we could have lost you! I called to you, but you didn't stop."

I felt terrible at putting myself in danger and stupid for causing such thoughtless trouble. "I heard a call, but I thought it was part of the children that I heard having fun," I said. "I am so sorry. Thank you for saving me."

Fannie said, "You can get in the boat."

"No thank you," I answered. "I'll swim back."

Later that day, during rest period, Fannie asked me if I would like to join her and Jeanne away from the crowd. I was pleasantly surprised and said, "Yes." Fannie had taken Jeanne under her wing to help her adjust to camp.

I was surprised, again, when we went down to the dock and got in the boat. Fannie said we were going to row to the far side of the lake where it was nice and quiet and relax. She brought her little wind-up record player and some records. Fannie rowed to a shady spot and we stretched out in the boat as it gently rocked in the water.

I apologized to Fannie again for causing her so much worry and told her how stupid I felt. She let me know how upset she had been and how surprised she was to see that I could swim. However, it was all over and we were going to enjoy ourselves.

Fannie's records were Ella Fitzgerald's recordings. She and Jeanne know all about Ella and her music. In the 1930's, I had heard some of her music, but I knew very little about her. On this day and many following days when we relaxed in the boat on the lake, I received a liberal education about Ella Fitzgerald, one of the greatest singers the world has ever known. I learned to love and understand her music.

This was the beginning of a lifelong friendship between the three of us. We called ourselves "The Triangle," and our emblem was

In the years that followed when we wrote to each other, we always added this sign to the end of our letters.

I thoroughly enjoyed my nature study classes. Fortunately, the girls came to camp in age groups; the first were the youngest and proceeded up to high school teenagers as the last. This made it easy for me to gear my instructions from simple, short periods to more complicated, longer periods while I was still learning.

One day the children and I were walking in the woods gathering samples of plants and trees, when we came across a patch of earth with many tiny squiggly pink objects no more than one or two inches long. I had no idea what they were. I was a little frightened of them, but one of the girls exclaimed, "Oh, look at the little newts." I had never heard of a newt. We had had a heavy rain the night before. I found out later that these were a type of tiny lizard that lived in the ground and came out when there was a soaking rain. I was relieved to know they were harmless!

I had a map of the area: hiking trails, roads, museums, special mountains, etc. so one day I planned to take my middle aged girls on a hike following a trail through the woods.

We had been hiking and occasionally stopping to enjoy our new surroundings for an hour or more, when we saw a group of white girls approaching on the same path. As they neared, the tall leader reminded me of someone I knew who walked like that. It was Ruth Dougherty with whom I had spent my college days in physical education and sports! We graduated together in 1935 and she became the physical education teacher at West Denver High School when I was assigned to Whittier Elementary School.

We were amazed at meeting way out in the middle of the New York Catskill Mountains, so far from home. We hugged. We told our girls about our friendship. She introduced her girls to mine and I did the same. Her children and my children had never had any contact with those of another race, so they just looked at each other at first. Since Ruth and I were so friendly and enthusiastic, the girls began to talk to each other and found out that they had many common interests. Before we parted, the children were laughing and talking with each other and each waved a friendly "goodbye" as we left. My girls said, "That was fun!"

I thanked the Good Lord for providing this surprise meeting in the middle of no place, that helped a small group of young people to learn a bit of racial tolerance, acceptance and understanding.

Our hiking trail ended at a road along which were bushes of ripe wild raspberries. We had learned about some of the wild plants that were edible, so we enjoyed eating these sweet raspberries. We were late getting back to camp. The girls were happy and tired and so was I!

A notice was distributed throughout the area that there would be an exhibit of snakes at the nearby little museum. I am deathly afraid of snakes, but I thought it would be good for the girls to see the exhibit. There were many kinds of snakes, small and big, and they were alive! The man in charge gave a wonderful lecture on the characteristics of each snake: some of which were poisonous, some were not, how to identify one from the other, and what to do if bitten. The information was interesting and invaluable, but I was glad to get back to camp.

A few days later, a child came running up to me happily exclaiming, "Look, I found a snake!" In her hand was a little garter snake which she was gleefully handing to me. I knew that garter snakes were harmless, but it was a SNAKE! As Nature Counselor, I had no choice but to bravely take the squirming little reptile. As I wrapped my hand around it just below its head, it wrapped itself around my arm. I wanted to scream, but I kept a straight face. I congratulated the child for knowing this was a harmless snake and told her since we had no place to keep it that it would be best if she took it back to where she found it. I uncoiled it from my arm, gave it back to her and she happily took it back to where it belonged. I was relieved and prayed that no one would find another snake. No one ever did!!!

After dinner there was a period of free time before our usual get together with the girls in the recreation hall before bedtime. We would play games, tell or read stories, sing and just have fun. One evening, after a very hot day, Fannie asked Jeanne and me if we would like to go skinny dipping to cool off. I had never been skinny dipping, but it sounded like an exciting, cooling experience.

"How are we going to do that with the others and the kids around?" I wanted to know.

Fannie grinned and replied, "We'll go after everyone is safely in bed." Fortunately, we three Activity Counselors had our own cabin with no children. The campers were housed with the Junior Counselors.

After ten o'clock that night, all was quiet, so the three of us went down to the lake in our robes with our towels. It was a beautiful, pleasant, moonlit night after a broiling hot day. Jeanne could not swim so she splashed in the shallow water at the edge of the lake. Fannie and I dove off the dock into the deep water. I had no idea how soothing the water could be without a swim suit. It felt like a soft, velvet glove had enveloped my body. I wondered why the water felt comfortably warm in the cooler night air, since it felt so cool in the daytime. Fannie explained that the water felt so cool in the day because the air was so hot. At night, when the air was cooler, the water felt warm from the heat it had absorbed during the day, but that was only on the surface.

Sure enough, as I dove deeper, the water became cooler, just as it became cooler when I dove deeper in the daytime. However, I tried that only twice during the day. The water not only got cooler, but it also got darker and the little fish gathered around me; one of them nipped me, so I decided to let the fish have their deeper unnerving darkness! I just swam above.

Fannie and I went skinny dipping several times, but Jeanne gave up after the second time since she was not a "water baby." She would sit on the dock and visit with us as we swam. We would keep our voices and our giggles low, but we always had fun together.

Our little director seemed to be in semi-hibernation. We saw her at meals and occasionally at evening activities. A few times she checked on our individual activity groups, but most of the time she was "love sick" in her room in the main hall. If anyone had a question, they usually asked me.

One day, the Director seemed to be very upset. After lunch she blew up over all of us for no reason at all. Afterward, we took care of our afternoon interest groups, but the Triangle decided to take a hike and get out of the confusion.

I told my friends about the road I had discovered when I took my nature study children to the nearby museum and I wondered where it went from there. We decided this was the time to find out. The cook liked us since we seemed to be the ones to be keeping the camp on an even keel, so we got some bottles of water from her and took off.

We stopped at the museum and looked at the nature exhibits; then we continued on the road to see where it would lead us. I do not remember what we saw as we walked along until we happened upon a little store where we bought some candy bars. We were talking constantly about our Director and tried to analyze what had suddenly brought her to life in such a vicious way.

We forgot about time and did not realize how far we had walked, until we noticed that the sun was getting low. It was mid-afternoon, approximately three o'clock, when we left camp. By the time the three of us finally reached camp, it was getting dark; dinner was over, but the cook had saved some for us and told us she was getting worried about us since we were gone for so long. We thanked her for saving our food and let her know we appreciated her concern.

Woody wrote to me to let me know she was still in Buffalo. She had been back to the apartment to get some more clothes, but the National Board was keeping her busy. She wanted me to know that she doubted that she would be in Newark when camp was over, but for me to make myself at home in her apartment. I wrote back to her to let her know that Fannie and Jeanne might be with me for a day.

The middle of August came and we had a farewell celebration with the camper before they left. The Director left the next day! The staff and the cook stayed an extra day to close up camp. It was really peaceful and relaxing. We received a monetary honorarium, so the three of us decided to celebrate in New York!

When we arrived at the apartment, we were so tired that all we did was sit down and rest. Woody called soon after we arrived, and told us to eat the food that was left in the cupboard and refrigerator. She did not know when she would be back and it looked as though she would be moving to Buffalo.

We fixed something to eat, cleaned up the dishes and decided to get some sleep. There was a problem, since there was only one small bed. We decided that we had had two months of togetherness at camp, so we could manage one night sandwiched in this one bed. Jeanne was quite small, Fannie was husky and I was somewhere in between. The three of us lay on our sides jammed together like sardines in a can. I was in the middle and there was no way to move unless someone fell out of the bed. We laughed about our unique situation and finally fell asleep for a few hours.

Fannie and Jeanne were leaving the next day, so we took the train into New York City early. They would take trains to their homes in late afternoon from Penn Station, so we would have a good part of the day in the "Big City." Fannie had been to New York before, but this was Jeanne's first time and she was as excited as I had been. They stowed their luggage in lockers at the station.

We had a great time wandering around Times Square, visiting Rockefeller Center and eating at the Automat. We watched our time so we would get back to the station in time for my friends to catch their trains.

When we went down to the subway at Times Square, I said we should take an express train to get to Penn Station quicker. It must have been rush hour. When the train arrived that we expected to take, it was almost full and many people were waiting with us. When the doors opened, there was this mad rush to get on board. I said to Fannie, "Let's wait for the next train." I turned around to tell Jeanne, just as I saw her get on the train with the crowd!!

The doors closed and the express train left! Fannie and I looked at each other in shock and said, "Why would she do that?" We were scared to death at losing Jeanne in the New York City subway on her first day in the famous city.

Fannie and I got our heads together and prayed that Jeanne would get off the train at the first stop and wait for us. We took the very next train, which was a local. It stopped at every station. We did not know where the express stopped, but we knew it was a long way away. However, at every stop of this local train, we looked for Jeanne. We did not sit down; we stood holding the pole by the door so we could get off quickly. We were praying together that we would find our little friend who was wearing a pretty little hat with colorful flowers on it.

What seemed like an eternity riding the slow local, we rolled to a stop at a station where we saw that "flowery" hat atop Jeanne's head as she sat alone. Both of us exclaimed, "There she is!!" When the doors opened, we were the first ones out. We rushed to Jeanne, hugged her and told her how scared we were when that train door closed and she was gone. The three of us shed tears of relief. We asked, "Why did you get on with all those people?"

Jeanne said, "I thought you were right behind me, and I was surprised when the door closed and you were not there. I knew that if I got off the train and waited that you would eventually find me."

We sent up our prayers of thanks to the Good Lord for taking care of us. We took the next train to Penn Station where we said our goodbyes and promised to keep our Triangle friendship alive. I left them and went on back to Newark.

The next day I returned home to Denver with some of the greatest memories of my life!!

Eleanor and I were active members of Alpha Kappa Alpha Sorority (AKA). Eleanor was initiated into Alpha Kappa Chapter in 1931, and I was initiated in 1932. Since our chapter was so small, we had both undergraduate and graduate members. Since most AKA sorors at that time were in the field of Education, it was convenient to have the Boulé, (the annual meeting of the National Officers) during the Christmas break in December each year when everyone was free.

Away out here in the Rocky Mountain West, Alpha Kappa Chapter had not been able to send delegates to Boulé. In 1939, with more working graduate members, the chapter voted to send a delegate since there were members who could afford the trip (with what limited help the chapter could give). Eleanor was selected as the delegate and I was the alternate. The Boulé was meeting in Louisville, Kentucky. Eleanor and I were excited about taking the long train trip to a new adventure.

I told Mrs. Price (member of a women's group from church) about our upcoming trip to her home town. She immediately said, "I have a girlhood friend who lives in Louisville. She is an AKA and I am sure she would be happy to have you stay with her." Her friend was Caroline Blanton, a dedicated active Soror who had held a national office at sometime or other!

After Mrs. Price called her friend, she told us that Soror Blanton would be delighted to have Eleanor and me as her guests during Boulé, so we did not have to worry about our accommodations. We would be well cared for.

We changed trains in Chicago for the short trip to Louisville. Eleanor had said earlier that she wanted to stop in Chicago to visit relatives on the way back from Boulé. That was fine with me because I had two aunts in Chicago, (my father's sisters) whom I would like to meet. I wrote to let them know.

When we arrived at the station in Louisville, Kentucky, Eleanor had the shock of her life when she saw the signs, "White Only" and "Colored" on seats, doors, fountains, etc. She had never been South. I knew about Southern segregation from my childhood days in Texas, but facing it as an adult, I was resentful. I explained to Eleanor that this was the way it was in the South and we needed to be careful.

Caroline Blanton was a delight to know. She welcomed us to her home and said she felt that she already knew us from what her friend

Josephine Price had told her. (She called her Jo.) It wasn't long before we felt like a part of her family. Her children were grown. She was a community leader and a member of Boulé Planning Committee. We had arrived two days before Boulé so we could get rested and oriented before attending meetings.

We had a delicious southern dinner and we slept well that night. The next morning we couldn't believe breakfast – cereal, eggs, bacon, ham, grits, biscuits and fruit!

Soror Blanton let us take it easy that day and clued us in on what to expect at Boulé, when we would attend the opening session the next day. Back then, it was a very special honor to be a delegate to this meeting of Supreme Officers. We were still suffering in the Depression, so it was also a special privilege to be able to attend.

When we arrived at the meeting, I was surprised at how few members were there. There were the National President, Secretary, Treasurer, a couple of past National Officers and a few delegates. Our Alpha Kappa Alpha Sorority Founder was there and in charge. Meeting her was the thrill of our lives, for Eleanor and me! I expected to see a tall, demanding individual and was surprised to meet a short, pleasant, friendly, down-to-earth personality - Ethel Hedgeman Lyle! She seemed especially interested in the two of us, since we had come from the far away west where they thought we still had Indians, Cowboys and buffaloes roaming around.

At the Boulé I attended during the following years, Soror Lyle did not remember my name, but she always called me, "The Soror from Colorado." I felt honored that she always remembered me!

In those days, the Boulé was strictly an annual business meeting for National Officers to deal with problems and make decisions for the Sorority. To be a delegate to this meeting was truly an honor because no lay members were permitted to attend Boulé. Delegates took information back to their chapters. Since there were so few chapters in 1939, there were only a few representatives and only those who could afford to attend.

I have watched the Boulé grow from these intimate, small meetings where you got to know the national leaders personally, to the massive conventions of thousands where there is no way to meet these leaders.

I called my friend, Margaret Mackey, to let her know I would like to visit her in her small home town. Her aunt, Mrs. Price, and I kept in touch with her. She lived farther away from Louisville than I realized, so we set a day for our get together. Eleanor would take care of Boulé meetings while I was gone.

Caroline Blanton told me what to do about going by bus. The bus depot was not far from her house, so I walked over there. When I entered, there was someone being helped at the window, so I sat quietly on the bench and waited until they left. I went to the window and the young fellow in charge was visiting with his girl friend. They ignored me as I stood there. There was an early afternoon bus I wanted to take. I said something, politely. No response. I could feel my temper rising and I knew I had better get out of there.

I returned to the house blazing mad. I was seeing my dangerous red! Eleanor and Caroline were there and I exploded as I told them about the insult of being completely ignored because of my color! They agreed with me, then Caroline calmed me down and suggested that I call the Bus Station. I was willing to try anything.

I called and a pleasant voice answered. I told him what I wanted and since he could not tell who I was from the sound of my voice, this young man answered, "Yes, ma'am" to my every request. I began having so much fun that I kept him on the line, enjoying the fact that he had no idea that he was talking to the person he had just ignored. Unfortunately, the next bus for me to get to Margaret's home left about midnight. I called Margie to let her know I would arrive the next morning.

When I got to the depot, I bought my ticket. There was no one there but me to take the late bus. When I boarded the bus and gave my ticket to the driver, he did not say anything. There was no "colored" sign anywhere; I figured the bus wasn't segregated, so I sat near the center. One man did get on, but he paid no attention to me. It was an all night ride to Knoxville, so I slept off and on. We arrived in Knoxville about 8:00 a.m. I went into the station, ate the little snack that Caroline had made for me and waited for the ten o'clock bus that would take me to

Margie' home town.

I was one of the first people to get on the bus, and since there had been no discrimination on the night bus, I sat in a seat near the front. Others getting on looked at me, but said nothing. Soon a woman boarded, looked at me in awe, got off the bus and started waving her arms as she seemed to be fussing with the bus driver. The driver came on board, pointed to me and told me to move to the back of the bus. I looked around as though I did not know to whom he was talking. He yelled and pointed at me again, "YOU move to the back of the bus!" I answered, "But there are plenty of empty seats." He started toward me and I began to see red. I also realized that I was the only brown face on the bus, so for my own safety I moved. For the half hour ride to my destination, I was steaming mad!!

Since I was the only one getting off the bus, and Margie was waiting for me, as the doors opened I let go in a loud voice about how insulted I felt and just what I thought of that bus driver. Margie hurried me away <u>fast</u>!

She was still living in her old family home. We had a wonderful visit bringing each other up to date on our past activities over the years. The next morning I took the bus back to Louisville. I calmly sat in the back of the bus and rode peacefully back to the city to complete my attendance at the Boulé.

When Eleanor and I arrived in Chicago, her cousin met us at the station. She told him where I wanted to go and he said he would gladly drop me off. I gave him the address of my aunt's wig shop on the south side of Chicago. He knew where it was; but when I saw the tiny shop, I wasn't sure what to expect when I entered "Shaw's Wigs."

My Aunt Isabelle had married Mr. Shaw who owned a successful wig-making business. My Aunt Marie had come to Chicago to be with her sister during Mr. Shaw's illness, and to help with the business since she spoke English and Aunt Isabelle only spoke French. When Mr. Shaw died, Aunt Marie took over handling the business connections and orders, while Aunt Isabelle continued to make the wigs.

Aunt Marie was happy to see me. Her bubbly personality made

me feel at ease. She was small, no taller than I, and she introduced me to Aunt Isabelle in French. She called her Belle, and acted as interpreter between my English and Belle's French. Aunt Marie talked fast and with her French accent, I had to listen very carefully to her English. It was quite a new experience!

She explained to me the intricate skill of wig-making. They imported the best hair, usually from Italy. Because of the quality of their wigs, the business was very good. Most of their orders were special. It was interesting watching Aunt Belle weave the long strands of hair into the wig base. She did not talk much, just kept on working.

About four o'clock, Aunt Marie told Aunt Belle to take me home. Now, I think Aunt Belle understood a few English words. I spoke very little French, and they spoke so fast that I understood even less. My spirit hit bottom when I wondered, how were we going to communicate without Aunt Marie?! She had another hour or more before closing the shop. I didn't say anything; I just silently prayed that the Lord would help me through.

They had no car. They rode the bus or the trolley, so it was going to take a while to get to their home. Aunt Belle and I caught a bus near the shop. We tried to communicate. I managed to tell her (in French) to talk slowly, and with hand movements we gradually began to understand bits and pieces of our conversation. We had to transfer to another bus. While we were waiting, a black and white couple went by. Aunt Belle said, "*Elle est blânche.*" I answered, "*Oui.*" I surprised myself that we were beginning to understand each other!

By the time we got home we were laughing and talking with gestures in a combination of French and English! Aunt Marie was a bit worried about how Aunt Belle and I would get along, but when she got home, she was happy to see that we were doing just fine.

The next morning Aunt Marie's son, Octave Rainey, came over. He was about twenty-one years old. He spoke accented English, but very little French. I was glad to have a young person to talk with, and my cousin Octave was most interesting, lively young man. He had graduated from Xavier University in Louisiana and knew some of our Creole cousins. He said he would like to show me some of Chicago and that gave me a good lift because I was beginning to feel a bit depressed since my two lovely, caring aunts lived mostly for the wig business, and talked of attending Mass at their church.

Octave and I took the bus or trolley. Chicago was not as concentrated in 1939 as it is today. I wanted to see the "Loop," and the elevated trains that I had read about, so that was where we went first. I was amazed at the hustle and bustle of people and traffic in the center of the city. I had my first exciting ride on the El! I do not remember what else we did, but it was late afternoon when we returned home. Octave and I developed a close friendship which we maintained for many years.

Cousin Octave

That evening I called Eleanor to find out our schedule for leaving the next day. They came for me the next morning. I told my aunts and Octave how much it meant to me to have met them, and I would let my father know all about our visit. Eleanor and I took the train back to Denver, and thus ended my 1939 year's adventures!!!

A few years later the Boulé met in Philadelphia and I had the thrill of my life when Marian Anderson was made an Honorary AKA! I loved her music and had some of her recordings, so I was anxious to have the opportunity to meet her. When I introduced myself to her as Marie Anderson from Denver Colorado, this gracious, down-to-earth, pleasant celebrity smiled and said, "Our names are similar." She told Eleanor and me that during her upcoming tour she would be in Denver for a concert. Of course, the night of the concert, Eleanor and I were there. I could listen to this world-wide singer's beautiful voice forever!!! After the concert, we went back stage to greet our famous Soror. To my surprise, before I could re-introduce myself to her, Marian Anderson broke into a broad smile, extended her hand and exclaimed, "Marie Anderson!" That was one of the greatest thrills of my life to think that this great artist remembered little me from one meeting at Boulé!!!

106

CHAPTER 6

Young Billy Greenwood

On July 15, 1919, William Rivers Greenwood was born in Los Angeles, California. His parents were William Ridley Greenwood and Vivian Rivers Greenwood. They called their little son Billy. When his parents separated, little five week old Billy traveled with his mother Vivian back to Denver to live with her parents, Joseph and Richie Rivers.

Joseph Daniel Dorsey Rivers was a graduate of Hampden Institute (now Hampden University). He had been a student under Booker T. Washington, and they developed a lifelong friendship. Mr. Rivers migrated to Colorado in the 1890's because there were more opportunities for minorities out here in the West. He and a friend established *The Colorado Statesman* newspaper, but the only way they could get news for their publication was to be members of a class system for minorities that had been set up by the City and County of Denver. Their newspaper grew in volume. Joseph D.D. Rivers became such an outstanding member of this class system that he was graduated to the State House as Sgt. at Arms. He became a highly respected citizen in Denver. *The Colorado Statesman* flourished with community

William Rivers Greenwood
– 6 months old

Joseph D.D. Rivers and
Richie Rivers

news and business ads. He eventually bought the newspaper from his partner.

Eliza Smith, Richie Rivers' mother

Mack Bryant, Pullman Porter

In the meantime, Mr. Rivers married Richie Smith from Kansas, and brought his bride to the home he had built on the edge of the city on West Eleventh Avenue between Bannock and Cherokee Streets. In the 1890's that was across the street from the city dump; it is now almost a part of Civic Center. They were a beautiful couple. He was a handsome, dark-skinned man and she was a pretty, white-skinned, young woman. Vivian was their only daughter and she was brown like her father. They belonged to Shorter A.M.E. church and were a part of the growing Colored society, even though they did not live in the Northeast community.

Little Billy was a happy, white-skinned, baby with blue eyes like his father. His mother used to laugh and tell the story of how people would stop her when she was walking with him in his pram to ask her whose lovely baby she was caring for. It was hard for them to believe that she was his mother.

Vivian divorced William Greenwood and eventually married Mack Bryant when Billy was a little boy. Mr. Bryant was a Pullman Porter on the railroad. He became the only father the boy ever knew. William Ridley Greenwood became "white" and made no more contact with the family.

My father read *The Colorado Statesman* every week and developed a great respect for Mr. Rivers, whom he eventually met. My parents and

I got to know about this outstanding family, and when we moved to the West side of Denver we lived only a few blocks from them. That's how little Billy came into my life and developed into quite a story.

J.D.D.R., Vivian, Richie Rivers- The Colorado Statesman newspaper printers

*I had seen him occasionally since he was a little boy. When I was in high school, believe it or not, he was in grade school. I used to tease him. He was kind of a shy little boy. A funny looking little kid. He was very pale-skinned: He looked anemic. He was so white, and had blue eyes. He also had sandy-colored hair. His mother kept him in knee pants and long socks. He was an only child. He had a little dog named "Buddy." Occasionally he would pass our house. Every time I saw him, Buddy was with him, and I would say, "Hi, Billy. How are you?" he would say.

Bill, age 2

Vivian & Bill

Bill - age 6

"Fine," I'd say. "How are your mother and your grandmother?"

He would say, "Fine." And by that time, he was out of speaking distance.

When I graduated from West High School in 1931, he finished elementary school and went to Baker Junior High School. He was the last person in the world I would have thought I would ever marry because he was just a kid. When he graduated from high school in 1937, I had been teaching for two years. His mother called and said, "Billy wants to go to college. We don't have much money and he doesn't know want he wants to do. We thought maybe you could help him decide." She brought him over and I couldn't believe how he had grown. I hadn't seen him since he was a little boy. He was this tall, pale guy, thin as a rail and I thought, "I have no idea what his interests are."

He said he wanted to be a pharmacist, he thought, simply because he was working at Park Hill Drug Store and he had helped the pharmacist in his free time. He was a delivery boy there. I told him, if that was what he wanted then go for it.

Billy entered Colorado University at Boulder. Gilbert Cruter got him into the wealthy fraternity house where many Negro boys worked for their room and board. I used to go to games up there. My boyfriend, Luther White, was still at Colorado State College in Greeley.

I knew Gilbert as a kid in Y.P.D. at church. He was quite an athlete at Colorado University. His girlfriend, Mary Martin, and I had become good friends since her parents and my parents were close friends. She had just graduated from high school. When Gilbert wanted me to drive Mary to Boulder for football games, I told him I would be glad to bring her, but I felt like an oddball without a boyfriend since Luther was in Greeley.

Gilbert said, "Billy Greenwood doesn't have anybody. I'll team you up with him." I figured that's safe enough since he's so young. I found out Billy had a great sense of humor and we had a good time when I attended the games, but that was it. He had to leave C.U. after a year and a half for lack of money.

(Luther and I had become engaged. When he graduated in 1939, he got a job as a high school coach in Dayton, Ohio. When he came home for summer vacation in 1940, our relationship was not the same. I broke the engagement.)

In August of 1940, Billy's mother and grandmother were going to drive to California and they called me to see if I would like to take the trip. I figured, "Oh, what the heck. Why not? I needed to get away for a while." That was the year that Bill turned twenty-one. I got to know him better. He was so much fun! We got to be better friends, but as far as I was concerned he was still just a young fellow. [1]

The trip turned out to be quite an adventure. Mrs. Bryant and Billy did the driving. We drove to Salt Lake City, Utah, which took a long day – before interstate highways. We arrived late evening and went to the only Black-owned hotel in the city. We were taken to a room with beds or cots covered with red wool blankets. The room was dimly lit and it was hot. We were so tired that we bedded down as best we could. I had just fallen asleep when something crawled across my forehead. I woke up with a start, brushed it off and in the dim light was a cockroach! I yelled. There was no more sleep for me or anyone else. We were out of there early the next morning.

It was a long drive across the great Salt Lake Desert. The sun rose hot and the heat became almost like an oven as the day wore on. Cars did not have air conditioning in the 40's. It was a relief to drive out of that desert and into Nevada where the heat was bearable!

---

[1]* excerpt taken from Trail Blazers Oral History Series transcript, courtesy of Denver Public Library, Blair-Caldwell

Mrs. Bryant decided that we were going to find a decent place to stop for the night. When we stopped at a motel, she went in but was told they could not accommodate us. At the next motel she told Mrs. Rivers and Billy to go in; she and I stayed in the car. I had to smile when she told her son to keep his cap on. Since the grandmother and grandson had white skin, a reservation was made. We drove to our assigned unit. Mrs. Bryant and I got out of the car and went in quickly so no one would see our brown faces. This way, we had a comfortable night's rest!

The World's Fair was in San Francisco in 1940. We planned to spend a few days there and our hotel proved to be very pleasant. The first day we drove around San Francisco, went down to Fisherman's Wharf and took it easy. The next day was the big one – the World's Fair!!! We did not know what to expect, but it was exciting! On the way, we drove past a theater that was showing the fabulous movie, *King Kong*. I really wanted to see that show, but I didn't say anything. We had a wonderful time at the Fair. With all the walking and excitement, by mid-afternoon Grandma Rivers was tired and ready to take a rest. So we decided to go back to the hotel to relax.

While Billy and I were wandering around at the Fair, I told him that I wished we could go see *King Kong*. We really wanted some time away from his mother and grandmother. Since they were both tired, we presented to his mother something that we wanted to do that entailed more activity. It had nothing to do with the movie. Mrs. Bryant was happy to give Billy some money and let us go.

It was evening and we arrived at the theater. *King Kong* was almost over, but no one was admitted to see the ending. We had to wait for the next performance, which was the late show. We thoroughly enjoyed the exciting movie, however, we were very late returning to the hotel and Mrs. Bryant was not pleased. We told her that we had decided to go to the movie at the last minute while we were out.

The next day we drove on down to Los Angeles to visit Mrs. Rivers' niece, Mrs. Ethel Prioleau. Mrs. Prioleau was the widow of a retired Army Chaplain who had organized a church in Los Angeles. She had two married daughters, Sue and Mary, who had families of their own and one young daughter, Lois, at home. There was a big house with plenty of room for everyone.

I had a former Denver friend who was married and lived in Los Angeles. Her name was Cerressa Stroud. I called her and we arranged for me to spend a day with her and her husband. They had a lovely home with a big swimming pool in the back yard. Cerressa had graduated from Colorado Teachers College as a Physical Education major at the same time as Eleanor, two years ahead of me. I do not know where she learned to swim, but she was a pro. She had a successful business teaching private swimming lessons in her pool at her home.

We had a wonderful time renewing old memories and updating our lives since we had last met. She said they were planning to attend a fabulous show at the new, huge arena that evening. They had two extra tickets and would like to take me. Cerressa asked me if there was anyone in the family I was with who might like to go, since they had the extra ticket. I told them that Billy might be glad to go, especially since he had been stuck with the old folks all day. When I called him I could hear the joy and relief in his voice.

When we stopped to pick him up, Billy was waiting for us on the front porch. The huge arena was awesome with thousands of people and brilliant lights. We witnessed one of the most spectacular programs we had ever seen. When it was over, it took forever to get out of the parking area. It was after midnight when my friends dropped us off.

Our car was parked on the street in front of the house and, as we passed it, Billy said, "Why don't we go somewhere and see some night life?"

"What do you mean?" I asked.

"On the other side of town there are some night clubs run by colored people. I've heard that they are great." We were on the opposite side of Los Angeles from the black Watts area. Billy had the keys to the car in his pocket. I thought why not, this could be another adventure, so I said, "O.K. let's go!"

We found the area and it was alive with activity. We entered the first club that we came to, had drinks and enjoyed the jazz for a while. Then we went across the street, had more drinks and watched a floor show. At the third night club, things were a bit slow, so after drinks there, we decided we had better head for home. By that time, we were feeling a bit high and happy.

It was about three o'clock in the morning by then, when Billy suggested that we stop by the famous Olvera Street and see if the shops were open. (At three a.m.?) I reminded him that we would be bringing his mother and grandmother down to Olvera Street soon, but it seemed like fun to see if any shops were open all night. We were on a roll!!

Of course, the shops were all closed and only the moonlight lit the street. All merchandise had been taken in. As we wandered through this short block of shops, we saw one with a small object still on display. It was a little raffia man on horseback about eight inches tall. In my happily, fuzzy mind I giggled and told Billy that I wanted that souvenir. It was the only shop with a dim glow of light that we could see from a partly open door at the back. We called, but no one answered. We called several times – nothing.

Since I wanted this small object so desperately, Billy wanted me to have it, but we wanted to pay for it in person. We couldn't just leave money on the ledge. Billy came up with this solution: that when we brought his folks to Olvera Street within the next day or two, we would pay for our prize. I joyfully took my little souvenir and we headed for home. I called it "The Little Man Who Wasn't There."

When we got back to the house, the sky was beginning to show the first signs of daylight. Billy had been given the key to the back door – an old fashioned skeleton key. In our happy, inebriated condition, we could not find the keyhole. We took turns trying and with every miss, we giggled. After approximately twenty minutes, and the sky getting lighter, the key slid into the keyhole and we unlocked the door.

As we entered the house, we agreed that we had to be quiet so as not to arouse anyone. As we tiptoed up the steps, I slipped and we giggled softly. When we reached the top of the stairs, Billy went to his room and I quietly entered the room I shared with Mrs. Rivers and Mrs. Bryant. How I managed to get undressed and into my pajamas with only the faint early morning light filtering through the window, and not awaken either of them, I do not know. There were two beds in the room; Mrs. Rivers slept in the single bed and Mrs. Bryant and I shared the double bed. Since I slept on the wall-side, I had to get into bed without climbing over her, so I carefully climbed over the high footboard and eased down under the covers.

Oh, the bed felt good. I closed my eyes and I felt as though I were floating. It was getting daylight when I finally fell asleep. The next thing I knew I was being shaken with Mrs. Bryant saying, "It's time to get up and get dressed for breakfast." I did not want to get up. I did not want any food. I just wanted to sleep, but I couldn't let her know that.

I crawled out of bed and I had a king-sized headache. My head felt like a balloon about to burst! I managed to get dressed and follow them down to breakfast. There was food like I had had in Louisville, Kentucky. Billy was sitting across the table from me. We looked at the food, then looked at each other. We had to keep straight faces to avoid making eye contact during the rest of breakfast. I nibbled at food that I really didn't want, and prayed that it would stay down. I had my first hangover.

A couple of days later, we did go back to Olvera Street with Billy's folks. We tried to find the little shop to pay for our little raffia souvenir, but with all the multitude of colorful wares out in front of every shop, it was impossible to identify one from another. I always felt guilty for not paying for "The Little Man Who Wasn't There."

One day the family planned to have a picnic at the beach. I was really excited to finally get to see the ocean. It was a big family get-together – old folks, young folks, children, grandchildren, a huge merry crowd, all new to me. The most awesome sight for me was the vast expanse of endless water – the Pacific Ocean!

Some of us were prepared to swim, but I was the only one who dared to go in the ocean. There was a big swimming pool where many people were enjoying themselves; only one or two swimmers were off the beach in the waves. Of course, I had to have my first experience in the ocean, so away I went. I had to wade out a few steps before I found water deep enough for swimming. It was a new experience maneuvering in moving water, but I was proud of myself and I was enjoying it. Suddenly, a big wave which I did not see coming, hit me and submerged me. As I swam up toward sunlight, the undertow caught me and was dragging me seaward. Fortunately, I was not too far from the beach, but all I could think of was being washed out to sea and drowning. I was terrified! As water flowed away from me, I frantically swam for the shore. Another wave hit, and this time I dug my feet and hands into the sand as I hit bottom, held my breath and let the wave recede over me. I had reached shallow sand by the time the third wave hit, and ebbed back into the ocean.

I ran out on the beach. Everyone was standing watching me. Billy said he was afraid I was going to drown. Everyone was relieved to see me coming safely out of that dilemma and remarked about my strong swimming. I was shaking and scared to death as I realized how close I came to drowning! I swam in the pool with Billy and enjoyed the rest of the day safely on shore with the family. By the Grace of God I was still alive!!

We had a wonderful time with their family, but I was glad to get back to Denver and resume my usual activities – working in my church, teaching and volunteering at the Y.W.C.A. where activities had increased to the point that the Executive Secretary needed more help.

When the Assistant Secretary arrived, I had the surprise of my life. It was my "triangle" friend, Jeannie! I asked her why she did not tell me she was coming to Denver. She said she wanted to surprise me. Even thought we wrote to each other often, renewing our friendship in person was great. Of course, she worked with the girl Reserve Secretary, Frances Gordon, who was a friend and Soror of Eleanor and me. The four of us soon developed into quite a friendly foursome.

Eventually I needed some information and Mrs. Bryant was the only one whom I thought might be able to help me, so one day I stopped by their house. When I walked in, Billy was sitting in the living room. I said, "Hi, how are you?"

He replied in a dull voice, "O.K." He did not look like his usual happy self. Mrs. Bryant quickly said, "Come up stairs with me. I have something to show you."

That was unusual. I had never been past the living room. When we got up to one of the bedrooms, she told me that Billy was coming out of a disastrous marriage of less than two months and he was very depressed. She was glad that I stopped by and she hoped that I could help to cheer him up. I was flabbergasted and felt sorry for him, but I told her I would see what I could do. This was a real challenge for me to try to help this young man with whom I had had so much fun on our trip.

I do not remember if I got the information for which I stopped in that day, but I did get Billy to talking and he seemed to feel better when I left. Periodically, I would get in touch with him. We would talk about how his divorce was going, exchange "for fun" ideas, go to the movies. I had him go on a picnic with me with some friends. He seemed to be happy when he was with me and I enjoyed his company, laughing and talking with him.

*We became good friends and I could always depend on him if I needed him. If there was a party or a dance, and I didn't have a date, I would call Billy. Billy would be ready to go. Then we discovered that we had a common interest in photography, and he had all this equipment for developing pictures and enlarging them. Once every week or two, I would go over one evening and we would have a ball developing and enlarging pictures and doing all kinds of things just to see what we could make.

Then it got so that I would call him for any kind of date, and I'd have so much fun with him. We just gradually began going together because most of my peers, who were men, were either married or they just seemed "old."

I was still skiing and doing all these active things. If I could get into a baseball game, me and the bat would have it. Picnics and hiking and camping, I just loved all that. Billy would go on a picnic with me, or just do any of those fun things.

In the meantime, he had taken the Civil Service Exam. He was still working at Park Hill. He worked at the old Orpheum Theater until they closed it. After taking the Civil Service Exam, and passing, he was hired as assistant to the custodian. No grade, just an assistant to the custodian at Lowry Air Force Base. He told me that he had this job and that he was cleaning the accounting offices. He would call me two or three times a week just to tell me what he was doing. He talked to me if he had a question or would ask me for advice. He didn't dare talk to his mother or grandmother about these things. They did not understand. He salvaged discarded manuals in the accounting office, and would take them home and study them.

He told me that he was going to Emily Griffith Opportunity School to take some clerical courses, and I encouraged him to do it. This was in 1942. He frantically called me one day after I got home from school to tell me that there was an opening for a clerk in the accounting office. The women in the office had gotten to know him because Bill was the kind of person who would help, no matter what. He would clean the office, and he would get his job done, then if they needed someone to do a little filing and a little typing, he would help them out. Here in the middle of the war, male help was very rare. He had a bad heart, so he was 4F. He said he didn't know whether or not he ought to apply for it. I said, "Well, you don't have anything to lose. You're on the bottom already and you can only go up. Go ahead and apply."

It always bothered him that he had to drop out of college and never got his degree. I told him not to worry. Eventually he "outstriped" some of those Ph.D.'s! He applied and, sure enough, he was hired. It was supposed to be as a GS-2, and he was hired as a GS-3. He called me and said, "Guess what? I got the job and I'm a GS-3!" Finally, he had a grade. I told him how proud I was of his raise in grade!

We had begun to go out together very steadily now. I got to thinking, "Look, Marie, you're almost thirty years old, and you want a family." I had always said that I was going to get my Ph.D. and be this great teacher, but I had always wanted a family so I began to weigh this out. I realized that I'm not the kind of person who would be my best at furthering education, and having a family at the same time. I was going to do one or the other, and having a family won out. I got to thinking, "Gee, Billy and I have so much in common, but he's just a friend and awfully young."

Finally one night, we'd been out on a date. We'd been to a show or somewhere, and on the way home he was so quiet I said, "What are you thinking about?"

He said, "I was just thinking that if I asked you to marry me, what would you say?"

I answered, "If you ask me, I'd say 'Yes'." He was dumbstruck. I thought, "Well, you blew that one, Marie."

He said, "Do you really mean it?"

"Of course I do. I was wondering if you would ever ask me!"

Well, that was it, and we began to plan. I did not tell my folks right away. I had vowed to make sure that my parents had a home before I married. My father had a good job at Remmington Small Arms Plant (now the Federal Center), so I told him I wanted to buy a house so we could stop paying rent, and we would have a home of our own. He knew a little realtor who was quite a "go-getter." He found a house for us at 245 Lowell Blvd., where a woman needed to sell her house for a few thousand dollars. It was worth much more on 2 ½ lots, a garage and sheds in the back yard where my father could raise chickens. We settled on it. My dad and I shared the mortgage payments.

One evening, when Billy was at our house, he told my father that he and I were planning to get married. My dad said all right, but he hoped we knew what we were doing. My mother was not happy at all.

Bill and I planned very carefully, but trying to find a place to live in the middle of the war was difficult. So many people had moved to Denver because many government offices were transferred here for the inland safety against the Rocky Mountains, and Lowry was an active Air Base.

Well now, I believe in planning. As far as Bill was concerned, we could go on and get married and worry later about where we were going to live. I was NOT going to live with my folks, and I sure wasn't going to live with HIS! We were going to find some place even if it was one room. It was going to be OURS!

We did find a place. We contacted the realtor who had helped my folks find a house. He told us about a house on 25th Avenue between Williams and High Street. Some bank had it and they were trying to get rid of it. They couldn't get the tenants out (who had trashed that house like you wouldn't believe).

Billy and I decided we would check into it, so our friend took us to the bank to talk to them. They told us that they wanted to get rid of this place for about $1800. I was, at that time, at the top of what teachers earned. We asked if we could see the house. I'll never forget the night we went to see that house. I never saw such a dump in my life. I don't know how anybody would live in a place like that. So we weren't too sure about buying it. The windows were broken. The bathroom had been painted black and blue for some reason. It was a mess. Oh, to get rid of it. They had said they would re-do everything. They'd replace everything. Clean it up and really put it together all for this $1800. Remember, in 1942 we were just coming out of a BIG Depression and work was cheap. The bank wanted desperately to get rid of this load.

I said we can handle that. Bill wasn't making a whole lot because he had just gotten his GS-3 a few months ago, but I was doing all right. So we worked it out and signed the contract. They did everything that had been promised. They had to replace about fifteen panes. They had to put on a new roof because the roof was leaking. We found out when they sanded the floors, and got the grime off, they were A-1 oak, beautiful floors! We didn't tell anybody, not even our folks. We went down and looked at rings. (I still wear my original wedding band, and I wear Bill's ring which he wore for forty years.)

House on 25th Avenue

We would go to the house periodically to see how they were doing. We finally set our wedding date for April 17, 1943, and we were hoping the house would be ready. About two weeks before that, we let our folks know the date and our plans. Well, they knew that we were planning to get married, and of course my mother really was not for it at all because her friends had said what in the world does this teacher, this first black teacher, think of marrying this silly kid. He was twenty-three and I was thirty. I told my mother at thirty years old, if I couldn't make my own decisions that was my problem. If I made a mistake, I couldn't blame anybody but me, so this was going to be.

My mother had always wanted her daughter to have a big wedding. Eleanor and I had been bridesmaids at Elaine Brown's wedding, when she and Howard Jenkins were married. With all the dressing up, rituals and social activities involved, I vowed that I would never go through a big, formal wedding again. I was thrilled to death when it became impossible to have this event in the middle of the war. So, sure enough, in April they had the house finished and it was so nice with chandeliers and everything.

On April 17, 1943, just Bill's mother, grandmother, stepfather and my mother and father went to the parsonage. At that time, Shorter's parsonage was down the way on 23rd Street just half a block from the church, and we were married by Rev. Bryant with his wife as witness. Then we took the family over to see the house. They couldn't believe it. So that was our "married life" beginning.

Bill & Marie, circa 1940's

"Beverly Gardens" - 1940's (L to R) Olietta Moore, Richie Rivers, Vivian Bryant, unknown, William Greenwood, Marie Greenwood

CHAPTER 7

Life with William R. Greenwood, Sr.

Since we needed to get our clothes from our parents' homes, I took my mother and dad home and Bill went with his folks. A few minutes after I got in, Eleanor called. She was surprised when I told her that I had just gotten married to Bill. I had told no one of our plans, not even my best friend! I told her about our house and gave her the address.

After I got some of my clothes together, I loaded them in my car and went to pick up Bill. I had a little blue 1936 Chevrolet sedan named "Suzabella." (I don't remember where the name came from, but that car had personality!) This would be our family transportation for many years.

Baby Louise in front of "Suzabella"

A friend of ours who owned a restaurant had planned a special dinner for us, so we went there since it was late afternoon or early evening. He made us so happy with a candle-light setting just for the two of us. After this wonderful dining, we took our clothes home to our sparsely furnished house.

Our house had a living room with a fireplace, a dining room, small kitchen and an entry from the front door with a stairway to the two bedrooms and bath upstairs.

We had gone to a wholesale discount furniture market, a short time before our wedding, and bought a bed, a kitchen table and two chairs, a little side oven gas stove, and a small couch. From Montgomery Ward, we purchased the smallest refrigerator I had ever seen, and it was not electric. During the war it was impossible for manufacturers to obtain refrigerator units so many had been converted to old fashioned ice boxes with a shelf in the top section of the refrigerator to hold a large block of ice. Fortunately, for our little ice box, Montgomery Ward provided a written guarantee that an electric refrigerating unit would be installed as soon as they were available. Eventually I brought my mahogany dining room table and six chairs to our home. (My folks had an extra beautiful solid oak table for their use.)

We just dumped our clothes in the bedroom and took off for a movie at the Denver Theater. For many, many years this became our anniversary celebration for just the two of us, dinner and a movie.

The next day was Sunday and we stayed home, enjoying our new home together. Suddenly, the doorbell rang and we wondered who on earth could that be?! To our surprise, when we opened the door, there stood Eleanor and Jeanne! Since I had surprised her by getting married without telling her, Eleanor told Jeanne and they decided to surprise us by coming over after church. I showed them through our house and we all had to laugh at the joke my friends pulled on us.

There were four houses in the short half-block to the alley between Williams and High Streets. There was barely enough space to walk between the houses. Our house was on the alley so we had a small garage attached to the kitchen. The door opened directly into the garage. Bill usually drove the car to work and I walked the five short blocks down 25th Avenue to Whittier. Bill became friends with some Lowry workers living in Northeast Denver, so they carpooled. However, I enjoyed the walk so I seldom drove to school.

One cool day we realized that we had not checked to see where the furnace might be. There was a door in the kitchen we had never opened. We opened the door to see steps going down to a basement we didn't know we had. We were shocked to see it had been a "catch-all" for trash! It was unbelievable!

Bill would not let me go down there. He wore a mask as he shoveled the trash and dirt out through the little basement window into the alley. The furnace was there and some coal in the bin, but it was getting warmer so we did not need the heat. The fireplace was sufficient when needed. It took days for him to finally find the concrete floor. After it was cleaned up and aired out, Bill took me down to see what a nice basement we had with a good furnace for the winter. We used the space for storage.

Mrs. Bryant surprised us with a beautiful bedroom set – bed, chest of drawers and mirrored dresser. My mother and dad gave us a complete sterling silverware service for eight. Eleanor surprised me when she took me to the elite Denver Dry Goods store to select my desired design of china service for six. It was open stock, so I could add to it.

We planned to have "Open House" on May 2nd, two weeks after our wedding. That would be on a Sunday afternoon from 2:00 to 5:00 p.m. When I got up on the Friday morning before, I was not feeling well but I went on to school. As the day wore on I began to feel quite ill. I don't know how I managed to teach. By the end of my day at school, I could barely make it home and go to bed. I was worried about not being able to complete my plans for Sunday. I had sent out many invitations, gave a special one to Miss O'Boyle and posted an invitation on the bulletin board for the faculty. Bill and I had shopped for the refreshments for my planned menu. Of course, I had discussed my plans with Eleanor and she knew I was not feeling well when I left school.

Saturday morning when Eleanor called to see how I felt, I was too sick to get out of bed and Bill had no idea of what to do. My best friend came over and proceeded to prepare for my party with the help of Bill. Since he was in a worried haze, he just did everything Eleanor told him to do. By the end of the day, the food was prepared, the house was in order and they told me to stay in bed and reserve my strength for Sunday.

I was still quite weak on Sunday. Eleanor came early and took care of the last minute preparations with Bill's help. I managed to get dressed by two o'clock, and when I slowly made it downstairs they had a special chair for me and Eleanor took complete charge as a lovely hostess.

I was pleased to see that practically everyone whom I had invited came to my new home. My astonishing surprise was the gifts they brought that conveyed such warm messages: two sets of beautiful crystal stemware, matching additions to my china service, sets of bed linen, bath towels, silver pitcher and tray, new on the market Pyrex cookware and many, many other wonderful items; many of which I still have.

The party was a happy affair. I was especially glad to have my coworkers meet my friends and family. After the last guest left, I thanked Eleanor for making my party a success and she insisted that I go upstairs and go back to bed. She and Bill put the house back in order - my two BEST FRIENDS!!!

Bill continued to advance in the accounting office. He needed to learn more about accounting so he took some night courses at Denver University Business School. He really enjoyed his work, but he was concerned about the disorganization and the inefficiency he was seeing in the operation of the office, as he learned more about accounting and organization (in his classes).

The officer in charge of accounting was eventually transferred and with the obvious, dedicated progress that Bill had shown, he was promoted to Chief Accountant. He reorganized the office and within a few months had it running smoothly and efficiently.

Bill joined the Masonic Lodge, Rocky Mountain #1. He enjoyed the ritual and the brotherhood, but he was concerned about their not owning the building that they had been renting for years and years. It took time and a lot of hard work for Bill to convince the members of Rocky Mountain #1 to buy the building and collect the rent from the store on the street side. The lodge met upstairs and the meeting space was also rented by other lodges and the Eastern Star chapters. Bill loved

Masonry and became quite a leader.

The first time that Bill and I were invited to a formal affair, Mrs. Bryant called that afternoon to make sure I had laid out all his clothes for the evening. When I said, "No, I haven't." She said she always did.

I replied, "His tux and shirt are in the closet and his tie and jewelry are in the drawer. He knows where they are. I am his wife, not his mother." That settled that!

Since we were both "only" children, I wanted a family of two girls and two boys. In early 1945 I took maternity leave. Eleanor had married Noel Daniels in 1944, a year after I married. Now, both of us were expecting our first child within weeks of each other. Unfortunately, Eleanor lost her baby a month or so before her due date. I immediately drove to the hospital and stayed as long as possible. I consoled her as best I could. I was expecting to deliver soon on July 28, 1945.

Believe it or not, a first time father-to-be can be nervous, excited, frustrated, disoriented and a bit off balance. Early on the morning of July 28th, I woke Bill to tell him that we had better get ready to go to the hospital because I was getting signals. As I was dressing, Bill was sitting on the bed in his undershirt and boxer shorts. He put on his socks and shoes, reached for his hat and put it on. I thought, "Hat?" He put on a dress shirt and tie. "Why are wearing a tie?" I asked.

"Oh, I have to look nice," he replied.

This was one of the hottest months we had had all summer and a sport shirt would have been fine. He told me to take my time and go on downstairs; he would bring my little bag. He kept telling me to keep calm.

When I got downstairs and heard him coming, I looked up to see he had added a jacket, but still had bare legs and was wearing the striped boxer shorts.

With a grin, I said, "Honey, aren't you going to wear any pants?"

(Who was the calm one?)

He looked down, said, "Oh!" and went back upstairs. He returned dressed as though he were going to church and said to me, "Now, keep calm. Everything will be all right." That was approximately 7:00a.m.

As we drove Suzabella out of the alley onto 24th Avenue, he turned east toward City Park. "Where are you going?" I asked after a few blocks.

"Honey, I'm taking you to the hospital. I know what I'm doing," was his frustrated reply.

"Well, you're going the wrong way because Downing Street is the other direction and that's where we have to go to get to Porter Hospital."

This hospital (a wonderful institution today) is located far south on Downing Street. In 1945 it was a lone building sitting in the prairie away out on the edge of Denver. It was usually a half hour or more drive from our house to Porter, but this morning it seemed like forever! It was after 8:00 a.m. when we finally arrived. The sun was high and it was getting HOT!!!

In those days, Denver had little or no air conditioning in its buildings, only fans for cooling. I was well taken care of, but I could feel the heat even with the fan going. I wondered how Bill was getting along, so I asked the nurse to check on him. When the doctor came in I asked if he had seen my husband and he said he had talked to him and he was fine.

Early afternoon, Bill came into the room and I was so glad to see him. However, I was a bit concerned when I saw that he looked so strained. He no longer had on his hat, jacket, tie or his buttoned up collar. He was sweating heavily and very nervous. Fortunately, he had called his mother and she was there keeping him company.

When the doctor came in again, I told him that I was worried about my husband since he had a bad heart. He laughed and said, "I am taking care of your husband. He is fine. We have never lost a new father yet!!

128

Marie with grandparents, Sarah (with Louise), Joseph Anderson

Great grandmother, Richie Rivers & step-grandfather, Mack Bryant, Bill (with baby Louise) & grandmother Vivian Bryant

July 28th, 1945 was the hottest day of that summer. Our daughter, Louise Yvonne, was born about four o'clock that afternoon with the temperature at 104 degrees! She was the only one of my children who arrived right on the predicted date.

Since I had no idea of what to do with this pretty little baby, we moved to my parent's home for the next two weeks. My mother loved her little granddaughter, and helped me learn how to care for her.

Grandmother Vivian Bryant, Marie with baby
Louise, Great-grandmother Richie Rivers

Bill, baby Louise, grandpa Joseph
Anderson

After we returned to our home, Bill became the greatest father.
He could calm her when she cried, feed her, burp her and change her
clothes. There were no disposable diapers in those days, only cloth
diapers that had to be properly folded and pinned to fit the baby. Louise
was so tiny that Bill's first diapering fell off when he picked her up, so I
had him pin it to her shirt. When she spit up on him, the first few times
he had to change his shirt. After that he would just wipe it clean. Finally,
he said, "This is my daughter and if it smells at the office and they don't

like it, that's just too bad!" What a father!!!

Bill was a chain smoker, which did not help his breathing or his bad heart. One day when he came home from the doctor he didn't say anything, went upstairs, came down and said he would be back, as he went out the door. I was worried because he didn't look well and I wondered what the doctor had said.

When he returned I asked, "What happened at the doctor's? Where did you go without saying anything?"

In a strained voice he replied, "The doctor told me that he could do no more for me unless I stopped smoking. Otherwise, I had six months to a year to live. I came home and gathered up all of my smoking materials. I took my cigarettes to your dad and my pipes and tobacco to Bryant. I thought of my baby and I want to live to see her grow up, so I am going to stop smoking!" Louise was only a few months old.

He had a tough time fighting the nicotine urge with the temptation of office smokers, but he substituted packs of chewing gum. He never smoked again; his health improved and he lived to enjoy our family.

At the end of my maternity leave I resigned to stay home and have my family. I wanted to give my children the kind of start I had been giving other children for ten years.

After the war, things that had been unavailable or rationed were once more on the market. To our surprise and great relief, we received a notice from Montgomery Ward that they had the electric unit for our refrigerator and would be out to install it. This was like a blessing from Heaven – no more ice box, automatic refrigeration!!!

The Triangle still kept in touch with each other, but not as often since our lives had changed. Activities slowed down at the Y.W.C.A. after a year, so the assistant was not needed. Jeanne went back home to West Virginia, married, and they moved to Cleveland, Ohio. Fannie and Emerson married after he completed medical school. They had a baby girl a few months before Louise was born.

Eleanor and Noel moved to California with his five year old son, Noel, Jr., to whom Eleanor became a devoted step-mother. In January of 1947, they had another son, Wayne. I missed my friend, but we kept in touch. We got together when they came to visit her family. Bill and Noel developed a strong friendship, so the four of us had great times together over the years.

By the time Louise was a toddler, Bill would take her with him for rides on the street car, to visit friends, even to the barbershop to get his hair cut. He enjoyed showing her off!

Our son, Richard Joseph, was born April 20, 1948. When the nurse brought him to me to take him home, his breathing was erratic and he had lost a whole pound from 71/2 pounds to 6 ½ pounds. When I asked the nurse about his condition, she took him away, finally brought him back, but could not explain what was wrong. He sounded as though each breath would be his last. I was frantic! When we got home, Bill's mother and grandmother were waiting to see their grandson. They were shocked. I called the doctor immediately. He told me to bring him in right away.

When we arrived at the doctor's office, he was furious that he had not been called from the hospital about this baby. With every labored breath you could hear a rattling in his throat. The doctor looked and listened, said nothing and gave him a shot of penicillin. Then he told me that my baby had bronchitis. He gave me a small syringe and told me to use it to pull the mucus out of his throat whenever I heard the sound.

Baby Richard's bassinet was beside my bed and every half hour or so I was using the syringe to relieve his breathing. This went on day and night. Bill moved into Louise's room so he could get some sleep to be able to go work. We had moved our original bed into that room. Louise still slept in her crib. Gradually, Richard's breathing improved and I could get some sleep. However, I must have kept an ear tuned to my baby because I would be wide awake immediately if there were the slightest sound in the change of his breathing.

One week later, when I took Richard to the doctor, he could not believe that this baby was still alive and breathing normally. That was when he told me that bronchitis was 99% fatal in newborns, so he had given him a full shot of penicillin since he really did not expect him to live. This little, scrawny, two week old baby had developed a slight cough that loosened the mucus enough for me to extract it. The doctor said it looked as though Richard would be all right, but he needed to get some weight on him.

I sent up my prayers of thanks to the Good Lord for saving my son. I was sure that God must have had a special plan for him!

Richard – 6 months

Richard & Louise

Lousie, Marie & baby Richard

In 1940 I had bought six lots for $100 a lot on West Sixth Avenue in the far Western Barnum area, almost in Lakewood. We wanted to move back to West Denver where there was more open space to bring up our family, so in 1947 I started planning to build a house on those lots. I studied floor plans, talked with contractors and learned about sizes of rooms, thickness of walls and general construction of houses. On graph paper, I drew my floor plan to scale. I wanted a brick house. Unfortunately, during the war bricks were unavailable with shortage of help and great military demand. It took years for bricks to be available to build houses, since business buildings took priority after the war. I never gave up. I just put my plans on hold when I was told my house could be built with siding and a brick facing added later. No Way! I just kept improving my plans.

Louise started walking at ten months old and never stopped. At two years old I took her to the nursery class at church and I returned as a Sunday School teacher at Shorter, just as I had been before. It was then that I met Mrs. Ira Slack, who was the Sunday School Superintendent.

We attended two churches. Bill belonged to Holy Redeemer Episcopal Church and I was a member of Shorter. Every other Sunday we attended each other's church. Since I wanted to have communion at Shorter, we went there on first and third Sundays, so second and fourth Sundays were Redeemer. Fifth Sunday was tossup.

I wanted all the children brought up together in one church, Shorter or Redeemer. We decided that if our first child were a girl, the children would be brought up in my church; if the first were a boy, they would be in Bill's church. Of course, with Louise being our first child, our children were reared in Shorter, but the family continued to attend both churches every other Sunday for a long time.

Our house had no yard, and with Louise almost three years old and being "little perpetual motion," we needed space for her to play. It so happened that Mrs. Rivers wanted to be closer to her friends in Northeast Denver and Mrs. Bryant would not have to drive clear across town so often if we just swapped houses. They would have no yard to take care of on 25th Avenue, and we would have play space for Louise at the old home on West 11th Ave. Richard was still a baby. We made the exchange and it was perfect.

When Louise was three years old she had a tonsillectomy. The doctor said to keep her quiet so the incision would heal. Trying to keep this three-year-old quiet was almost impossible! After the first day, she was laughing and playing with her baby brother. The third day she was jumping, running, squealing and making Richard laugh. That night, after midnight, I was awakened by a sound of choking and crying. When I rushed into her room, Louise was gasping and bleeding from her mouth. I was scared to death! I called Bill and he called the doctor who told him to bring her to Children's Hospital right away. We wrapped her up and away Bill went with our daughter. I had to stay with Richard, and I prayed.

After what seemed like an eternity, they returned with a very quiet little girl. Bill said the doctor was really upset with Louise. She had torn the stitches loose in her throat and could have bled to death. He made it very clear to her that she was to keep quiet, as he cleared out her throat and repaired her damage. She got the message, because we had a very quiet, inactive little girl for days as her throat healed.

On January 22, 1950, William Rivers Greenwood, Jr. was born.

Louise, baby Bill, Jr., & Richard

Louise, 5, Richard, 3 1/2, Bill, Jr.,1 1/2

Two days after little Billy's birth, Bill arrived at the hospital with a grin on his face. "Honey, I think we are going to get our house built!"

"Really? A brick house?" I asked.

"Yes, I was talking to Earl West and he said he had a contractor who was building houses for him and he was sure he could build our house."

"Who is Earl West?" I wanted to know.

"Oh, he is a realtor who has an office near Five Points and has built a number of houses for some of the people we know," was his reply.

After I got back on my feet, we met with Earl West and the builder and made our plans to build on my property at 4700 West Sixth Avenue. When the city widened Sixth Avenue from Federal Blvd. west to Remmington Small Arms Plant (now the Federal Center) during the war, they took three of my lots so I had three lots left. We were told our house could be ready by mid-summer.

I took my graph drawn plans to an architect to have the blue prints made. He was amazed at my accurately detailed drawing. He asked me if I had ever had any architectural drawing. I told him no; I had studied floor plans, talked to builders and drew up my plan to scale.

We applied for a Federal Housing loan and received an okay for $13,000 – the cost of building our brick home in 1950!!! It would have three bedrooms, a full basement and an attached garage.

Unfortunately, after we had signed the contract to build in early Spring, there was a huge construction strike. We had sold our house on 11th Avenue with the stipulation that we would move out within three months, when our new home was scheduled for completion. Weeks went by with no end in sight, so we moved our family to my parent's home. We were thankful that there was room for all of us and my folks really enjoyed their grandchildren.

We finally received word that they would be able to excavate for our basement and for pouring the foundation. That was all that happened because the concrete workers were still on strike, so the open excavation baked in the sun while waiting for the foundation to be poured. When the concrete workers' strike ended, I was there to watch them pour the cement for the foundation, two inches thicker than normal and corners reinforced with steel rods.

Summer moved on and eventually the carpenters came back to work and laid the sub-floor so that the bricklayers could build the walls. Another delay was waiting for the bricklayers' strike to end. Summer was coming to an end and we were beginning to wonder if the house would be enclosed by winter. When they finally came, I watched them build the brick and cinder block walls. On every seventh row of bricks the fifth brick was turned to tie into the inner cinder blocks. It was amazing to see the strength of that construction in the 1950's.

At last the windows were in and the roof completed. It was early Fall. The house was enclosed and interior work was begun. I was there every day to be sure my plans were carried out: two inch thick plastered walls and solid mahogany doors throughout the house, with A-1 hardwood floors.

We were still living with my parents. Louise was in kindergarten at little Perry School on First Avenue while Newlon School, two blocks from our house, was being built under the same construction delays that we were facing. It was due to open in 1950, but was not completed for opening until 1951.

One day, when Bill came from work, he told me that he had been offered a promotion to Budget Director at Lowry Air Force Base. The Colonel in charge of Budget was being transferred. Since Bill had developed Accounting into such a smooth running office, he was asked if he would be interested in taking over the Budget Office (since it was in need of organization.)

Bill wasn't sure he wanted to give up his comfortable Accounting Office and take on the problems he knew were awaiting in the Budget Office (although it meant quite a promotion). He wanted my opinion, so I told him to analyze the situation and make his decision with whichever position he felt comfortable. After a few days, he decided to accept the Budget offer.

Since it was a Colonel's job and Bill was civil service, a civilian, there would have to be a dispensation made for him. The dispensation came through and Bill became the first civilian Budget Director at Lowry in the history of the U.S Air Force!

The Budget Office was in bad shape: incomplete records, workers with no responsibilities, no schedule or organization. It was worse than Bill had expected. However, within six months he had that office running smoothly. Over time, Bill balanced out the shortages in the budget. A new General came on Base and demanded new furniture for his housing. Bill told him that was not in the budget. When the General insisted that he be accommodated, Bill told him there were all kinds of furniture in the warehouse, both new and used, so he was sure he could find what he needed. The General was furious, but he could do nothing about Bill since he was civilian, not military. The General must have found his furniture because Bill heard no more from him.

Over the years, Bill was able to have a new chapel built at Lowry that could be scheduled by all faiths. He updated and refurnished the NCO recreation facility. He remodeled the Officer's Club and became a member since his position as Budget Director was that of a Colonel.

In December 1950, our new house was finally ready for occupancy, so we moved into our beautiful home and settled into family life. I spent weeks making lined draperies for the picture windows. At last, <u>by the Grace of God</u>!!!

Family home designed by Marie

Bill, Jr., Louise, baby James, Richard, & great-grandma Richie Rivers

Our fourth child, James Lee Greenwood, was born April 16, 1952, one day before our ninth anniversary. Bill took a week's leave to take care of the children. Our house was a mess and he said he would get it organized. I thought, "Good luck!" When he came to visit me in the hospital, he was exhausted and could hardly stay awake. He was learning that organizing a household with three small children, 6, 4, and 2 years old, was not the same as organizing an office. It does not happen! He was happy to get back to the office.

I loved our family. I kept them clean, but no ironing. I kept them well fed, although I did not like to cook. I kept them happy, but I was no housekeeper. My time was full taking care of my children and my husband. Our house was clean, but cluttered. My mother would straighten up the house and once she said, "What if someone would come to visit?"

My answer was, "This is my house and anyone who drops in without calling ahead, so I can prepare, must take what they find. If they are offended, they need not come back again." My mother just shook her head and never asked again.

My father raised chickens and had customers for eggs and fryers. Bill and I would deliver across town for him. We always had plenty of food – chicken, eggs, milk by the gallon, etc. I handled our family budget by shopping for sale items and paying our bills on the "pacifying system": pay what needed to be paid and "pacify" others with minimum payments. It worked with our limited budget. When Bill was asked how he managed to stabilize Lowry's budget, he said he used some of his wife's plan of paying bills. I felt complimented!

Bill always wanted the best for me and our family. Everything we did was for **us** and almost everything we had was **ours**. We made decisions together, shared problems and joys, solved our differences agreeably, and always presented a united front to our children. Dinnertime was family time when we communicated with each other – good, bad or indifferent. Life nor marriage is perfect, but solving problems and disagreements <u>amicably</u> accentuates the good and the understanding that strengthens love and respect in any relationship. Life in the Greenwood family was building up to be quite an adventurous experience!!!

Louise, age 9   Richard, age 7   Bill, Jr. age 5   James, age 3

(L-R) Louise, Bill, Sr., Richard, Marie, Bill, Jr., James

In their "Sunday Best"

CHAPTER 8
Family Experiences, Activities and Achievements

Since we had so many grandparents, we had to identify each one so we would know whom we were talking about. Mrs. Rivers became "Big Grandma," and Mrs. Bryant was "Little Grandma." My mother was "One Grandma." My father was called "Grandpa," and Mr. Bryant was called "Granddaddy."

Louise Yvonne walked at ten months. She was so tiny that she could walk under our kitchen table. She grew very slowly, but one day her head bumped the table; she sat down, looked up as though to say, "Where did that come from?!" After that, she ducked under the table only a few more times.

Mrs. Josephine Price was Louise's godmother. She took us to Fontius Shoe Store to buy the first hard soled shoes for her. Louise's feet were so small that their smallest shoe had to be stuffed with tissue to fit her feet. Mrs. Price bought two pairs – brown for everyday and white for dress-up.

One day when Louise was about a year old, I took her downtown shopping in her little stroller. In Woolworth, I stopped for a few seconds to look at something and when I turned around the stroller was empty! I looked around the counter, down the aisle, but there was no Louise. I panicked!!! I called her name and frantically asked the few customers if they had seen a tiny child running by. No one had seen her and I was shaking with fear. Suddenly I heard someone call out, "Here she is!"

On the far side, two counters down, a clerk had rescued my little two-foot tall daughter. I thanked the clerk profusely and blessed the Lord for saving my child. (Louise was very quick and ran more than she walked.) I took no more chances with Louise. I bought a little body harness with a detachable strap which I put on her for safekeeping when we went shopping. I got a few strange looks occasionally with my child on a leash, but others had not experienced the trauma that I had gone through. Since she did not like the harness, she soon got the message to stay by me – no more harness!!

After we moved into our new home on West 6th Avenue, Louise was still in kindergarten at Perry School while Newlon School (two blocks away) was being completed. Her Grandpa would take her down to Perry School on First Avenue and bring her home for me. She was the only little minority in the kindergarten, but blended with all the other children. One day when I was combing her hair, and we were talking about school, she said, "I'm sure glad I am light."

"What did you say?" I asked.

"I am glad I am light," she repeated. I almost popped her on the head with the comb, but figured I had better find out why she said it. "Why?" I asked.

"Oh, I don't know. I'm just glad I'm light." I presumed there had been some racial talk among the children at school. This was time for a good lesson!

"Do you mean you love Big Grandma more than Little Grandma because her skin is white and Little Grandma's brown?"

"Oh, no!" she said. "They are my grandmas."

"Do you love your brother, Billy, more than Richard because he is lighter?" I asked.

"Oh, no!!!" she exclaimed. "They're my brothers!"

"Do you love Daddy more than me because he is light?" That did it! She was almost sobbing, "Oh, NO!!!"

My next remark was, "Remember, you do not choose your friends from the way they look on the outside. You find out what they are like on the inside. I know you may not understand this now, but just tuck it back in your mind and some day, when you need it, you will have it." I continued," I had a friend who was dark-skinned and not pretty on the outside, but was such a nice person. She was honest and enjoyed the same things that I like doing; I never thought of her as how she looked. We were good friends." I smiled. "I had a mother of one of my first graders who was light skinned and pretty, but she was selfish, pretended to be more that she was. So I wanted to be near her only when necessary. Remember, being light-skinned does not make you any better than anyone else."

I taught this to all my children and they have friends of all colors, races and ethnic backgrounds.

Since she was the only granddaughter, her grandmothers loved taking her shopping and buying her pretty clothes. Louise loved being dressed up – unlike her mother!

It wasn't until third grade that I realized my daughter was a born "dancer." The Denver Public Schools had an annual Play Festival each spring at the City Auditorium. The same dances were taught in the schools and the best dancers from each school were selected to dance with their grade level at the big Festival. Louise was one of the few selected from Newlon School to perform with the third grade dancers. We were thrilled! However, when the Newlon third graders danced at our PTA meeting, one little girl in front of Louise was out of rhythm trying to keep up; Louise just pushed her out of the way without missing a step and kept going. She was a natural dancer with a perfect sense of rhythm.

Louise had friends at school and friends at church. She was the smallest and the youngest of a group of girls in Shorter's YPD, but she was as active as the older high school girls, although she was still in junior high. Mrs. Ira Slack was in charge of the Young People's Department of Shorter A.M.E. Church.

In the summertime of 1959, there was an A.M.E. Youth Conference being held in Detroit. Mrs. Slack was planning on taking a group from Shorter, including Louise who was excited about going. Mrs. Slack told me she would need some help chaperoning, would I like to go with them. I helped with YPD often and teenagers were not a level with which I was comfortable, but I was learning since my daughter had just become one of them.

With Louise's enthusiasm and the prospects of her being away from me for the first time, I told Mrs. Slack I would go with them. There would be five girls and one boy. It was a relief to know the boy would be staying with relatives in Detroit.

When we arrived at our hotel, it was crowded. A large top floor room had been made into a dorm for our girls. Mrs. Slack, the minister's wife and I were assigned to share one large bedroom. We truly had "togetherness." The three of us adjusted to our differences. Our sense of humor kept us laughing. We got to know each other very well. In fact, Mrs. Slack and I developed a life-long friendship which included my family.

The girls took Louise as their little sister. They made her up, and dressed her as cute as could be. Since my daughter had personality and was no little "shrinking violet," she was attracting most of the boys. Mrs. Slack laughed and said the girls were wondering if they had made a mistake dressing up Louise. However, those girls bonded into a close friendship that lasted for years.

Louise graduates from high school

Lincoln High School opened the year that Louise would enter high school. Our area had a choice of going to Lincoln or going to West Denver High School. Since Bill and I were West High graduates, we chose to send Louise there. Ruth Dougherty was still gym teacher at West and she was elated when she found out Louise was my daughter. She almost smothered Louise with attention, although my daughter was more interested in dance than in sports. Louise danced in one of the big musicals featuring Denver Public Schools' talent. She was an Honorary Cadet, a member of the National Honor Society, sang on the famous West High School Christmas Tree and graduated in 1963.

The Owl Club, an organization of Black men, for many years has sponsored a Deb Ball for outstanding girl high school graduates. Louise was selected as one of the 1963 Debs. Finding a dress to fit my tiny daughter was a big problem. She was about the size of a sixth grader, so nothing was small enough for her, except in the children's department. At almost eighteen years old that would not work. Finally, at one of the expensive shops, we found a beautiful dress that she liked, but with the alterations it would have cost too much. I decided to make her dress since I had made so many clothes for much less.

We found a pattern quite similar to the dress she liked, so I bought the smallest size. The skirt had seven yards of material to attach to a fitted top. I had to adjust the pattern down to her size, which was somewhere around <u>zero</u>. The skirt was double, silk crepe like the top with an over skirt of tulle. That was the style! After making the waist to fit Louise, I spent days gathering the skirt material down to size to attach to the little waist. The finished dress was beautiful, fitted her perfectly, but my arms and shoulders ached. She was a beautiful little Deb.

At one time Louise had said she wanted to be a nurse, with her sensitive personality and a very "squeamish" stomach, I doubted this decision; so the summer before her senior year in high school, I had her enroll as a Candy Striper at Denver General Hospital. On her third day, she was placed in Emergency to help. When a bloody accident victim was brought in, the medical team wound up picking my daughter up off the floor as she passed out. For the rest of the summer she was assigned to the office to deliver records. She got the message that nursing was not for her.

Although, she wanted to be a dancer, she enrolled at Colorado State College in Greeley (now U.N.C.) and majored in Education. However, she made a record as a dancer in college. When she auditioned for the national Orpheus dance organization, she was taken in immediately. She danced in every musical that the music department produced, even choreographed many of the dances.

Her junior year Louise was the first Black **ever** to compete for Miss C.S.C. and became the second runner-up! This was the college competition for Miss America contest! After observing her in the competition, an United Airlines representative offered her a job as their first African-American airline "stewardess" (now called flight attendant), but she refused because she wanted to graduate. She was also in the C.S.C. Air Force Angel Flight Unit.

She received her B.A. Degree in 1967, and taught in Colorado Springs for a year. We had a little Volkswagon which she drove. One day, after a hard rain and a wet pavement, she was driving home for the weekend. A Semi passed her and splashed water on the little car as she approached a curve which Louise could not see. The car rolled into the median and the windshield shattered. The lap seatbelt saved Louise as she was thrown over the passenger seat which prevented her face from being cut from flying glass. The High Way Patrol called Bill at work and he was a nervous wreck when the patrolman met him. He calmed Bill down and told him Louise was all right. She was taken to Denver General Hospital where the nurses picked glass out of her hair. She had a small cut on her cheek and was scared, but otherwise all right. Her Guardian Angel was definitely riding with her that day!!!

Since she needed transportation, we took her to find a car. At our first stop, the salesman showed us a sporty little Chevrolet Camaro. This was a brand new model. Louise's favorite color – yellow! Since it was a "standard shift," it was being sold a t a discount. Louise drove standard and could afford the payments. The deal was done. She drove that little Camaro for many years!

United Airlines contacted her again, and she began thinking seriously about accepting. When she asked my advice, I told her since

Lousie as a United Airlines stewardess

she was "foot-loose and fancy-free" to try any adventure she found interesting. She accepted United's offer in 1968 and became the *third* Black stewardess hired in any airline in the United States. She barely made the minimum high of 5 feet, 2 inches. She was based out of Chicago, but after a year and a half she had had enough of following orders and back-breaking rules with no opportunity to express her own ideas. She had some "for fun" times, and learned a lot, but she resigned and went back to teaching - in Chicago!

Wherever Louise was and whatever she

was doing, Bill and I were always there to encourage her and support her!

Richard Joseph was born brown like his great grandfather. In fact, he looked like Joseph D.D Rivers. He walked at 10 ½ months, but unlike his speedy little sister, Richard took his time and walked very carefully and cautiously.

Bill, Sr. & Louise

When I put him on solid food, I became quite concerned because his system seemed to be intolerant to most foods. Mashed potatoes came right back up and he refused to swallow many vegetables, fruits and pureed meats. He drank a lot of milk, ate cooked cereal and occasionally a bit of other foods and juices. I told our pediatrician, Dr. Gardner, about my concern since Richard was so small and needed adequate nourishment. She told me to keep a list of everything he ate or drank for a week, no matter how much or how little. When I took the list back to her, her analysis was that through this strange diet, he was getting everything he needed. We were both very surprised!

Richard was a quiet thinker, had a subtle sense of humor, learned fast and had a mind of his own. As time went on, he developed his own diet of cinnamon toast, crisp bacon, dry cereal, waffles and pancakes, banana, carrot, occasionally orange juice (or a taste of something else), and lots of milk. He was small, but he was healthy!

We continued to take the children to the library and I was amazed at the books Richard chose when he was in first grade. His favorite series was about "Cowboy Sam" which was third grade level!

In second grade, he tested with an IQ of 120. I don't know where it went from there, as time went on, because he seemed to learn very fast and remembered everything!

When he was five years old, he said he wanted to play the violin. I had all of my children take a year of piano lessons in third grade before taking another instrument so they could learn to read music. At the end of his year of piano Richard still wanted to play violin, so when he was in fourth grade I told Gwen Beeler, the instrument teacher, about him. He was too small to play a full sized violin, so Gwen found a ¾ sized school instrument for him. I told Gwen I wanted to be sure that he really could play the violin before we invested in the instrument.

About six weeks later Gwen met me in the hall one day and said, "Marie, I have been intending to talk to you about Richard."

"What has he been doing?" I asked, expecting to hear that he had been goofing off.

"Oh, he's just fine, but I can't keep him busy. I give him music to work on while I help the other children, and in a few minutes he isn't doing anything. When I go to check on him he plays the music perfectly. This happens all the time and I love having him, but I think he really needs to have private lessons."

"Then you think he can play the violin!" I exclaimed.

"Oh, yes, he is talented and I want to keep him in my class in addition to having private lessons. He is playing better than some of the children I registered in the Denver University beginner's competition, but the deadline for registration has passed."

"What is that?" I wanted to know.

"Every year Denver University conducts a competitive music program for Denver Public Schools' students who play instruments and I can see Richard playing the violin," was her reply.

We contacted Mr. George Morrison, Sr., one of Denver's greatest violinists, musician and teacher. Richard and Mr. Morrison bonded into a lifetime friendship through which my son developed his amazing talent as a violinist, a performer and a composer.

In fifth grade, Gwen registered Richard in the Denver University competition. He was still quite small and still played the ¾ sized violin. He had memorized his composition and Gwen accompanied him on the piano. He was wearing a brown suit and he looked so tiny on the stage that I just prayed that he would make it through the competition. His performance was absolutely perfect – every note clear and on key! The only criticism the judges had was that he played looking straight at the audience instead of his violin, otherwise a perfect score!

When Richard's hands were large enough to handle a full sized violin, Mr. Morrison gave his star pupil one of his violins, which Richard played for the rest of his life.

My son was a born leader. He was on Student Council at Newlon School. He and three other outstanding boys, Hal Pierson, Jim Nushy and Chuck Davis, developed a close friendship that lasted beyond high school. At Rishel Junior High School, Richard played in the orchestra and taught himself to play big bass so he could play in the jazz band. In ninth grade he became "Head Boy" backed by his buddies. He even developed some slight-of-hand magic tricks! Richard and Hal developed a special friendship. Mrs. Pierson was like a second mother when he was at their house!

He became a winning debater at West High School. He played violin in the school orchestra, All City and State Competitions as one of the best performers. His friends encouraged him t o run for "Head Boy," but he hesitated since his popular friend, Jim Nushy, was planning to run. The buddies got their heads together and Jim Nushy decided not to run, but to back Richard. These friends had been supporting each other like this since elementary school! Richard won the election. He and the "Head Girl" worked as a team to improve their school's reputation. They did such a good job of developing positive publicity for West High School that the Rocky Mountain News wrote an article complementing these two leaders for their good work.

Richard was active in Shorter YPD. He sang in the Youth Choir with his sister and he played his violin at church programs.

He became quite a "flyer" on the trapeze at a class set up at the Y.M.C.A. When a troupe came through and practiced there, he was asked to join them, but he said no because he was just having fun. He set up a tight-wire in the back yard, and walked it with an umbrella. I don't know where he got that idea!!!

When the ski areas opened again, and we had given our children ski lessons, of course Richard excelled as usual. When he was sixteen, he heard about Jr. Ski Patrol training at Loveland Ski Area, so he enrolled – the first teenage Black to do so. All winter he drove himself up to Loveland Pass every Saturday and completed the course. He became such an expert that he was assigned to the Junior Patrol at Loveland Basin the following winter when he was seventeen.

His youngest brother had not learned to ski and wanted the exciting experience. Richard would take thirteen-year-old Jimmy with him and taught him the proper technique of the sport. Jimmy became an excellent skier and enjoyed every minute of the outdoor thrill with Richard.

One bright, sunny Saturday after they left for the slopes, the clouds gathered and by afternoon a sudden snowstorm was moving in. By the time the ski slopes closed at four o'clock, there was a massive blizzard in the mountains that moved into Denver by evening. From the weather report, the visibility was so poor in the blowing snowstorm that mountain highways were being closed. How were our sons going to get home? Richard had never driven in such extreme weather before. Would he be able to handle it safely? Bill and I could do nothing but wait and pray that there would be no accident.

Hours went by and finally the phone rang. It was Richard's voice letting us know that they were safe in Georgetown where the Highway Patrol had stopped all traffic. We breathed a sigh of relief. We could not go to sleep, so we stayed up, watched the blizzard outside, listened to the highway reports and prayed to the Good Lord to keep our sons safe. He must have heard our prayers for to our amazement, about midnight through all the snow we saw the car drive into our driveway. Our sons were safely home!!!

They had quite a story to tell. When they were permitted to leave Georgetown, the snow was still coming down thick and blowing. The windshield wipers could not keep the snow cleared so they could see the road, so Jimmy had to open the window on the passenger's side, stick his head out in the storm and tell his brother how to stay on the highway. He said it was scary! However, we praised our son, Richard, for his expert driving in getting them back home and again sent up our prayers of thanks to God for bringing our sons back safely!!!

Richard graduated from West Denver High School in 1966, and enrolled in Macalester College in St. Paul, Minnesota. With his sharp mind, his leadership and his decision-making abilities, he had talked with us about the possibility of trying Political Science. However, in college, his artistic talent and his intensive love of music took precedence. No matter what he did, playing his violin was his life, his joy, his relaxation. His instrument was like a part of his body so he became a part of the music department, played in the college symphony orchestra and held first chair in second violin section. In high school he had taught himself how to play guitar, so in college he developed a unique teaching plan by which he said he could teach anyone to play the guitar. It worked for him!

He added art to his music, and with his vivid imagination and his dexterity, he decided to major in Art. As usual, he excelled in this medium.

"Why aren't you majoring in music?" I asked in dismay.

"Music is my life, my joy, my relaxation. It makes me happy. I love it," he replied. "I want to keep it that way, so I will major in Art and minor in Music."

Richard graduated from Macalester in 1970 with honors for his music. He did part-time teaching, had an active combo in the St. Paul-Minneapolis area and married right after graduation. That proved to be a disastrous mistake, and ended in divorce.

He returned to Denver and his music career of teaching, composing and playing. His career was building up when the United States entered the Vietnam War. Richard was of

Richard

draft age and he told us he would never go to war because no one could put a gun in his hands to kill someone. He would leave the country. With his good health, he passed the physical, but when he was drafted he did leave the country. He went to London and then to Denmark where he became quite a performer with his band. He also walked tight wire playing his violin, until the ban was lifted here for deserters. He returned to Denver, taught violin and guitar, played bass in a band, renewed contact with his friends and enjoyed skiing all winter.

Richard had the amazing ability to communicate with people. No matter what the subject might be, he seemed to know enough to be able to discuss that topic! One day, I asked him how he happened to know so much. He smiled and said, "I just read a lot.

William Rivers Greenwood, Jr. (Billy) was a happy, husky baby. Unlike his brother and sister, who would cry and go to no one but family members, little Billy liked being with people.

We had a "Teeter-Babe," a canvas seat in which the baby could bounce. Louise and Richard would not stay in it when they were babies, but Billy loved it! He would bounce and sing, fall asleep, wake up and continue bouncing. When not in the Teeter-Babe, he would crawl all over the house. By the time he was a year old, he could stand up well balanced to play with toys, but would crawl to where he wanted to go. He could crawl faster than his sister and brother could walk, and if they ran, he was close behind! At thirteen months he began walking, happily with his brother and sister.

There were early signs of his being an audio visual learner. We had a View Master with which we all enjoyed looking at the three dimension pictures, but Billy used it constantly and talked about what he saw and why the three dimension viewing made them seem so real.

Billy wanted to play the saxophone, so after his year of piano lessons, we enrolled him with an instrument teacher and bought him an alto sax. He played in the school band and enjoyed his music.

His audio-visual skills became quite evident at Newlon School where he became proficient at handling projectors and recorders. By the time he was in fifth grade, teachers would ask for him to help them if they had problems with the equipment. He thoroughly enjoyed doing what he knew best to do. By the time he was in sixth grade, he was called from class so often for emergencies that his grades were suffering. The principal and I decided to curtail this activity until his grades improved. He had made such a record as an audio-visual trouble-shooter that when he entered Rishel Junior High School, he was assigned as an assistant to the Audio-Visual director.

Billy continued to play his saxophone in the school band at Rishel Junior High School and at West Denver High School. He played in All City Band, and when they needed a Baritone Sax player, Billy was the only one big enough with enough strength to blow it! He was also a stage assistant for plays and programs at West.

Bill, Jr.

He was the biggest defense player on the West High football team, but he did not want to hurt anyone, so he avoided tackling hard; however, he received a back injury and a broken nose. He remained on the team in charge of equipment, which was fine with him.

Billy had (and still has) a happy, pleasant, friendly personality that opens many doors for him. With his expertise in communication, he was hired to work at Channel 2 TV in December 1965 before he was sixteen years old and still in high school. It was a weekend, late night schedule so his grandpa would pick him up at midnight after he closed down the station. During his senior year, he worked part time at Channel 4 TV and radio.

After his graduation in 1968, he worked full time at Channel 6 and part time at Channel 4. During this time, he was enrolled at Metro State College as a full time student majoring in Music, until 1970. He had organized a ten-piece band, "The Team," and a four-piece combo of saxophone, piano, bass and drums so he dropped out of college and devoted his time to his music.

When called in for the draft during the Vietnam War, he was exempt from service because of the back injury and the broken nose (which he received from playing football) and from which he still had periodic pain.

As a young entrepreneur in 1975 he got the idea of chartering buses to ski areas to save car drivers the expense of gas and provide easy transportation. His dad and I helped our son with the deposits on the buses. He cornered the market that winter. With the help of Dave Cook Sporting Goods, the buses were rented through Bill's (no longer "Billy"), "Sports Forum Cooperated."

In 1979, Bill continued his education at Denver Community College and University of Colorado, Denver. He received his AA degree from Denver Community College.

Our son, Bill, was always the family helper. After his sister and brothers moved away, he would look after his grandparents and take care of any needs when his dad and I were away. He was always "Mr. Dependable"!

James Lee (Jimmy) Greenwood was born hours past midnight, my biggest baby – 8 pounds 5 ounces! The morning following his birth, I was anxious to see my new son, since all I remembered was a crying, very red-faced new born. When the nurse arrived at my room, she looked at me, looked at the baby in her arms, backed up and looked at the room number, then left. What was the problem? Soon she returned with little Jimmy who was white skinned like his dad's baby picture, and the nurse was confused when she saw my brown face.

Little Jimmy was his sister's living doll. Although she was a tiny seven-year-old, she was strong and would carry him like one of her dolls. He was growing so fast that I wondered how long it would be before he would be almost as big as she was.

One day as she carried him to her room, his feet barely missed the floor and soon I heard him cry. I rushed to see what was happening and found her trying to twist his arm into one of her doll's sweaters. "What are you doing?" I asked.

"I can't get this sweater on him," she cried. "I put it on him the other day!"

"Louise, he is growing. He is a baby and getting bigger; he doesn't stay the same size as your dolls." I gave her a baby sweater for him.

Jimmy grew very fast, was standing at ten months, and began walking soon after. I was glad when he could play outside in the sunshine and get some color. He had an engaging smile and bright, mischievous eyes. He was smart and with an outgoing personality, he could turn on the charm and be most convincing about anything. I called him my little "con" man, but I was usually ahead of him to keep him in line.

Jimmy wanted to play trumpet, but one day when he and Billy were playing and "rough housing" in the basement, Jimmy fell on his face and broke his front teeth. Since they had to be replaced, no way could he blow a trumpet. He decided to play drums, so after two years of piano lessons we let him have drum lessons with Bill Warner the Denver Symphony principal percussionist drummer who was recommended as one of the best. We bought him a snare drum and eventually a drum set. Bill Warner told me, one day, that Jimmy was one of his best pupils. Since he had piano lessons, he could already read the notes and rhythm, so he just had to teach him the technique of playing the drums. Jimmy's coordination in using his hands, feet and eyes was excellent.

He played in school bands at Newlon, Rishel and West High. When he played in All City Band, he was the only drummer who learned to play the timpani; because of his piano lessons he could tune the kettle drums. He played drums in his brother's band, "The Team," and filled in in Bill's combo when the drummer could not be there.

I made sure that all of my children learned to swim. At five years old I took them to Barnum Park in the summer for swimming lessons. Jimmy became the expert! He swam on the team at Barnum Park. When he was in junior high school, he took the bus to North High School to swim on their summer team and became a Junior Life Guard. He was in charge of the waterfront at Boy Scout Camp Tahosa, (the only Black staff member). He was captain of the team at West High and lettered in swimming.

He was on Student Council all three years at West, and became President of All City Council his senior year.

His teachers loved hm. With his charm and his intelligence, he managed to get by without actually working too hard academically. Occasionally, I would check on him or a teacher would call to say he had not completed an assignment. I would get on him about the problem; he would take care of it and go merrily on his way. He graduated from West High School in 1970, and enrolled at Colorado State University in Fort Collins.

James

I warned Jimmy that he would be on his own in college. There would be no teacher to remind him if he did not turn in an assignment and no mother to check on him. He, alone, would be responsible for getting the work done.

With all the new freedom, he was having a great time at C.S.U. and classes were secondary! When I would ask him how things were going, his answer was always, "Just fine. I have everything under control!"

At the end of the first semester his grades were terrible. When he failed one class he wailed, "That's not fair. He didn't tell me the final paper was due!"

"Weren't you given an outline or schedule of the class in the beginning for the semester?" I asked.

"Yes, but he didn't remind me," was his reply.

My answer was, "The professor wasn't supposed to remind you. You are now a young adult who is expected to assume responsibility.

You had all of the information for the semester and it was up to you to take care of assignments. Now, you settle down and bring those grades up next semester."

Jimmy's grades improved some, nowhere near up to his ability. In the spring when he was playing Rugby, he had a disabling accident. He destroyed the cartilage in his knee and was taken to the hospital in Fort Collins. Bill and I were in New York when we got the message, after midnight, from our son Bill that Jimmy was injured and would have an operation that day. We called the hospital and arranged to have the operation delayed until after our return that afternoon. On our arrival at Stapleton Airport in Denver, we drove to Fort Collins to see Jimmy. The operation was scheduled for the next morning, so we stayed overnight in a motel so that we could be with him the next day.

It took quite some time for recovery. His dad advised him to take "incomplete" in one of his questionable classes since it was so late in the semester, but our son said, "No. I have talked to the teacher and everything is fine." He was shocked when he failed the class.

A short time after school was out for the summer, Jimmy received a letter from the University. He took it downstairs to his room. Soon he came stomping up the stairs to the kitchen absolutely furious! "This isn't fair!" he shouted as he sat down and pounded on the table.

"What happened?" I wanted to know.

"They don't want me back at C.S.U.!" The letter was from the Board of Directors telling him he was being dropped because of his poor grades and suggesting that he enroll in another college or junior college. If he improved his record in a year, they would be glad to consider registering him again at C.S.U.

I let him blow, wipe his tears and settle down, then I quietly said, "You know, if I were on that board, I would have put you out, too. They did not know Jim Greenwood. You were only a number among thousands of students, and your grades were so poor they did not meet their standards." He looked at me in disbelief that his mother showed no sympathy!

I continued, "We have let you do it your way and it didn't work, so now you will do it THE GREENWOOD WAY. You get yourself into another college or junior college, and buckle down to work or get a job and take care of yourself. I recommend a junior college like Western State in Gunnison, Metro State in Denver, or Northeastern in Sterling. I have read a lot about Northeastern; it is rated one of the best junior colleges in the country. If you don't make it there by the end of freshman year, you are **out.** If you get in school and bring your grades up, we will help you. If you get a job and live at home, you will pay rent. The choice is up to you." He had to do some thinking!

One day Jim said to me, "I think I'll go to Denver University. I have a friend who is planning to go there and we could rent an apartment near the University."

"Who is going to pay for the apartment?" I asked.

"Oh, you and dad would help me!" he exclaimed.

"Oh, no, if you go to Denver University you will live at home."

"Well, his dad is going to pay for him," he said in surprise.

"That's fine for him , but you will live at home or get a job to pay for the apartment," was my final reply. That ended that idea.

Jim had a summer job at Public Service, and soon after that episode he called me from work to see if he could have the car the next day. (He use to ride to work on a little motor scooter.) He had called Northeastern Junior College and made an appointment to meet with the Dean. They would let him off from work since it was for education. I was so pleased to see him take initiative to get back in school; I told him he could have the car for the day.

Sterling is over 70 miles from Denver, more than an hour's drive. The interview with the Dean ended with our son being enrolled in Northeastern Junior College for the fall of 1971. Jim was so happy because he did it all by himself!!!

He made a complete turn-around and settled down to taking his classes seriously. One day when I was bringing him home for a weekend, he surprised me by saying, "Mom, you were right when you

160

told me I should have worked harder in high school. If I had, I wouldn't be taking 'dumbbell' English now!!"

His grades were great and he was on the Dean's Honor Roll both years. A professor, Mr. Bailey, became his mentor, advisor and close friend like a father.

In the spring of his second year at Northeastern, Jim and Paul (one of his buddies) were working at a Pizza restaurant. The weather had been miserably cold, windy and rainy for more than a week. Finally, the clouds cleared away, the sun came out, and the days warmed up. We had let Jim have a car, so one day on their break from work Jim and his friend decided to take advantage of finally being able to get out on a beautiful day. They were happily driving on a country road that went up a hill and appeared to go down the other side. At the top of the hill there was no road so the car went off into space, crashed and rolled. By the Grace of God, our son was not injured, but his friend Paul was killed! Jim tried to revive his buddy with artificial respiration which he knew from life guarding, but it was too late. In desperation, Jim ran back to a farm house which they had passed and called the Highway Patrol. He was in shock! There was no sign that the road made a sharp turn at the top of the hill. Because there was no sign, and Jim was driving carefully, the Patrolman said it was purely an accident and Jim was not at fault. There should have been a sign indicating a sharp, unseen turn at the crest of the hill.

When I arrived home from school, Bill and son Bill were waiting for me to tell me that Jim had an accident and was in the hospital so we had to get to Sterling. We got into the car and away we went – fast! We forgot to check the gas gauge! When we arrived at the hospital, we were amazed to find that our son had been checked out by Mr. Bailey and taken to his home. We called Jim's mentor, got the address and drove to his house. When we arrived, Mr. Bailey and his wife had bedded Jim down and were taking care of him as though he were their son. Jim was in severe shock, crying and glad to see us. We could not thank the Baileys enough for what they had done for our son. However, we knew we had to get going so we could get back home before night.

As we drove out of town, there was a black cloud to the north and a warning on the radio that a terrible storm was developing in Wyoming and heading fast for Colorado. As we drove along I-76, I happened to look at the gas gauge – almost empty! The storm was catching up with us and we had to get some gas. It was getting darker and began to rain. We got behind a semi and followed it. Bill said it might lead us to a truck stop for gas. After what seemed like forever, in the distance off the highway appeared some lights. It was a semi truck stop, so we were able to fill up. We heard on the radio that the storm had developed into a blizzard and the highway was being closed. We managed to get back on the highway, stay ahead of the closures, and get safely back home just as the blizzard hit Denver. The Lord took care of us!!!

In Jim's devastation, three of his "hippie" friends came to comfort him. I was not comfortable with the stringy-haired, scroungy-dressed, trio, but every day one or all three came to cheer him up and sometimes take him with them.

Paul was cremated and a memorial service was planned for him. Paul's mother liked Jim, but Paul's father was prejudiced and hated Jim (because he was African-American), so he did not feel welcome to attend. It hurt!! His friends came early that day, and convinced Jim to go to the memorial with them. They were all college friends.

The change in my son when he returned from the service was unbelievable! He was upbeat, talking and laughing. Paul's mother was glad that he came and assured him that the accident was not his fault. The last time Paul was home, she said he told her goodbye in such a strange way that she now knew it was his time to go. This relieved Jim from the pressure of blaming himself for the death of his friend for the rest of his life.

I had to put into practice some of the basic philosophy I had taught my children: do not judge people by how they look on the outside, but find out what they are like inside! These "hippies" were real friends who stayed with my son when he needed them the most. They were the ones who helped him to face returning to Northeastern to graduate! They also continued their college educations. Fall of 1973, Jim entered the University of Northern Colorado in Greeley as a junior majoring in Radio and Television Production.

He worked as a life guard at several pools in the summer. His first assignment was at Skyland Pool (now Hiawatha Davis Center). There he met the love of his life, young pool manager Jo Ellen Seymour.

One summer he was assigned as guard at 20th Street Recreation guarding the pool where I taught myself to swim during days of segregation!

He graduated from U.N.C. in 1975, and spent a year and a half at Wisconsin University in Madison, before going to New York City to work at Paramount Pictures on a graduate internship in marketing. This proved to be the beginning of Jim's successful professional career!

He was exempt from military service because of his knee injury.

We had "Greenwood Family Rules and Traditions." These are a few examples: there were no specific "his and her" chores or responsibilities. Everyone learned to do everything and to work together. Once when Bill and I were away, 17-year-old Richard was responsible for getting 13-year-old Jimmy to his band concert. The button was missing from the collar of his brother's only white shirt. Richard found a button, needle and thread in my sewing kit, sewed the button on the shirt and got his brother to the concert properly dressed to perform.

For the safety of our children when Bill and I were not with them, the oldest was in charge with no arguments. Any problems or disagreement would be taken care of by their dad and me when there was a complaint.

We took turns having one BIG birthday party each year. Whichever child we were celebrating, their friends and parents were invited, but everyone in the family prepared for the event and enjoyed the fun. Birthdays were important, so there were special family celebrations on each of the other birthdays.

Christmas tradition was exciting. A week or two before Christmas we would drive to the mountains to cut our Christmas tree, and small trees for the grandparents, and Mrs. Price. We would strap our big tree to the top of the car, fit the three small trees in the trunk or around the children. This was an annual adventure!

One evening we would go down town to see the lights and Christmas decorations in the store windows. Everyone would have a little Christmas money to spend for "fun gifts" for each other when we would go shopping on Christmas Eve after the stores had reduced merchandise to bargain shop and stay within their allotted funds. Bill and I always bought a big gift to surprise each child while they were young, like a bicycle or camera. When they were older, we would buy a surprise Christmas gift the entire family could enjoy – a color TV or pool table.

Everyone wrapped their gifts on Christmas Eve and placed them under the tree which we had all enjoyed decorating, but Christmas morning no one went into the living room until we were all together. It was exciting turning on the lights and opening gifts around the tree. After breakfast or early afternoon, we would take gifts to the grandparents and Mrs. Price to wish them Merry Christmas. Back home the rest of the day, we just enjoyed a tired, happy family Christmas!

Throughout these family activities we developed a close-knit family unit, but our children were free to develop their individual interests and personalities.

Richard, Bill, and James

CHAPTER 9
Family Trips and Adventures

Our children learned to adjust to traveling while still babies. On a bright, sunny Saturday or Sunday afternoon Bill and I would decide to drive to the mountains, to Colorado Springs or just follow an interesting road to see where it would take us. We started when Louise was three years old and Richard was a baby. Louise would get car-sick, but with our frequent trips she adjusted by just falling asleep. Billy and Jimmy were added as babies, so I would pack a bottle of formula and extra diapers, as usual, to have if needed.

As the children grew and looked forward to these excursions, one of our special treats was to stop at the <u>A&W Root Beer Stand</u> on West Alameda Avenue where they gave free "kiddy" samples with our adult purchases.

The children were small and fit on the back seat of Suzabella. Bill and I wanted to travel and take our children to see other parts of our country. However, I made it clear that short day trips in Colorado with young children were fine, but we would take no long trips with a baby in diapers!

The following stories are some of the highlights of our experiences. In 1954, when the children were two, four, six and nine years old, we planned our first big trip that summer to Yellowstone National Park to see the famous geyser, "Old Faithful." This adventure was truly planned on "Faith and Prayer," because we had very little money.

Suzabella had finally died and we bought another old used car. In those days, every gas station had free maps with parks, camp grounds and other information included, so we collected what we needed.

We figured we would need five days - one day to get to Yellowstone, three days to explore the Park and one day to return home. The only way we could afford the trip would be to camp. With no equipment of our own, we borrowed a tent with no floor from a friend. Another friend lent us a movie camera. We made menus and shopped for food, milk and drinks which we stored in our little cooler. We packed blankets for all of us and two folding cots for Bill and me to sleep on. For cooking and eating, we took a skillet, a pot and a bucket with paper plates and cups. We would cook on our little one-burner Coleman stove. We packed minimum clothes and decided that changing would be debatable, just enough to be reasonably clean – we would wear everything as long as possible. We bought a little one-wheel trailer in which to pack everything. With this inexperienced preparation for camping, we were ready to go. This was the beginning of the enthusiasm and anticipation of new adventures that carried the Greenwood Family through years of exciting experiences!

A few days before we were to leave, four-year-old Billy caught a cold and was coughing and blowing his nose. Since he was not sick in bed, we were sticking to our plan. The morning that we were leaving, my mother and father were there to see us off, and Mom was unhappy with Bill and me for going on this long trip with a sick child. The children were excited, and by the Grace of God, Billy's cold got better with the medication and his brothers and sister did not catch it!

We were driving along the highway in Wyoming when I heard Louise scream, "No, Richard, don't do that!" as I looked back, Richard was hanging on to the partially opened door of the car and Louise was holding onto his belt and pants. This was a four-door car, not two doors like Suzabella.

"Hold on to him Louise! Why did Richard open the door?" I yelled. He was so thin I was afraid his belt and pants would come off and he would be thrown out of the car. (In those days the rear doors opened from the front and not from the back.)

Louise was scared. "The door was not closed tight and he opened it trying to shut it," she answered. When he opened the door, the wind caught it and blew it open. Fortunately, he held on or he would have fallen out of the car. Bill had to slow down gradually, because a quick stop would have thrown Richard to the pavement. There was practically no traffic, so Bill slowly decelerated and as soon as he found a space on the side of the road he stopped.

Needless to say, we sent up our prayers of thanks to the Good Lord, complimented Louise for saving her brother and explained to Richard why he should never open a car door when the car was moving – tell us, and Dad or I would take care of it. It took me quite a while to relax from the trauma of realizing how close we came to losing our six-year-old son!!!

We made a few stops along the way to take in some of the beautiful and historic points of interest. It was late afternoon when we finally reached Yellowstone National Park. We eventually found the camp ground where we set up what was to be our "home" for the next three days. In setting up the tent we discovered it had no floor. We happened to have a tarp which we spread on the ground on which the children could sleep. Our only lights were our flashlights.

As the warm sun set and night moved in, it became cold! We were tired and ready to get some sleep, so I decided that, this first night, we would sleep in our clothes like the Camp Nizhoni camp-outs. We loosened our belts, put on fresh socks to keep our feet warm and the children snuggled into their blankets and slept. Bill and I wrapped ourselves in blankets on our cots. I think Bill slept, but for me it was one big mistake. I was so cold all night that I could not sleep, even when I put on my jacket. With all that cold air under me, I could not get warm. I learned a valuable lesson about camping, which we used on the rest our trips. Sleep on the ground; cots are not made for camping on cold nights!!!

The next morning I cleaned up the children, one at a time, starting with Louise and ending with Jimmy, while Bill prepared breakfast on the camp table. We took our time getting our campsite organized, so by afternoon we were ready to explore the Park. After driving around the beautiful lake and eventually finding out about Old Faithful, we were still tired. I was exhausted after the long drive and no sleep, so we headed back to camp and relaxed.

We had been warned to keep food securely locked up so bears could not get it. We locked our food in the trunk of the car. We had a visitor in the night, because there were big paw prints on the car the next morning. The food was safe.

The third day we were ready to see Yellowstone National Park. As I was finishing getting Jimmy dressed, Louise, Richard and Billy appeared with dust all over themselves.

"What on earth have you been doing to get so dirty?" I exclaimed. I had just cleaned them up and we were planning to head out after breakfast.

"Oh, we were just throwing some dust in the air," was Louise's reply.

Richard piped up with, "It was Louise's idea."

I could have swatted all of them, but I brushed them off as best I could and we had breakfast.

This proved to be our big day. We witnessed Old Faithful spout right on the hour – our big thrill! We followed the map to view the many hot mud pots and mini bubbling geysers. After getting in and out of the car numerous times to view these phenomena, we finally came to one where we all piled out of the car except Jimmy.

"Come on, Jimmy," we called.

"No," said Jimmy as he continued to sit in the car. "I ti-ed."

Bill and I looked at each other and broke into big grins. All of us had to laugh. We were all tired, but little two-year-old Jimmy was the only one with sense enough to quit when he had enough. We assured him that this was the last stop, but he refused to get off the seat until his dad backed up to the car door and told him he could ride "piggy-back." He climbed on his dad's back and we took our last look at a boiling, colorful mud pot before driving happily back to our camp.

The fourth day was an easy, relaxing day. I had noticed an elderly couple camping near us who frequently sat and looked our way. On this particular morning the old lady came over and greeted us with a pleasant smile.

"My husband and I have been watching you get your children ready each morning," she said. "We marvel at how you get them cleaned up and dressed and they are so well-behaved. We don't know how you do it! When you came the other day, and we saw the children we didn't know what to expect, since every time we had children here, they were noisy. I told my husband that I had to go over and compliment you two for the lovely family that you have."

I thanked her for coming over and told her how much I appreciated her compliment. I let my children know how important their good behavior had been.

We spent the afternoon driving around the Park to see some of the areas we had missed, then came back to get as much packed up as possible.

Early the fifth morning, we finished packing and took off. Along the way we stopped for a while at a lake near the majestic Tetons and the children had a chance to run and play. Late afternoon we were driving into our driveway on the last of our gas, no money, ready for a warm bath and eager for another happy trip!

We talked about where we would like to go next year and decided on going to the Black Hills of South Dakota to see the great Mount Rushmore Monument. This was the beginning of the whole family participating in the planning as we sat around the kitchen table. We got maps and information from AAA. For many months we discussed our plans and what we would need for the trip. The children learned to save spending money.

We traded the old car for a green Chevrolet sedan that had all four doors safely opening from the back. We decided to spend the fourth of July in the Black Hills and enjoy the spectacular fireworks which we had read about.

With the children getting bigger, all four of them on the back seat was getting a bit tight and they would argue about who would sit by the windows. I solved that argument by having them change places when they got back in the car whenever we would stop, no matter where we went – to church, to the store or on any outing.

However, I wanted them to be as comfortable as possible on our long trip to South Dakota. I figured if I could make the back seat into a kind of platform, the children would have room to sit or lounge at ease. Since apples came in small wooden crates in those days, the grocer gave them away or destroyed them. I brought home two crates and found they fitted perfectly on the floor of the car. Covered with a quilt, it made an adequate area of padded comfort.

They needed something in which to keep coloring books, crayons, small toys or small objects of interest, so they would not be scattered all over the car. When the boys wore holes in the knees of their jeans, I would cut off the legs, hem the pants for summer shorts and save the cut off legs. I devised these pieces of denim into four pockets, fastened them to coat hangers and hung them on the back of our front seat. It worked!

At the Army surplus store, we bought two double down-filled sleeping bags. Billy and Jimmy could sleep in the smaller inner bags; Louise and Richard would use the outer bags. Bill and I would still wrap up in blankets. We borrowed our friend's tent again, and the other friend was kind enough to let us use his camera.

We packed up our little one-wheel trailer and took off on July 1, 1955 for our second big adventure. After a hot day's drive, we were happy to find the camp ground indicated on the map and set up "home" for our stay in South Dakota. However, we were surprised to find that Mount Rushmore was farther from the camp ground than we had expected.

The next day we took a relaxing time familiarizing ourselves with our surroundings and meeting some neighbors. One pleasant couple was the member of a symphony orchestra and his wife, with whom we enjoyed talking about music. That afternoon we drove around sightseeing. We saw our first big buffalo herd, stopped at a quaint souvenir shop and visited the exciting Wind Cave.

On July 3rd, after breakfast, we took off to find the great Monument. As we drove along, we encountered some of the weirdest formations we had ever seen. They looked as though molten clay or lava had spewed up and hardened into odd-shaped images. Some were tall spires like deformed obelisks. One was called "the Eye of the Needle," because of the strange opening at the lower edge shaped like a huge needle's eye. Cars were permitted to drive, one at a time, through a narrow tunnel in the "Eye of the Needle."

Eventually, in the far distance, we caught sight of the white Rushmore Monument. As we drove toward it, the faces began to appear. Our greatest thrill was reaching the famous Mount Rushmore and taking pictures with the Monument as the background! This was before it became the commercial attraction of today.

On July 4th, we drove to the famous town of Deadwood and bought fireworks. We were told there was a big rodeo in Pierre, so away we went. It was hot and dusty at the rodeo, which reminded us of Cheyenne Frontier Days. We enjoyed the Indian parade and the cowboy activities. We even had cotton candy, but the heat and dust finally got to us, so we returned to our camp ground and that night enjoyed fireworks with the other campers. I don't know where the big display was, but we had fun.

The next day, we packed up and headed for home. After we paid for gas, Bill had 50 cents in his pocket. All the way back we laughed and prayed our car would have no problems – and it didn't. We arrived home safely, broke, happy and with the memory of another joyful educational experience.

Where shall we go next time? After much discussion, we decided on the exciting new Disneyland. Bill and I had relatives and friends in California whom we would like to see again, so this trip could be very special. However, a trip of this magnitude would take careful planning, so we decided to take a short trip in Colorado in 1956, and aim for the real Biggy Trip to California in 1957.

We had heard so much about Mesa Verde National Park in Southwest Colorado. We began making plans to visit the park in the summer of 1956 to see the fabulous cliff dwellings ruins.

I had gone back to work, so we had enough money to, finally, buy our own camping equipment. We invested in a 9 x 12 foot family tent, with a canvas floor in it. We also purchased a lantern. Bill and I finally acquired sleeping bags and we bought inflatable air mattresses for each of us. These were additional comforts for what I now called camping "Our Home Away From Home"!

One day Bill told me there was something he wanted to show me, so we left the children with their Grandma and Grandpa. As we drove south from Denver, I asked, "Where are we going?"

"Oh, you'll see," he answered. "I think you will like this."

As we drove into the little town of Castle Rock, Bill stopped at a small automobile dealership. As we entered, the owner greeted Bill with, "I'm glad you came. I think I have just what you want." Bill had told a friend how concerned I was about our growing children being cramped in the back seat of our car. I had seen other families, on our camping trips, with station wagons, and had said that I wished we had room for our children like that. His friend had recommended this dealer in Castle Rock for the lowest auto prices. Bill had called the owner and made this appointment.

I was completely surprised when I was shown a beautiful blue and white Chevrolet station wagon. Bill was beaming and asked if I like it.

"I love it!" I exclaimed. "But , can we afford it?"

"If you want it, we can afford it," was his reply.

Not only could I envision peace and comfort in our travels, but this would be the first brand new car we would have ever owned!!! The deal was done.

Bill drove the station wagon; I followed in the little green car back to my parent's house to surprise the children with our new purchase. The excitement of the children and the grandparents was overwhelming. We gave the little green Chevrolet to my dad to replace the ancient vehicle he was driving.

I assigned seating in our new station wagon. Louise and Richard had the middle seat by the doors. Billy and Jimmy had the rear seat. Now everyone had half a seat and a window – no more arguments.

On the morning that we left for our trip, my mom and dad were there to see us off, as usual. We made a few stops along the way. One of which was at a fish hatchery, where we watched officials replenishing the stream with hundreds of trout.

Our little one-wheeled trailer attached to our new station wagon slowed us down. It tended to sway unbalanced, at the speed of the new car. The result was that we did not reach our camp ground outside Mesa Verde until night.

In the meantime, Richard was complaining about an earache that was getting worse. We set up our tent by lantern light, bedded everyone down, except Richard who was quietly crying in pain. I was up all night trying to comfort him.

The next morning, Bill took Richard to the Ranger Station to see if they had some first aid to help him. I was surprised when they returned in less than an hour, both of them happy and laughing. There was actually a clinic at the Ranger Station with a registered nurse who knew, right away, what to do to ease Richard's pain. I sent up my prayer of thanks and relaxed.

In the meantime, the other children had discovered that we were camped only a few feet from a deep ravine, almost on the edge of a cliff! So much for setting up camp in the dark.

During the few days that we were there, we visited the many Mesa Verde ruins following Ranger guides climbing up ladders, going down into dugouts, walking on walls, you name it!

At the famous Spruce Tree House, when we were permitted to go down into the ceremonial *kiva*, the Ranger said that no child under five years old was allowed. Jimmy was only four, so I said I would stay out with him. I was disappointed and Jimmy began to cry. That understanding Ranger said we could all go down as long as his dad would be responsible for Jimmy. Our greatest thrill was going down the ladder, through that narrow hole in the ground into the underground Indian religious sanctuary.

One day, we drove into Durango to explore and see the scenic narrow-gauge train that is a tourist attraction from Durango to Silverton. We found out about the Million Dollar Highway #550 heading north. We checked it on our map and decided to return home by way of a new adventure.

The drive along the Animas River canyon was spectacular! This was the same route that the little train took. We said some day we would return just to ride the train to Silverton. We made a short stop in that little mountain town, then continued on our way. We expected to reach our designated camp ground before night, but we did not expect a terrific rainstorm and having to drive over treacherous Red Mountain Pass. Driving was slow and visibility was poor. It was night before we reached our soggy destination – too wet and late to set up the tent. Fortunately, there was a light at the near-by latrine. Bill took the children, one at a time, piggy-back. The back of the middle seat was hinged so it could be flattened out to make cargo space. We bedded the children in the car and Bill and I folded ourselves together on the front seat – not very comfortable, very little sleep, but safe and dry.

The next morning we drove into Montrose, had some breakfast and decided to drive to the near-by Uncompahgre National Forest. Bill had heard that a group of Basque sheepherders lived in those mountains, and he was curious to find out. We did not find them, but we saw some more beautiful scenery and groves of the biggest white-barked Aspen trees I had ever seen.

By late afternoon, we arrived at Grand Mesa where we planned to spend the next day exploring and relaxing in our "Home Away From Home." After this rest period we drove on to Grand Junction where we were told about the beauty of the new Colorado National Monument Park. It was late afternoon when we arrived there. I told Bill that it was still a long way to Denver; maybe we should camp here for the night, even though there was no organized camp ground. I had a strange, uncanny urge to stay there until morning; but Bill wanted to get home, even though it meant driving all night.

As we drove along two-lane Highway #6, (now I-70), it was dark and getting late. I still had that uncomfortable feeling, but I fell asleep. About midnight, I was awakened suddenly by a roar, and what looked like a solid wall moving to my right. Bill was driving in the on-coming lane to the left.

"Why are you over here?" I yelled. If a car were coming, we would have had a head-on collision!

Bill didn't say anything; no other cars were on the road, and the wall had disappeared. Bill drove back into the right lane and stopped at the edge of the highway; he was shaking. The roar that woke me up was a huge semi that was coming down the highway on our side of the road. Bill said when he saw that the driver was not going to move over, he avoided the fatal collision at the last minute by swerving over to the on-coming lane and praying that no cars were approaching.

Bill backed up to where the semi had stopped, got out of the car and walked back to see if the driver was all right. When the driver got out of the cab, he was scared to death and shaking all over. He told Bill that something had happened to his steering gear and he could not pull over when he saw our car coming toward him. He said, "I was scared and hoping you would pull over, and you did just in time to avoid a fatal collision!"

They looked under the front of the cab to find a deer had been hit and the antlers had jammed the steering mechanism!

When Bill told me what had happened, I knew why I had that strong urge to camp the night at Colorado National Monument. I told Bill Someone "Up There" was sending us a message that we should not be driving at night. It was only by the Grace of God that our entire family was not wiped out!!!

The sun was shining that morning when we drove into Denver and arrived at home. We thanked the Good Lord for saving our family and vowed not to drive the highway anymore at night on our trips.

We spent most of the following year planning for our 1957 trip to California. We were not going to use the little trailer again, so we checked Montgomery Ward catalog for camping equipment and were amazed at what we found. We bought a large overhead carrier that clamped onto the roof of our station wagon; a cook kit composed of an aluminum bucket in which was nestled a pan, six plates and cups, the lid converted to a skillet (and I added plastic knives, forks and spoons); a two burner Coleman plate for cooking added to preparing meals.

I went to various shops on Larimer Street and found small suitcases for the children, small 15 inch pillows and little fiber board "for fun" cases for each of them to put in whatever they wanted. I reinforced the edges with different colored tape to identify the owners. I wanted no arguments! I made small cases for the little pillows.

The back of the station wagon opened up and our cooler fit half of the space behind the back seat. I could visualize a small cupboard in the other half-space. I measured the area and designed a little cabinet to fit. Under my supervision, Bill built it and the back of our vehicle became a miniature pantry. It had a shelf on which fit a bread box, and the small hinged door dropped down against the open door of the car to form a cutting board and preparation area.

The trip was going to take three weeks – one week going to California, one week visiting friends and relatives, and one week coming back home. We wanted to have time to stop along the way to see some of the wonders we had heard about.

For our other short trips, the children had saved money in a glass piggy bank, but they would need more spending money on this long trip. At Colorado National Bank I picked up four little metal banks, one for each of them. I kept the keys. I didn't realize how serious they were until one day they came running into the house, upset because Jimmy wanted to spend some money to buy ice cream from the vendor going by.

"We told Jimmy 'No, we have to save our money for the trip'!" cried the three children.

We joined AAA and learned of the easy convenience of the TripTik.

We told them where we were going and the stops we wanted to make. The trip was mapped out with all the information we needed for camping accommodations and points of interest. We had an extra map for the children on which we marked our route and discussed our plans as we would sit around the kitchen table. Jimmy could follow a map before he could read.

The day before we were to leave we had the children empty their banks. Bill and I were amazed at how much money each one of them had saved. Louise would help Jimmy with his spending. That evening we packed the over-head carrier with our big camping equipment on one side, and suitcases, sleeping bags with smaller items fitted into the other side. The children would keep their little pillows and "for fun" cases in the car for their own use.

It was the middle of July 1957 when we excitedly drove away that morning for Salt Lake City by way of the (then) main route – Highway 40. Before we reached Salt Lake City that afternoon, we heard a loud thumping at our rear right tire. Part of the tread had come loose and was banging against the under carriage. We had never seen anything like this before! We slowed down, crept into Salt Lake City and found a tire repair garage. Fortunately, it had only partially deflated so there was no damage to the rim. We were told it was either a defective tire or a retread, and on inspection of the other tires, they appeared to be the same. This was hard to believe since these were the tires that came with the car! We couldn't take any chances, so we settled for a new set of tires.

It was going to take quite a while before we could have our car, so we took off to do some sightseeing. After visiting the museum and a few other sights, we wound up at the Mormon Tabernacle, which was open for visitors. It was fantastic!

Bill said he would get the car and we could wait outside the Tabernacle for him to pick us up. Since it was late afternoon, and we had had such a tiring, hot day, we had better stay the night in Salt Lake and plan to cross the Great Salt Lake Desert early the next morning. That was fine with me. I needed some rest.

The children and I waited. An hour went by, Dad had not returned. More time passed, still no Bill. Louise and I were really worried, hoping he had not had an accident. (Cell phones had not been invented, so there was no way to communicate!). All I could do was pray.

The sun was getting low when we were relieved to see the car arrive.

"Where have you been for so long?" I wanted to know.

"Get in the car. We are going to get something to eat and I will tell you all about it," was his reply.

After Bill got the car, he checked some motels; none of which would take colored people. He was not going to subject his family to the kind of accommodation we had endured in Salt Lake City in 1940! At last, he went to the Police Station to get help. The officer showed very little interest in helping him. Bill remembered an official letter of recommendation he was carrying from Steve McNichols, the Governor of Colorado. He pulled out the letter and showed it to the officer. Bill said he was amazed at the sudden change. Immediately, he said, "Oh, I'll see what I can do for you." He called a few places with no success, then he told Bill that he had a special friend who ran a motel who he was sure would take us in. He made the call, explained the situation and we had a place to stay if we came in after dark and left before 8:00AM the next morning!

It was a nice, big room with a comfortable bed and adequate space for the children in their sleeping bags. We thanked the woman in charge for accepting us. By sunrise the next morning, we left to cross the Great Salt Lake Desert before it got too hot. However, after the sun came up, the heat was unbearable. We were glad, when hours later, we drove into Nevada where there was a little less heat!

We drove into Las Vegas, a community with numerous clinking casinos in an area little larger than a wide spot in the road. We looked around for approximately a half hour, then continued on to Lake Tahoe where we planned to camp for a couple of days. From our camp site, the view of the Lake was awesome. It was an unbelievable deep blue! We discovered a little beach where people were swimming. One day we took one of our inflated mattresses with us and the children had fun floating, playing and swimming in the shallow water. It was so relaxing and beautiful at Lake Tahoe camp ground that we stayed an extra day.

It was a short day's drive to San Francisco. As we crossed the big new Bay Bridge from Oakland, toward the city we saw what looked like grey fog. When we entered that heavy mist, it was cold! We were in summer clothes, so we had to put on jackets and cover our heads for warmth. We found a comfortable motel. The children took off their shorts and put on long pants. We were dressed like this the whole time we were in San Francisco. The first night we visited Chinatown, had Chinese food and tried to eat with chopsticks. There were more bright lights than we had ever seen!

The next day we toured the city. We were fascinated with Fisherman's Wharf, rode the cable cars and thrilled the children driving up and down the hilly streets.

When we left San Francisco, we headed for Yosemite National Park where we spent several hours marveling at the awesome formations of *El Capitan,* Half Dome and the beautiful Bridal Veil Falls.

It was late afternoon when we reached Sequoia National Park, so we set up camp. The next day we drove among the ancient, giant trees in unbelievable wonder. The biggest thrill was driving through the mammoth tree called the "Grizzly Giant"!!! The next day we headed for Los Angeles.

We spent three days with my father's brother, Uncle Dave and Aunt Elizabeth Talamon. They had a big picnic at one of the small beaches and the children had fun playing in the shallow, gentle ocean waves. I enjoyed meeting some of my Creole cousins.

Eleanor and Noel had a barbeque out in their lovely backyard with friends and relatives. Noel was the chef. It was on July 28th, Louise's 12th birthday. Eleanor had a surprise birthday cake with candles for her. It was good to see Cerressa and her husband again, along with others whom I had not seen in years. The children were having so much fun with Eleanor's 10 ½ year old son, Wayne, that we paid

Los Angeles, 1957_Richard, Wayne, Bill, Louise, James

179

little attention to them as we visited.

Noel noticed Jimmy was getting tired, so he had him climb on his lap. Jimmy fell asleep. In a little while, Noel had a wet lap – surprise! The children said they kept telling Jimmy to stop drinking so much punch, but he kept on getting more. He was loaded! Eleanor gave me some of Wayne's outgrown clothes for him.

We were going to Disneyland the next day so we asked to take Wayne with us. Eleanor gave permission; her son was excited to ride in our station wagon and our children looked forward to having more fun with him. I convinced Eleanor to go with us, too.

Disneyland was the big, new amusement park geared especially for children. One of the first activities we encountered was the little cars that could be driven around a guided track. The child had to be as tall, or taller, than a measured minimum height. Wayne was tall – no problem. Richard barely made the height. Louise missed it by a fraction of an inch, and was quite upset not to be allowed to drive, since she was the oldest. Bill and I explained to the attendant that Louise was twelve years old and perfectly capable of handling the little car; she was just small for her age, so he consented. She got in the car and happily drove better than the boys.

There was another set of cars that moved along on cogs for the younger children so they could ride and pretend to drive. Billy and Jimmy had their fun driving, too.

By the end of the day, we had had a wonderful time and were completely exhausted. Driving back, the children had fallen asleep by the time we got Wayne and Eleanor home.

The next day we thanked Uncle Dave and Aunt Elizabeth for their gracious hospitality and family love, as we left to spend the next few days with Bill's relatives.

We arrived at the Prioleau home where Bill and I had been in 1940. Mrs. Prioleau and Lois were expecting us and greeted us happily with open arms. Lois was now a young woman still living with her mother. We settled into a more formal, organized environment, but felt completely at home.

Bill had a letter to Los Angeles mayor Norris Poulson, from Elvin Caldwell, President of Denver Board of Councilmen, introducing William Greenwood as Co-chairman of the Citizen's Budget Group for the City and County of Denver. It was a request for Bill to meet with the Mayor to study some of their budget operations that might be of value to the Denver Citizen's Budget Group. Bill called and made an appointment to meet with the Los Angeles Mayor the next day.

The meeting was scheduled for mid-morning. Bill wanted me to go with him, leave him and drive back so I could have the car. He would call when the meeting was over, and I could drive back to get him. He took with him both the letters from Elvin and the one from Governor McNichols. He arrived on time.

The children were with me and we enjoyed seeing some more of Los Angeles. However, I had not actually driven the freeways. Following freeway directions were confusing to me, so I decided to drive logically – a big mistake! I wound up in North Hollywood!!! I checked the map, which we had in the car, and carefully followed the proper freeways back "home." We were gone so long Mrs. Prioleau was worried about us.

When Bill, finally, called I made the way back to City Hall and was glad to have him drive. He and the mayor had had a great meeting for several hours. Bill was so excited; the first thing he said was, "Honey, you won't believe this. We are going to have a tour of Paramount Studios!!! When the Mayor asked me what he could do for me, I told him I'd like to see a movie studio. Immediately he had his secretary call Paramount and an appointment was set for us to be at the studio tomorrow morning!"

I was flabbergasted; I was thrilled. This was like a dream come true!

"We can take Louise. She'll love it," I said.

"No," replied Bill. "When I said I would like to take my twelve-year-old daughter, I was told the studio only permits children fifteen years or older."

When we got back to the house, we were telling about our

upcoming adventure, but we were concerned about leaving the children. Immediately, Lois said she would enjoy looking after them.

Sue Bowden, another daughter, was a lively, adventurous cousin, so we asked her if she would like to go to Paramount with us. Of course, she would love to go.

We were at Paramount Studio at 8:30 A.M. that morning, expecting to join a tour group. We were surprised when we were met by a uniformed official who said he was assigned to be <u>our special guide</u>! After a bit of orientation on some things to expect, we were on our exciting way by 9:00 A.M.

Our guide took us through the usual guided tour regime, but since we were special, we were shown some of the places that tourists never see: the costume room with hundreds of costumes for any era or needed event, and the locked weapons deposit where every type and vintage of gun is safely stored for use when needed in a film. After three hours, he told us how much he enjoyed being our guide, and we thanked him for the fascinating, informative tour. Bill gave him a generous tip. Our guide asked us if we would like to have lunch where the stars ate. It was not open to the public, but we were welcome. Another big surprise! Of course, we said "Yes!"

The guide took us to the door, turned us over to the hostess and said, "Goodbye."

As we entered, Cary Grant was having lunch with a friend near the door. The hostess took us to a table near the center of the room and told us that this would be a good place to see what was going on.

* [1] Sure enough, she pointed to Shirley Booth who was just leaving with her entourage. They were filming "The Matchmaker." That was a takeoff on what later became the musical, "Hello Dolly," and we got to see them go through in costume. The waitress was the one who really clued us in. We were told to keep our menus as souvenirs! She said, "You see that table by the wall? Cecil B. DeMille will be coming in. He comes in promptly…" At a certain time, sure enough, here he came.

---

[1]* excerpt taken from Trail Blazers Oral History Series transcript, courtesy of Denver Public Library, Blair-Caldwell

Cecil B. DeMille wasn't much taller than I am, and Henry Wilcoxon was with him. He's an old actor I had seen in early days' films. His secretary, and somebody else were with them.

Sue said, "I sure would like to have his autograph.

I said, "Why don't you go over there and ask him?"

I was surprised when Sue replied, "Oh, no, he is such an important man!" She was principal in a Los Angeles school and always a real "go-getter"!

She and Bill looked at me and said, "Well, will you?" and Sue said, "I dare you."

I picked up my menu and I went over to DeMille's table. I figured I had nothing to lose. He could just ignore me. I hadn't lost anything. I walked over and I spoke to him. He stood up and was just as gracious as he could be. When I told him who I was and from Denver, Colorado, he said, "From Denver. Have you ever been to Elitches?" Of course, we'd been to plays at the theater. He went on to tell me he had played there in the early days and his picture was among the hundreds in the lobby.

When I told him that my husband was Budget Director at Lowry Air Force Base, he knew the general out there. We stood there and talked. *

Mr. DeMille asked me if I had seen "The Ten Commandments" which he produced in 1956. I told him that we had seen it and what a wonderful story it was. It was shown at the Denham Theater in Denver in 1957. On our 14th anniversary in April, Bill and I took the children to see the fabulous production of "The Ten Commandments." Mr. DeMille said he considered this film to be his greatest masterpiece of all time! He spent six years planning it. We discussed various scenes and story parts of the picture. He explained how he made the awesome parting of the Red Sea sequence. Cecil B. DeMille was an example of a <u>Truly Great Man</u> who, in spite of his greatness, would take the time to talk with an ordinary citizen like me.

1* excerpt taken from Trail Blazers Oral History Series transcript, courtesy of Denver Public Library, Blair-Caldwell

*He introduced me to Henry Wilcoxson, his secretary and whoever this other person was, still standing talking to me. I was thrilled, and thanked him for his kindness. I told him I would like to have his autograph on my menu.[1]

When I returned to our table, Bill and Sue burst out with, "What on earth were you talking about? What took so long?" I told them about our wonderful conversation and showed them the autograph. I felt honored!

* I put it in the safe in my family home. It is still there. I finally had to put some scotch tape over the signature because his autograph was beginning to fade.

We had a cook-out with cousin Mary King's family, and a big family picnic in a park. One day we took the boat to Catalina Island. We saw flying fish for the first time, and marveled at young divers for coins. The trip on the glass bottom boat was awesome.

At Sea World, we watched the dolphins play and the Sea Lions Circus performance.

It was a hot day when we drove down to San Diego. We stopped along the way to play on the sand at the edge of the ocean. A wave washed the sand from under Richard's feet and he wound up sitting down in the water. As we drove down the highway, I held his wet jeans out the window blowing in the hot air and by the time we arrived at the San Diego Zoo, they were dry. That was a sight that made us laugh.

Touring the fantastic zoo was great, but when we got to the Snake House, Louise refused to go in. She wanted no part of viewing snakes, so she waited outside while the rest of us went in. The exhibit was fantastic – even a two-headed snake!

Since we were so near the Mexican border, we decided to cross over into Tijuana. It was a busy day with people arriving to see the bull fights. I bought a big sombrero. It was still afternoon so we drove on down the picturesque Baja Peninsula to Ensenada. By the time we returned to Tijuana, it was night. The traffic was heavy with people leaving the bull fights. I was tired, so I slouched down in my seat, put my sombrero over my face and fell asleep. I was awakened to find a flashlight shining on me and a border guard questioning my nationality. He insisted that I was Mexican! Fortunately, in those days, the driver's license had your place of birth. When I showed him my Colorado license had California birth date on it, we were permitted to cross back across the border. Bill kidded me about almost losing me in Mexico because of how I look. It was midnight by the time we got back to Los Angeles.

After our enjoyable time with Bill's family, it was time to head for home. We stopped at Hoover Dam and took the amazing tour down in the dam. We learned that there were workers and huge machinery deep within the concrete structure.

We made a brief stop in Prescott, Arizona to visit my parents' early best friends, Mr. and Mrs. Young. We took pictures of the house where I lived as a child and drove out to Fort Whipple Hospital where my parents had worked. It was fun introducing my husband and children to some of my early childhood life.

Our next stop was the awesome Grand Canyon. For the first time in my life, I discovered that I had developed acrophobia. I had never been afraid of heights before! I watched Bill and the children go out on the protruding overlook to view the magnificent gorge, while I stayed a safe distance away. Our greatest thrill was watching the Hopi Indian dancers perform in their spectacular feather attire.

Our last stop was Zion National Park where we set up "Home Away From Home" in the busy camp ground. Our neighboring campers were a family from Calgary, Alberta, Canada. We had a wonderful visit with them and learned about the beauties of their area near the Canadian Rockies. Their two children played with our children.

One day we planned to drive over to Bryce Canyon. After breakfast, we left everything neatly on the big table, as usual. We spent most of the day viewing the awesome expanse of colorful layers of red, orange, yellow and white in the gorge of unbelievable formations. Bill and the children hiked down into the Canyon. I did not go down because all I could think of was the long hike back up. I stayed above and watched them run down and walk back. It was a beautifully sunny day.

When we returned to camp in late afternoon, we were shocked to find our table empty – everything gone! We had left the flap into our tent open with just the protective screen closed. Now the flap was fastened down.

Suddenly, our Canadian neighbor came running over. "We had a shower," he said. "So I put your things inside the tent and closed the flap." We were so relieved and thanked him for his thoughtfulness.

This was a great example of what we had already learned about campers in those days. They might be friendly, or stand-offish, but you never had to worry about the safety of your belongings. Campers looked out for each other! On camp grounds everyone lived in a tent. Occasionally, someone had a small trailer. There were no huge mobile homes, like today. Camping was safe and fun!

After three days at Zion, we cheerfully made our way back to Denver. We had had such a wonderful time and exciting memories, we did not think about the next trip. We were just happy to be back home!

For two years we stayed home and were busy participating in Boy Scouts, exploring nearby areas, sports, Rocky Mountain National Park, church and school activities, and spending week-ends and holidays at our cabin, The Lazy "G", a few miles from Lincoln Hills. We began thinking about another trip.

In 1959, Bill and I drove to New York. I don't remember why. Our cleaning lady, Mrs. Pink, and my mother were left to look after the children. We stayed at a lovely little hotel in New York that we remembered later, attended shows and points of interest. Bill had planned to drive in the city, but I told him I didn't think he would. After we emerged from the Lincoln Tunnel into the New York City traffic, he was happy to park the car and use the subway.

When we returned home, we had our usual family session around the kitchen table to decide where we might go that was new. We had never been to Idaho or Montana, so we checked to see what was of interest in that area. We settled on going to Glacier National Park in northern Montana, and began planning the trip for summer of 1960.

The day arrived and we were off to another exciting adventure. As usual, we had a AAA TripTik with all the pertinent information.

When we finally reached Glacier National Park and set up our tent, we were tired from the long drive, so we spent a day relaxing. The children explored the area and found a small store nearby. They had been gone for quite a while, when here they came running back to camp. Louise, Richard and Billy were upset with Jimmy because he had spent all of his money on a pocket knife, and this was just the beginning of our trip. I felt sorry for Jimmy, but I warned Bill not to give Jimmy any more money. We could share things with him, but this was a lesson this eight-year-old had to learn about spending money.

The glaciers were not as impressive as I had thought they would be, but exploring the park was beautiful. We saw an exciting sight of stampeding wild horses! We also discovered that Glacier National Park extends into Canada, and the name changes to Waterton National Park.

One day we took a guided trip on horseback. I was afraid for Louise, since there were so many things she did not enjoy on our camping trips. To my amazement, Louise loved riding the horse and rode with the greatest of ease. As a young adult, she became the happiest, speediest rider I have ever seen! She and a horse seemed to become one unit.

Since we were right at the Canadian border of Alberta, we checked our map and found Calgary was not too far away. Why not extend our trip to visit the city that our Zion Park Canadian neighbors had told us about? We packed up our camp equipment, crossed the border into Alberta, Canada, drove to Calgary and spent the night in a nice motel. The manager was a friendly woman who told us about the wonderful camping in nearby Banff National Park. We took off for another unexpected adventure!

Banff campsite was well groomed, plenty of space for our large tent, a stone fireplace, but no table to set up our cooking and eating. To keep camp grounds clean, there was a big pavilion with tables and benches where everyone prepared their meals and ate. Sometimes there were few if any people, other times it was crowded. Of course, we met many people from many places.

One morning when we were there for breakfast, a friendly man came over to talk to us. He was a beekeeper and he was telling us about his bees, and his delicious honey. He had samples and gave me a small jar. However, he insisted on our tasting the honey, and somehow Jimmy became the objective taster. We did not want to insult him by saying no, so wide-eyed Jimmy opened his mouth and into his mouth went a tablespoonful of honey! I thought I was going to choke, just imagining what my son was going through! His eyes bulged, his cheeks ballooned, his face turned red, and I was afraid he was going to vomit all over the table. I was proud of my little son when he managed to painfully swallow all that honey.

One day we drove over to Lake Louise, beautifully nestled in the Canadian Rockies. It was not as big a lake as I had expected, but there was a quiet, serene peaceful, relaxing atmosphere that we all felt. The people in the hotel were relaxed and friendly.

We struck up quite a friendship with a neighboring family of campers from British Columbia. We corresponded with each other for many, many years keeping informed on our children's growth and experiences on into adulthood.

Someone told us about a famous glacier that was across the border into British Columbia. We were camped near the border in Banff, so we decided to take this one, last adventure before heading for home.

We were surprised to find a Ranger Station and many people at the glacier. Tourists were taken on the glacier in huge treaded vehicles. Of course, we took the tour. The guide told about the history of these icy formations. Somehow, they had measured the depth of this glacier to be over a mile deep in some areas, but there was a narrow crevasse that they were unable to measure; it seemed to be an endless depth. We were allowed to get out and walk on the ice, but were warned about the danger of the crevasse.

I wanted to see what that narrow fissure looked like. As I neared it,

Bill called out, "No, honey, come back!"

Just then, my foot slipped a bit and Bill grabbed my jacket pulling me back. From what I saw, the deep icy crevasse was blue and far down narrowed to interminable black. It was scary! Thanks to the Lord, and my beloved husband, I was saved! I began to shiver as I realized what a horrible death I could have had, all because of my insatiable curiosity. To this day, I can still see that crevasse and feel the horror of what could have happened to me. Again God was not ready for me!!!

The crevasse

Marie & Bill, Sr.

The next day we left for home and headed for Yellowstone Park to camp for the night. The next morning after breakfast, Bill and the boys were breaking up camp while Louise and I cleaned up after our meal. We needed water to wash the utensils, so I sent Jimmy with the bucket to get water from the tap a short distance away. Soon we heard a call in the distance, "Bear." We listened to see if the next calls would be louder or farther away. You could determine the direction of the bear by the sound of the voices as campers spotted the animal. The calls of "Bear" got louder so we knew the bear was coming toward us. Louise and I kept watching the road and hoping that Jimmy would get back before the bear arrived.

We could see Little Brother happily drawing the water and completely unconscious of the "Bear" warning. Suddenly, there was the bear heading straight for Jimmy! I was petrified and Louise was speechless. Jimmy looked around just as the bear arrived, and started running toward us. Fortunately, he did not make a sound, and the bear stopped at the trash container to forage for food. My son did not drop the bucket of water. He came as fast as he could with his mouth wide open and not a sound coming out. I was relieved, and to my surprise all he said was, "Mommy, I didn't spill any!" not a word about the bear scare. I was proud of him. The bear finally went on down the road and ignored the campers.

We arrived home safely and had decided on our next trips. When we were at Glacier camp ground, we heard about a World's Fair to be in Seattle, Washington in 1962, and another World's Fair that was scheduled for New York City in 1964. Those would be our next exciting adventures!

Summer Trips

CHAPTER 10
Two World's Fairs

Since we needed a place to stay at the World's Fair in Seattle, Bill acquired a list of accommodations and made reservations at a small hotel in early Spring of 1962 for our trip in August.

In July, Bill received a startling call from William Ridley Greenwood, his biological father whom he had never seen or had any contact. He knew him only from an old snapshot and what his mother had told him. He only knew that his father had become white, married and had a white family somewhere. He was calling Bill to tell him he was sick, down on his luck and needed help. He was in San Francisco. Bill was stunned! All he could think of telling him was that we would stop by in August and see what we could do.

A few weeks later, another call came from a woman to tell Bill that his father had died and she did not know what to do with his few belongings. Bill told her to put them in storage and he would do what he could when we stopped in San Francisco on our way to the Fair. This was a baffling situation!

We decided to camp again at Lake Tahoe. It was not quite as quiet and peaceful as it had been in 1957, but we lucked out with a camp space close to the beautiful lake and spent two days there.

We packed up and headed for Sacramento. As we were driving along, I happened to look at my right hand and was shocked to see that the beautiful blue turquoise stone was missing from my ring! I frantically looked on the floor of the car – no stone. When I was putting our cookware together that morning, my ring was fine. I had had it tightened once when the stone became a bit loose, but after almost 35 years of constant wear, the setting had become worn. The stone must have loosened and fallen out that morning when we were packing up to leave Tahoe. I was miserable! This was the ring that I had made in ninth grade.

When we got to San Francisco, we found a lovely little motel near the ocean where there was nearby bus transportation to the trolley into the city. Since Bill and I had to take care of his father's belongings, we were not going to drag the children through this unknown situation. We told them they could spend this time on their own. They were ten, twelve, fourteen and seventeen and thrilled to have this opportunity to take the bus to explore the city by themselves. Bill and I felt they would be safe with Louise in charge, since they had been to San Francisco before and transportation was near. In 1962, this arrangement was perfectly safe!

The woman, who had called us, told us where she had stored Mr. Greenwood's belongings. We had quite a time finding the place, and more time convincing them to turn the articles over to us. Additional time was spent going through and sorting out what was usable for Good will, and what to throw away. We finally finished and both of us were physically, mentally and emotionally exhausted, so we returned to the motel.

When the children arrived, they were thrilled and excited as they told us about their adventurous exploring of San Francisco.

That night we went to Chinatown for dinner, and this time I was able to eat with chopsticks a little bit easier. Bill had become quite adept at using the little sticks. The children gave up and used the fork and spoon.

The next day we departed for the Redwood National Park in northern California. Here we set up "Home Away From Home" to relax for a couple of days. It was peaceful among the skyscraper-tall evergreen trees. We explored the forest a bit, but most of the time we took it easy. On Sunday, August 5th, we drove to a small store to buy a few supplies and were shocked to see a newspaper with the glaring headline of Marilyn Monroe's death! We bought a paper, something we never did on trips. Our trips served as short, temporary refreshing "Get Aways" from the normal hassles, traumas and responsibilities of life; so we seldom checked on the news.

The drive through Oregon was miserably cold, heavy rain and slow driving. We stopped somewhere for the night – no camping.

The next day, as we drove into Seattle, it was bright and sunny. We felt upbeat and optimistic about our prospect of seeing the World's Fair including the Space Needle and the Monorail.

We had a minor problem on arrival at our motel when they couldn't find our reservation. However, it was cleared up by our being assigned a little apartment – living room, bedroom and small kitchen at no extra charge, instead of just one room. Having a refrigerator and stove made it easy for us to shop for groceries and prepare meals there; thus saving money!

We discovered another asset. Our motel was only two or three blocks from the entrance to the Fair! After we got our groceries put away, we decided to spend the afternoon at the Fair.

When we paid our fare, the back of our hands were stamped so there was "in and out" privilege for the day. We entered a large reception area with comfortable lounge seating and a color TV! We were excited because we had heard of color TV, but it was the first time we had actually seen one. Bill and I were tired from the long drive and getting settled, so we looked around a bit at the Fair and decided to rest in the lounge and enjoy the color TV. We told the children to go where they wanted to go, stay together and report back to us at a specific time.

Family trip, 1962

Bill and I thoroughly enjoyed the relaxation and visiting with other travelers as we watched TV. As we talked to one friendly person about our trips, we were asked if we had ever been to Victoria on Vancouver Island. Bill had heard about the famous Butchart Gardens near Victoria, but we had not planned to go to Canada this time. We were told Seattle was so near the Canadian border, that we could drive a short distance north of the city and take the ferry over to Victoria. This set us to thinking of the possibility of another adventure.

It was past time for the children to check with us and we began to wonder where they were. About fifteen minutes or so afterward, they appeared as happy as could be. They were a bit late because they had gone back to the motel, prepared themselves some lunch, then came to check with us before taking off again. Thanks to "in and out" privilege and a near motel! We continued to rest.

After having a good night's sleep, and after having breakfast the next morning, we were off to the Fair for the day. We spent the morning exploring the exhibits and concessions, took a break for lunch back at the motel, then back to the Fair for the rest of the afternoon.

After a few hours of walking and viewing, with so much more to see, Bill and I were ready to stop, but the children were eager to see more. Since the two of us were ready to go back to the lounge, I told the children that they could continue exploring, but it would be on the "Buddy System." There were some things that Louise and Richard were interested in seeing, and other things of interest to Billy and Jimmy. They could all go together to places that they all enjoyed, but for individual interests "Buddies" must stay together: Louise with Richard, Billy with Jimmy. We gave them a few hours to have fun; told them to meet us at a specific time and we would all go up in the Space Needle. Bill and I took off to spend the time to ourselves.

We were waiting in the lounge at the time we expected to meet the children. They did not arrive. Half an hour, almost an hour, and no children. By then we were really worried. I told Bill that I was going to look for them. Maybe they misunderstood us and thought they were to meet us at the Space Needle. I told him to stay in the lounge, in case they should come while I was gone.

As I walked in the direction of the Space Needle, I prayed that my children were all right. To my surprise, suddenly Louise and Richard were running toward me.

"Where have you been? We have been waiting for you for a long

194

time!" I exclaimed.

"We were on our way to tell you we lost Jimmy," they both wailed.

"What do you mean, you lost Jimmy?" I wanted to know, as the shock hit me. "Where is Billy?"

"He's waiting where we were to meet in case Jimmy comes back," was the answer.

They had a designated place where they would meet every hour or so to check on each other. (This amazed me!) This time, when Louise and Richard arrived, Jimmy was not there and Billy was frantic. When we got to the meeting place, Jimmy was still missing. Billy said he turned around and his brother had disappeared. He had no idea which way he went. Louise and Richard had been trying to find Jimmy, while Billy was waiting; that was why they had not met us on time. When I met them, they were on their way to tell us.

Louise and Richard took off again to look for their ten-year-old brother. Billy was so upset, I needed to stay with him. I was worried, thinking of the horrible things that might have happened to my youngest son – even possible kidnapping!

Suddenly, around the corner came Jimmy with a broad grin, a wave of his hand and "Hi!" I was so relieved to see that he was all right, then I was mad enough to strangle him.

"Where have you been?" I barked at him.

"Oh, there was something back there I wanted to see," was his reply.

"You didn't tell your brother, and we have been worried to death wondering where you were. Your sister and brother are out looking for you. When I said 'Buddy System,' that is what I meant. Buddies stay together for safety. Now, if you can't stay with your brother, you will have to stay with Dad and me!" That gave him something to think about.

I was sure Bill had wondered what had happened to us. As soon as Louise and Richard returned, I sent them to get their Dad. Jimmy got a bit of "chewing out" from his brother and sister, too. Then we settled back into our happy family together.

We went up into the Space Needle after Bill arrived, and awed at the fantastic scenery of the city of Seattle, the vast harbor and Mt. Rainier. We marveled at the much publicized Monorail, but we did not take a ride.

That night we told the children about possibly taking the ferry over to Vancouver Island to see the beautiful Butchart Gardens and the historic capital building in Victoria. We would visit a few points of interest in Seattle the next day before taking the late afternoon ferry to Victoria.

After breakfast we packed up and checked out of the motel. We could see the glorious snowcaps and wanted to go to Mt. Rainier, but it was too far away. We had heard that Boeing was building a Presidential Aircraft, so out we went to see where airplanes were being built. To our surprise, the first thing we were told was how proud the company was to have the honor of building Air Force One for the President; and, we would get to see it!

It was a Boeing 707, the first long range aircraft. It was the biggest plane we had ever seen. It was beautiful and awesome!!! The plane was delivered for Presidential use that October; and, it was the Air Force One in which President Kennedy's body was returned to Washington after his assassination!

We drove to Bremerton where ships were repaired. I had heard of "dry dock," but had no idea what it was. Sure enough, there was a ship in for repairs. It was amazing to see a huge ship, high and dry, completely out of the water. Now, I know what "dry dock" really is!

We realized that it was time to leave Seattle and the happy, informational time we had experienced, so we headed for the port where we were to take the ferry to Victoria.

We drove our car into the lower level of the ferry and followed everyone to the upper deck where we could see the scenery and enjoy the fresh air. The children explored the ship while Bill and I remained at the bow. Soon Louise and Richard joined us, but Billy and Jimmy were still exploring. As the port of Victoria came into view, Jimmy came running to us, all excited, "Mom, Dad, Billy is going to steer the ship to the dock!!!" and away he went. We could not believe this; but as we turned around and looked up to the window, there stood twelve-year-old Billy behind the wheel with

Bill, Jr. steering the ferry

the pilot to his right and Jimmy to his left, all of them grinning as the ferry gently docked for landing.! We would not have believed it if we had not seen it!!!

When we drove off the ferry we asked Billy how on earth did he manage to be "in" with the pilot and steer the ferry. He and Jimmy met the pilot while prowling around the ferry and while they were talking with him, he liked these two friendly little boys. He invited them to go up to where he could show them how he handled the ferry from this tiny little space with the big window. He let Billy stand with his hands on the wheel while we docked and that is why all of us were proud of Billy!

Bill had a list of motels and hotels, but we did not know any locations in Victoria, so he arbitrarily selected one and went into the telephone booth on the dock. Next door there was an open door to what looked like an office. Bill made the call. I heard a phone ring in the office. Someone answered and Bill began to talk. Louise and I began to listen to the voice coming from the office and it seemed to be meshing with Bill's speaking. He hung up and so did the person in the office.

"We have a place to stay," he said. Louise and I laughed.

"We know, because it is right next door!" we exclaimed. "We have been listening to your conversation."

Bill had to laugh. We went in the door, told the lady there what happened and we all had to laugh at the joke. She gave us a two room assignment. We asked her about restaurants. She recommended several and told us where they were.

We decided to try the Chinese restaurant. It was in a strange neighborhood. We went up a long flight of stairs to a nice oriental setting. As we sat by the window, we could see across the alley a building where men seem to be going in and out, and the open window showed a smoky room with some people moving around in it (where others were seated at tables). When the waitress noticed us looking out the window, she told us that was an opium den where men constantly came and went and played mah-jongg. The food was good, and the people were friendly, but we were glad to get back to the comfortable rooms for the night. We had busy plans for the next day.

Bill and I slept like logs. When we woke up the next morning, we could hear a little splashing and an occasional giggle or low voice just outside our bedroom window. The swimming pool was there, but we couldn't see who was having fun. Bill went into the other room to get the children up, so we could begin to get ready for our day. There was no one there. Those were our children in the swimming pool!

Bill put his pants on over his pajamas and took off to bring them in quickly. As he got out to the pool, the manager came out and stopped him before he could call to them. She told him that she had been watching them as they quietly had fun. She said it was the first time that she had children in the pool who did not yell and scream and disturb the tenants. She told Bill to let them alone; she was proud of them. When they finally came in we let them know we were proud of them, too!

We packed up our car. As we checked out we told the manager how much we enjoyed our stay and thanked her for her kindness.

Butchart Gardens

Our first destination was Butchart Gardens. It was a huge field of beautiful flowers of every brilliant hue and kind. As we walked among the colorful plants, reading the names and varieties, we saw a man coming toward us. He had a beard, was wearing khaki shorts,

T-shirt, sandals and a straw hat. As he met us, his face lit up and he cried, "Bill Greenwood!" Bill took one look, grinned and called the man by name. He was a retired General whom Bill had known at Lowry Air Force Base.

This retired General now lived on Vancouver Island and frequently came to the Gardens. What a coincidence that he was there at this time, the same as we were! He was glad to meet Bill's family and invited us to his home. We met his wife, had lunch and a wonderful visit.

Our next stop was the picturesque old stone British Columbia Capital building, and we learned some of its interesting history.

Somewhere along the way, we had heard about a nearby ferry from Nanaimo (north of Victoria) to the city of Vancouver, so instead of returning to the United States, we might as well return by way of the new Trans-Canada Highway (since we were already in Canada).

It was a short ferry trip and the only thing I remember was the sight of a sea gull that lit on the mast and rode most of the way to Vancouver.

Since this was the end of our trip, we did not plan to make any more stops than necessary. As we were getting into the mountains, traffic slowed down to a stop because of an accident. We had to stop right by the crash and an injured man was lying on the ground shivering from shock. His friends had nothing with which to cover him to keep him warm. We had an old wool blanket which they needed more than we did, so we gave it to them to cover him. They were so appreciative. Our children were so impressed that they talked for the longest, about how we helped someone in need. This was a positive lesson for them.

We drove Trans-Canada Highway #1 to Calgary, then headed south into Montana. We spent the night somewhere in Montana. We were anxious to get home, so we did not make our usual stop in Yellowstone. We just kept driving and made it home by early evening.

On my birthday, I had a surprise call from Bill inviting me to a "date" to meet him near the Brown Palace Hotel. (He was always surprising me, but this was unusual). He would meet me there when he left work at Lowry. He had not driven to work, so I asked him how he was going to get there.

"I will get there. You just drive there and park the car," was his answer.

In 1962 parking downtown was no problem, so I did as he requested, wondering what this was all about. Maybe we were going to celebrate my birthday by having a special dinner.

Sure enough, he arrived on time and told me to get out of the car. There was some place he wanted to go. We went around the corner, crossed Seventeenth Street to a small shop that specialized in Indian jewelry.

He said, "Honey, I know how badly you have felt at losing the turquoise stone, so I have been trying to find some place to buy another ring. I think you might be able to find what you like here. I have looked everywhere." He went on, "I hated to have you drive down here, but if I went home to get you we could not have made it here before they closed."

This was the biggest surprise of my life! There was no duplicate for the perfect stone which I lost, but I wanted another heavy silver ring, not a fancy little delicate setting. I found just what I liked, heavy silver ring set with three small blue turquoise stones. I still wear that ring. It is very special!

My husband was one of the most thoughtful, helping and giving persons I have ever known, not only for me, but for everyone we have ever known. He was also a lovable human being who could get mad, make mistakes and questionable decisions, which we usually could work out satisfactorily together. It was the same when I had a problem! We took care of each other and our family. We shared responsibility.

In 1963, as we made plans for our trip to the New York World's Fair in 1964, we realized that our station wagon was seven years old and this next trip would be the longest of all. With all the driving we had done, this wagon had held up well, but was beginning to show small needs for repairs. I hated to see the pretty blue and white vehicle go, but we traded it in for a new brown station wagon.

Eventually, I let Woody know that we would be in Buffalo so the children could see Niagara Falls on our way to New York City. Woody and I had kept in touch over the years. I asked her to recommend a hotel for us, but she wrote back and insisted we stay with her. I wondered how that was going to work with four children at twelve, fourteen, sixteen, and nineteen years old; and, Woody had never married! I explained the situation to the children, laid down a few rules of expected behavior, and reminded them to be as helpful there as they were at home.

In the summer of 1964, the day finally arrived for us to leave for our first family trip back East! There would be no camping, which made Louise happy. She was now 19 years old, had just finished her freshman year in college, so I knew this would be our last big Family Trip, after ten adventurous years!

Along the way, we made a short stop near Hannibal, Missouri to see the area where Mark Twain had lived and wrote the stories of _Tom Sawyer_ and _Huckleberry Finn_. We crossed the Mississippi river and drove to Springfield, Illinois to visit the historic site where Abraham Lincoln is buried. By late afternoon we were on our way to Chicago.

It was night when we settled into a nice little hotel away from the busy center of the city. The next day we toured Chicago: The Loop and marveled at the El trains, Soldiers Field, the Chicago River (that runs through the center of the city), the Aquarium (which fascinates me to visit in every city!), the Museum and everything else for which we had time.

There was a baseball game that night at Wrigley Field. Bill and the boys wanted to see it, but Louise and I were not interested. Bill said for us to take them to the game and they would return to the hotel by bus. Louise and I could have the car. We had passed a small theater showing a movie I wanted to see, so after depositing the four males at the game, Louise and I went to the movie. I don't remember what it was, but we enjoyed it.

Unfortunately, when we came out of the theater, I lost my sense of direction to the hotel and we became completely lost. I drove around forever, until I wound up in a horrible section of the city under the El tracks. We were scared! I found a phone booth, called information for the hotel number. The clerk at the hotel gave me directions. We were a long way from our destination, so it was after midnight before we returned.

Bill and the boys had arrived at the hotel late (after the game). Bill was worried about our not being there when they arrived. Then he began to panic when we didn't show up. To say the least, we were all relieved and happy to be safely back together and sent up our prayers of thanks!

The next day we left Chicago, headed for Buffalo, New York, and hoped all would go well on introducing our family to Woody.

Our few days with Woody were wonderful! Upon arrival she let Louise and Richard know that she had a friend whose children were the same ages as they were. That evening she took them over to meet these young people. These young friends agreed to meet my children later in New York City while we would be there for the Fair.

The next day we went sightseeing and drove out to see the spectacular Niagara Falls. When we returned later that afternoon, Woody had cooked a delicious dinner. (She was a good cook). She was surprised when, after dinner, my children cleared the table, washed the dishes and put them away, just as they did at home.

Louise and Richard contacted their new friends, again. Bill took Billy and Jimmy some place. Woody and I enjoyed visiting together, like old times, on our last day in Buffalo.

It was night when we arrived in New York City. We found the little hotel where Bill and I stayed in 1959, but the area did not look the same. We entered the hotel to find it had changed management that was not as pleasant as five years before. We were assigned a large, dimly lit, not too clean, room on the top floor. If it had not been so late, we would have left. The bed was terrible. We were afraid to breathe. There was very little sleep.

Before seven o'clock the next morning, Bill left to find decent accommodations for us. An hour later he called (there was a phone in the room!), and told me he had found a place for us to stay. Have everything packed and ready to go. He was coming to get us.

A new Sheraton Hotel had just opened on the docks of the Hudson River. They were still doing some last minute work on it. We had the large unfinished, partly furnished, lovely room (which would be a penthouse), overlooking the docks and the river. It even had a bar. A nice little restaurant was next door to the hotel. Bill said all of the hotels were booked up because of the Fair. He was getting pretty discouraged at seeing "no vacancies." Somehow, he heard about the new Sheraton just completing construction, checked it out and we became one of the first customers. We relaxed from the trauma of the night before. The Lord does provide!

The next day was the big day we were waiting for – the World's Fair! A bus came to the docks, right by the hotel. This bus made a direct connection on the other end with the train that would take us to the Fair in Queens; so away we went!

Riding the train was part of the excitement of going to the Fair. We arrived with hundreds of people to the huge expanse of activity. After hours of prowling in and out of exhibits, exploring interesting and amazing sections of this World's Fair, Bill and I were exhausted by late afternoon. We were ready to go back to the hotel. Louise and Billy were ready to quit, sixteen-year-old Richard and twelve-year-old Jimmy wanted to continue the adventure.

Since the days were long, and the transportation by train and bus back to the hotel was so simple, we told Richard to take care of his brother and they could stay, but to be back at the hotel before dark. The four of us went back to rest.

We relaxed until it began to get dark and the boys had not returned. Ten o'clock, still no boys. We weren't sure what to do to try to find them. We got in bed, but could not sleep, hoping to hear from them. Bill made some calls, but nothing! About midnight, here came Richard and Jimmy with the story of how they stayed on the train into the city to see the bright lights. They didn't realize how late it was. A policeman stopped them, put them on the train back to catch the bus to the hotel. Jimmy said his brother really took care of him all the time. I was relieved to see them safely back with us. Bill had been so worried that he blew up all over Richard for not getting back to the hotel early. On the other hand, I was proud of the fact that my son did not get lost or panic in this first trip into the Big City, which could have been disastrous for him and his brother.

Bill apologized to Richard the next morning for being so furious when they returned, but explained how worried he was. However, he was glad they were safe, but they should have kept their word to come to the hotel as planned. He was right!

One day Louise went shopping. Without telling me, Bill gave her a credit card and she had a ball buying clothes at Macy's and Saks Fifth Avenue.

We took the boys sightseeing: Times Square, Rockefeller Center, Guggenheim Museum, Harlem, and ended up at Radio City Music Hall where Louise met us for the matinee to see the fantastic Rockettes. She had purchased so many clothes that she had them sent to the hotel. After the show, Louise and Richard went to meet their friends from Buffalo for an evening on the town. This was 1964 and these young people could do things safely on their own.

Bill and I took Billy and Jimmy back to the hotel where they had fun exploring. I knew Louise would be late getting in. I was tired so I finally went to bed and went to sleep.

Louise took her sixteen-year-old brother to all the night spots she and her friends could find in New York. They were older than eighteen, so they could get in. When they finally returned to the hotel, about 4:00 a.m., her dad was waiting up for them. When he asked if they had a good time, Richard said, "Yeah, we went to bars!" Louise did not expect this revelation, so she explained to her dad that they did go to some bars, but they did not drink. Fortunately, Bill knew enough about the results of alcoholic drinking that he could tell that Louise was telling the truth.

Our daughter had bought a complete wardrobe of expensive fashion clothes for the coming school year, on her shopping spree! When Bill found out how much she had spent, he told her, "Don't tell your mother!" She would have been in trouble because I watched the budget.

204

They did a good job of keeping me from finding out. Bill told me that there was something he had to ship back home because there wasn't enough room in the car. For once, I didn't ask for an explanation!

On our last day, we took the subway to lower Manhattan and boarded the ferry to the Statue of Liberty. A thrilling experience!

On this trip, we had a relief driver - Richard. It made this long trip easier for Bill and me. Louise was a good driver, but she still tended to get drowsy at highway speeds, so we took no chances with her driving. (Fortunately, she eventually overcame the problem and became an excellent driver).

We left New York and made a short stop in Philadelphia to browse in Independence Hall Square (now a park), and see the Liberty Bell.

We continued on to Washington, D.C. with Richard driving. Bill planned on letting him drive until we neared D.C, then Bill would take over because the traffic would be heavy. Unfortunately, it thickened before we expected, and with no way to pull over and stop, Richard kept driving on into Washington. Bill and I were amazed at how well he drove that station wagon in the thick city traffic. We finally found a place where we could pull over and park so Bill could take over. We were proud of Richard, and complimented him on his expert driving!

We had made reservations to stay at the Sheraton Hotel. This hotel was new when discrimination was outlawed. It was here where Alpha Kappa Alpha Sorority Boulé was held, and for the first time we were permitted to stay in a big hotel. At that time, I was so impressed with the luxury that I wanted to return to this hotel with my family.

We checked into the Sheraton, had dinner, and the children explored the hotel while Bill and I relaxed in our comfortable room.

The children found the swimming pool, so the next morning they put on their swimsuits and were off to have fun before breakfast. When they returned to our room, they said they had a great time. When they arrived at the pool there were only a few people. Most of them left when they saw these four brown faces, so they had the pool to themselves, with the exception of one or two other swimmers.

Our days in Washington D.C. were spent sightseeing, which included: the Lincoln Memorial, where Marian Anderson performed when the D.A.R. refused to let her use their hall, and, where Martin Luther King, Jr. gave his famous "I Have a Dream" speech; the massive Washington Monument; a day at the Smithsonian Institution; across the Potomac River to Arlington Cemetery; a view of the White House; visiting the awesome Capital Building with a stop in the office of Colorado Representative Byron G. Rogers (with whom we had a pleasantly welcome visit).

I called my friend, Fannie Williams, to see if she knew anything about Jeanne. I had been unable to get any answers when I had written to her. Fannie said she had written, also, with no results from the third of our "Triangle." Eventually, we learned that Jeanne had died of cancer.

After all this activity, we were ready to return home to our beautiful, peaceful Colorado mountains. Thus ended the last of our ten years of family travelling!!!

These trips proved to be educational for all of us, especially our children as they were growing up. In National Parks we sat around campfires listening to Rangers' stories, or attended illustrated lectures in Ranger Stations or at museums. On fishing trips, at picnics, outings in Rocky Mountain National park and other outdoor activities, I took the family on nature hikes as I did as counselor at Camp Nizhoni. When we would read about or see pictures of places we had been, they became real experiences.

We met people of different races and cultures, learned about them and accepted them on their merit, just as they learned to accept us. Not once did we see any African American campers. We were the only brown faces in every campground in which we stopped!

We learned to get along with each other in good times and in bad times. Dad could "blow his stack." I could get tired and irritable. The children could have loud disagreements, but no matter what, we were one bonded family who accepted our individual differences and looked after each other!

CHAPTER 11
Back to Work and Other Events

When Newlon School opened in 1951, my daughter entered first grade. We were the only Black family in the school; however, the Principal, Mildred Biddick, remembered me from early teaching days and welcomed me warmly. I asked her if there would be pre-school for my three-year-old son, Richard.

She said she had not thought of pre-school since the school was so new. Before Newlon opened there were only scattered houses in the area, but with the many new homes being built, and young families moving in, there might be enough young children.

"Mrs. Greenwood, if you are willing to be in charge of organizing the pre-school, I will check on possible enrollment, and if there are enough children I will see about getting a pre-school teacher. It will meet only once a week," she told me.

"That will be fine with me," I assured her. "I certainly will do all I can, because I want my three-year-old son to have pre-school experience just as his sister had. It definitely is excellent preparation before entering kindergarten.

There were enough young, stay-at-home mothers in the Newlon area who were delighted to have their children in pre-school, so I helped organize the mothers in helping with the children every Friday, along with the professional pre-school teacher. For approximately an hour, I would take the mothers to the auditorium to discuss problems, answer questions and exchange ideas. It made no difference that I was the only brown face in the group (and definitely the oldest and most experienced). We became a closely bonded team of mothers.

When Newlon PTA was organized, I was elected President.

In 1953, when Jimmy was a year old, I decided to return to teaching as a substitute in kindergarten, first and second grades. My mother loved being with her only grandchildren, but I wanted my time to be flexible so I could be home when my children were ill or needed me. This way, I could gauge my teaching schedule accordingly.

Louise was in third grade and Richard was in kindergarten at Newlon. Little Grandma enjoyed taking little Billy to pre-school on the Fridays that I was working. My children were being well cared for, so I was at ease in going back to my teaching.

All African-American teachers were assigned to schools in Northeast Denver. Not one had ever been placed in a Denver Public School outside of that area – not even to substitute. The excuses given by the Administration were: <u>we could not adjust to working in an all white school; the teachers would not accept us; and, the parents would object.</u>

When Miss Biddick found out I was substituting, she asked for me when she needed a substitute in first grade. In two years Newlon had become so crowded that first and second grades were on double session, so I taught reading in a classroom with another teacher for part of the morning, and she taught reading with me in my class for part of the afternoon. I was accepted as just another substitute.

When I am teaching, no matter what the ethnic make-up of the class might be, those children are <u>MY</u> children. I have control, and I get desired response. My first day at Newlon went smoothly.

As time went on, I was called often to Newlon. I was told that the primary teachers would ask for "Mrs. Greenwood" when they knew they were going to be absent, because they knew their classes would be kept in order.

I had several weeks of back-to-back long assignments in Northeast Denver, so I did not hear from Newlon for awhile. I was beginning to wonder why. One day when I came home from work, my mother said, "You have been called to report to Newlon tomorrow." I was delighted and relieved.

When I walked into the Newlon office that morning, the secretary greeted me with, "Mrs. Greenwood. We are so glad to see you. We have been calling, over and over for you, but could not get you." I explained how busy I had been and how happy I was to be back at Newlon.

In the spring of 1954, I had a Newlon kindergarten for so long that I felt as though it were my own. I was treated like part of the faculty – even asked to attend faculty meetings!

I was so well known in Northeast Denver at Whittier, Mitchell and Gilpin Schools that I had very few days off. When Whittier's Principal, Jack Boyd was promoted to administration, Jessie Maxwell became our first African-American principal in the Denver Public Schools. She was the best! Soon after her appointment, I was sent to Whittier. I was thrilled to congratulate her and we laughed about the early beginnings.

My assignment was a new experience for me. I had never taught a complete class of special education children, and this was the loudest, most unruly, undisciplined class I had ever faced. The teacher was out of town at a conference, and there were no plans or schedule. When I took them to the lavatories, which were in the middle of the building from our room at the end of one wing, they were yelling, shoving and disturbing classes as we passed. I couldn't believe that any teacher could let a class become this disruptive! This first day was a disaster and I knew I had to do something to maintain my sanity. The teacher would be gone for a week or more.

The second day was spent on discipline, rules and behavior. One big boy continued to be disruptive. When I lit into him, he whined, "I'm going to tell my mother."

"Be sure to tell your mother," I replied. "Tell her to come to see me. I would like to talk to her." I really wanted to meet his mother, but she never came.

That day when we lined up to go to the lavatory, I warned them that there would be no talking or shoving. We would walk quietly so as not to disturb other classes. Of course, as we left the room there was chatter and disturbance at the end of the line. Immediately, I had them turn around and return to the room. I told them they were acting like little wild animals instead of nice boys and girls. They were to "zipper" their mouths, keep their hands to themselves, and we would walk quietly in the hall, or we would not go anywhere.

When we reached the lavatories, I let a few go in at a time. I told them they could talk quietly to each other – no yelling or screaming. When I heard loud noises in the boy's lavatory, I went in, pulled out the two noisemakers and put them at the end of the line. The class got the message.

There was very little material to work with. I found some pre-primers, but no one was reading, so I made some charts, found a few children who were ready to read, and began teaching them. I always carried a little case full of material I could use whenever needed in my substituting assignments. I had word and number flash cards, simple picture games, a simple set of duplicator material that I could run off on the machine in the office, and a few other things.

Now that I had a quiet class under control, I began teaching them some of the basics. Their learning skills varied, but they were happily learning as much as possible. The little reading group was working hard.

One day as we were lined up at the lavatory, a first grade teacher came out of her room to tell me that since she had heard no noise in the past few days, she decided to check to see if we were really there!

Another day, Mrs. Maxwell came to the room. The door was open, the class was busy and she was amazed at how quiet it was. I had the little readers show her what they were learning. As she was leaving, she started to shut the door, but I told her to leave it open, since we now had a quietly working classroom. I was there for over two weeks, and was proud of the progress we had made. This was one of the varieties of substituting experiences I had.

One day in the spring of 1955, as I entered Newlon School, Miss

Biddick met me with a wide grin. "Mrs. Greenwood, the P.T.A. mothers have asked me why you do not teach here as a regular teacher. They are so impressed with your teaching their children." This topped it all, having the <u>mothers</u> asking for me!

She continued, "I have a second grade opening coming up this fall. Would you be interested?"

I was so amazed! I hardly knew what to say. "You mean the MOTHERS asked for me?! That is wonderful, but I will have to think about it since I hadn't planned on going back to work regularly just now. I'm not sure I would want to teach second grade regularly; I actually prefer first grade."

"Oh, I also have a double session first grade opening. The teacher says she knows you and would enjoy sharing the room with you."

This was another surprise!!

"I will check with my mother and see if she feels up to coming every day. I will let you know," was my reply.

My mother was delighted to come every day; three-year-old Jimmy would be the only child at home all day.

I let Miss Biddick know that I would like to take the first grade assignment, but I wondered if I would be accepted at my age, since I had been off contract for ten years. She assured me that all would go well and clued me in on a few helpful pointers to remember in my interview with Mr. Bennett, the Superintendent in charge of elementary education.

Mr. Bennett had my file from my early teaching days. He mentioned that I had an excellent record. He asked me if I would be interested in taking an assignment in Northeast Denver.

"No," I told him. "I will only consider a school close to home like Newlon or Cowell. Otherwise, I will remain a substitute teacher, rather than drive all the way across town every day."

Mr. Bennett picked up the phone, called Miss Biddick, and my assignment to Newlon, as of September 1955, was settled. This made me the first African-American teacher to be placed in an all white school in the history of the Denver Public Schools.

If I had returned to teaching on contract within eight years after resigning, I would have re-entered at the level at which I left. Since I was off contract for ten years, I returned as a probationary teacher. I felt like an old lady attending the probationary meeting with those young beginning teachers, led by a first year coordinator! My surprise came when the coordinator asked me to give some advice to these beginners.

"How did you know about me?" I asked.

"Oh, I was told about you and your experience, so I think you can be of help to these new teachers," was her reply. What a shock for the opening of my second go-round of teaching!

On one of her visits, the coordinator observed me teaching Phonics with my reading. At our little evaluation session, afterward, she told me that Phonics was no longer being taught because some educators said sounding out words slowed down reading. I would be criticized if a supervisor came in and saw me teaching Phonics.

"If a supervisor came in, I would know absolutely nothing about Phonics." I sarcastically answered, "Thanks for letting me know, but I will always teach Phonics. It is the key that unlocks word."

"You are right," she smiled. "I just wanted to let you know."

One day I asked her why sometimes she seemed to be paying no attention to me.

"This is the only time I can relax. You know what you are doing and I gain a lot of information which I can pass on to my beginning teachers, but they keep me busy," was her reply. This was quite a compliment!

Every week Mr. Bennett called to see how Mrs. Greenwood was getting along. Miss Biddick would tell him, "Mrs. Greenwood is doing just fine. She is one of my best teachers." This became a weekly joke between Miss Biddick and me. By spring of 1956 he stopped calling.

The administration got the message that qualified, dedicated teachers come in all colors and can be accepted to teach in any school. I had disproved the discriminating excuses given all those years. In the fall of 1956, two of the best minority teachers were placed in schools in white areas and were praised for their excellent work. The door was now open for teachers of varied ethnic groups to be placed in schools wherever needed.

I was in a unique position as I began teaching at Newlon School in 1955. Louise was in fifth grade upstairs. Richard was next door in second grade. Billy was across the hall in kindergarten. Little Grandma brought Jimmy to pre-school downstairs.

I told Miss Biddick, "Do not put any of my children in my room. It would not be fair to my child or to me because I might be too easy or too hard on him in trying not to show favoritism."

I informed the teachers, "Treat my children the same as all the others. You will be doing them no favor by letting them get by easy. Whatever your discipline methods are, use them! At school I am just another teacher. I become mother when I get home." I made the same information clear at home.

Several times I was asked to become a coordinator. No way! I made it clear that I loved teaching first grade, laying a sound beginning foundation and I did not want to deal with anyone over eight years old!!

After many years of being asked to move into administration and refusing because she loved being near the children, Miss Biddick finally accepted a position at the Administration Building. Our new Principal was Egon Hanson.

Mr. Hanson and I developed a surprisingly

Marie with her Newlon Elementary School first grade class & Miss Biddick - 1960

pleasant relationship. He told me that he had been hired in the middle of the Depression, just as I had in 1935. We were two of only ten new teachers hired that year! We had a remarkable understanding of each other. We could discuss joys and problems, family experiences and plans for the future.

Whenever I needed timeout for a trip with Bill, or any other reason, there was no question; I had a substitute.

A new wing was being built to enlarge Newlon School. I would be moved to one of the new rooms. Of course, I kept checking on the progress of finishing my room. The chalk boards were too high, so I reported to Mr. Hanson. They were lowered to primary level. There were no storage cupboards, only open shelves under the windows. A wall of cabinets and drawers were installed after I pointed out the omission.

Our first grade in this wing was assigned to use the kindergarten playground instead of the big playground, but we had no way of getting there, and the entrance to the kindergarten grounds had been fenced off. I reported to Mr. Hanson that we needed a door from our wing to enter the playground. Why had the steps to the playground been fenced over when it was the only way the first grade and the kindergarten could enter? Our wing got the necessary door. The fence was removed from blocking the steps.

I made plans for my retirement to be at about 60 years old. I had seen too many teachers stay in the classroom until retirement age, and just vegetate or die before they could enjoy a free life. I intended to do some of the things I had on hold that I did not have time to do while raising a family and teaching. I told Mr. Hanson about my plan and he was interested in seeing how it would work, since he was looking toward retirement. Since I would get no credit for my unused days of leave, I planned to "ride them out" first. One could take a one-year leave of absence, without pay, for education or travel, and return to teach for at least two years. I applied for 1970-71 leave for education, but I was not going to take any credits. I just wanted to freely enjoy taking courses in Creative Writing or anything else of interest. It was a very busy year.

In 1966-67, DPS Superintendent Oberholtzer organized a committee to study <u>Equal Education in the Denver Public Schools</u>. There had been criticism from minority areas, questioning why they lacked many of the advantages found in more affluent DPS districts – especially less in Northeast Denver. I served on that committee, and it was a shocking "eye opener" for me! There was a lack of supplies and equipment that other schools had. Many beginning teachers were placed in poorer schools for training, then transferred to better areas. Some buildings were not kept in the best condition as others. We spent an exhausting year visiting schools and listing the many inequalities that we found.

We even worked through the summer. For the first time in my life, I developed high blood pressure from the stress and strain of teaching, family responsibilities and serving on that valuable committee during that year.

In August of 1970, we had Louise's big wedding to Ray Weathersby. Bill and I got it together in three months! I sent out 500 invitations. Bill took care of most of the plans. Louise finally arrived from Chicago to help finalize arrangements. Shorter A.M.E. Church was full and the service was beautiful. The reception was at Lowry Officer's Club with Bill Jr's combo playing; Jim was the drummer – quite a family affair!

At Metro State College, I enrolled in a Creative Writing class. I learned so much about expression and the impressive use of vocabulary. I was told that I had a talent for writing for children, and one of my stories, "A Ten Cent Miracle," was published in the college magazine! I took a course in Script Writing, and another in Rachel Noel's Black History class.

In the spring of 1971, I flew to London to visit Richard. It was a five-day AAA trip that only covered flight and hotel, so I was free to fit my son's schedule. When we arrived at Heathrow Airport, all luggage showed up except my little vanity case. I waited and waited until I was the only person left. I was just about ready to give up, when there it came down the ramp. I grabbed it and rushed out to find the bus to the hotel. I spotted it and ran to the right side; there was no door! The passengers were waving to me to go to the other side. Of course, the door was on the left, since Britons drive on the left. When I entered the bus, everyone began clapping and I was told the bus driver had gone looking for me. In a few minutes he returned and was told that I was there. To my surprise, he said he wanted to meet me since my name was Greenwood. His name was Greenwood, too, and in England it is as common as "Smith" and "Jones" in the United States.

I spent the rest of the day resting from "jet lag." Richard came to see me that evening. The hotel was comfortable with free Continental Breakfast each morning. I had to get used to the funny little "bring-bring" of the telephone. It took me a while to relax when riding on the left hand side of the road with Richard seated at the steering wheel on the right side of the car.

I had three full adventurous days with Richard. We saw the changing of the Guard at Buckingham Palace, and drove along the Avon River. We went out to visit Windsor Castle, but repairs were being made so it was closed to visitors. We just drove around. I was thrilled to attend "The Mousetrap" by Agatha Christie, the longest running play in the world. Richard took me to an Indian restaurant for the first time where I enjoyed delicious, spicy native food. Those were some of the highlights I remember. Soon after my visit, Richard returned to Denmark and settled in Aarhus.

My father was past 90 years old when he fell out of the apple tree and broke his arm. My mother called to tell me that he was at Denver General Hospital, just as I was leaving school. I called Bill to meet me at the hospital, since I wasn't sure how badly he was hurt. As we entered the emergency room, we were amazed to see my father sitting on the table, with his arm in a cast, talking and laughing with the nurses as he told them humorous jokes!

A year before, I had told my doctor about my plan for retirement. The summer of 1973, I had taught the two years after my leave, so I told my doctor that I wanted to use up my unused leave days before retirement. What health reason could he give? He put me in the hospital for a complete check-up. I was in such good health they could find nothing wrong with me, my blood pressure was under control.

The only advice my doctor could give was that because of the pressure of some of my family responsibilities which I had recently endured, I needed a little more rest time before returning to teaching in the fall. He wrote this assessment for me. In August, I contacted Mr. Hanson and explained to him. I did not return to school in September 1973. I was on full pay without returning to school until my days of leave ran out on January 10, 1974.

When I applied for retirement, they tried to convince me to continue teaching until the end of the school year, but I refused. Although the pension was small, I refused the offer and retired. I had achieved my goal.

After eighteen enjoyable years at Newlon School, I retired in January 1974. Mr. Hanson followed my example the following year.

The following letter from one of my students is one of my greatest rewards for teaching first grade:

August 28, 1993

Dear Ms. Greenwood,

I was in the second year of my first grade when I met you. I called you Mrs. Green at that time. Reading was a struggle that I thought I could do without. To this day I can remember the patience and understanding that you displayed.

As I finished school, I was told that college was not a good place for me. I accepted this for many years, until my son started having reading problems in the first grade. It was me all over again and he did not have someone special like you.

I was determined to help my son. First I needed to go to

an adult education class to spruce up my skills, then I attended Eastern Montana College. There I received a BS in Education and majored in Special/Elementary Education with a science emphasis.

In between going to college and family life, I tutored my son in school. He is now in 6th grade and still struggles in reading, but he is following my footsteps.

As I think back my eyes still tear up when I think of you. And I still get that determined stubborn streak when I think of that counselor's advice. I would love to show him my diploma which reads WITH HONORS.

When my mother sent me the article out of the Denver Post, I know I needed to thank you and give you an update of a past student. Now that I am a first year Resource Room Teacher, I relish the thought of one of my students doing the same thing.

I admire you and thank you for what you have given me. I hope to do the same for my students.

Thank you for being there.

D.G.

I am also proud of another one of my students who entered my first grade in 1956. He was a brilliant little boy who presented me with one of the greatest challenges of my teaching career.

Robert Tweedell is now an attorney representing abused and neglected children. He keeps in touch with me, and I am pleased to have had a small part in helping to lay his early foundation. The following excerpt from one of his letters made me feel warm all over:

I was elected to the Delta County School Board in November. I had been thinking of running for the School Board for many years and I finally did it...I am going to have a lot to learn in order to do this job well! As I do my work on the School Board, no doubt I will be applying some of the things you taught me in first grade!!

He is now President of the Delta County School Board.

By the time I retired, we had an "Empty Nest" – Hallelujah!! We loved our children, and kept in touch with them, but now I could finally relax! It took me two months to stop falling asleep about two o'clock in the afternoon. I had time to read and do puzzles. Crossword puzzles and the dictionary helped me bring my primary vocabulary up to adult level. I still do all kinds of puzzles.

A whole new vista of activity that we could do together opened up to Bill and me: travel, entertainment, social activity, community and religious services.

The secret of successful retirement is to have something to which to retire. Now, I could enjoy doing some of the things I had put on hold for years!

CHAPTER 12
My Amazing Husband

William R. Greenwood became such an outstanding Budget Officer at Lowry Air Force Base that Budget Officers from other Air Bases were sent to him for training – American and foreign: Ethiopian Air Force, Korean Air Force, Dominican Republic Air Force, Greek Air Force and many others. The following is an excerpt from a letter of appreciation sent to Major General Charles H. Anderson, Commander of Lowry Air Force

> *While Major Stephanos Bushen of the Imperial Ethiopian Sir Force was at OJT training at Lowry, Mr. William R. Greenwood was assigned as his instructor and supervisor. Mr. Greenwood, besides giving the normal OJT training to Major Stephanos, was also very helpful in the preparation and printing of a budget manual which Major Stephanos brought back to the IEAF for use in his work here.*

> *General Ayene requested that his thanks and appreciation be conveyed to Major Finley, the Foreign Training Officer and Mr. Greenwood.*

Bill brought foreign officers home so we could meet them. Our interesting experiences with two of them are still outstanding in my memory, Major Stephanos Bushen from Ethiopia and Officer Panayotopoulos from Greece.

Major Bushen brought a Sergeant with him whom he treated as a servant. On base the NCO had to "jump to the music,"

A training session

but Bill made it clear that off base, at our home they were two young fellows that we were having for dinner. Bill purposely sat them next to each other at the table. The poor Sergeant was not accustomed to being on an equal basis with his officer, but we just carried on a conversation with both of them. Sometimes we would ask questions about Ethiopia in such a way that they had to refer to each other for the answer. Little by little, they discovered that they both came from the same general area in Ethiopia; they knew some of the same people, and, their families were similar. They actually began communicating man to man.

The second time that we had them at home, after dinner we took them to our summer home in the mountains, the "Lazy G," for the rest of the day. By the time we brought them back, they were laughing and talking with each other as though there was no difference in rank. In fact, the Major told Bill later that it was the first time he had been able to communicate with his Sergeant. He was happy.

In appreciation for what Bill did for him, Major Bushen sent one of Ethiopia's most cherished gifts to us. It is a small circular rug, approximately two and half feet in diameter, made of precious skins of five Colobus Monkey hides. These little black and white monkeys are highly honored, and the Major had to have government approval to send this precious gift out of the country. We still have this special present!

Our children were still growing up, and we learned so much about people of foreign cultures from these special visits.

One day Bill came home absolutely furious. He told me that the Officer from the Greek Air force had been at Lowry for two weeks, living in the BOQ, and not one officer had taken him anywhere! When Bill asked him if he had been to the mountains, he said, "No. I have ridden the bus around Denver a few times."

Bill had Officer Panayotopoulos for training only, and presumed that some BOQ officers would have been hosts to an officer from a foreign country like Greece. (However, he had not expected it for those from Ethiopia.)

"Honey, I'm going to have him over here for dinner and we are going to take him to the mountains," Bill declared.

222

Within a few days his wife arrived, a doctor who spoke no English. Instead of dinner at home, we decided to take them to the mountains and have dinner at a famous restaurant in Conifer. Jim was still in high school, and the only one of our children left at home. When we told him our plan, he was eager to go with us. Bill brought them to our home and away we went.

In the car, Bill and the Officer sat on the front seat, while his wife was between Jim and me on the back seat. As we drove up Turkey Creek Canyon on Highway 285, I indicated points of interest and her husband would turn around and interpret for her. After awhile, he and Bill got to talking and we were left on our own.

I heard the Greek Officer make an interesting observation. He was surprised to see racial discrimination in the United States. They have none in Greece. It is such a short distance between Africa and Greece across the sea that many Africans have migrated to Greece. There has been so much inter-marriage that Greeks are all colors and all are equal Greek citizens.

I used my hands a lot to express what I was saying, and somehow his wife began to understand and occasionally repeat a word. Even when she asked something in Greek, I got the meaning. Jim joined us talking, and by the time we got to the restaurant, the three of us were communicating in the two languages. She couldn't speak English and we couldn't speak Greek, but somehow we had developed a system of conversation. Bill and the Officer were surprised.

We took them back on what I call "The Loop," by returning through Evergreen and ending by way of Highway 6 (now I-70). On the way back to the Base, Bill dropped Jim and me at home. While we were discussing our pleasant adventure, Jim said to me, "You know, Mom, we were communicating by osmosis." I hadn't thought of it that way, but it was a perfect explanation!

Officer Panayotopoulos gave us their address in Athens and invited us to come to visit them in Greece.

When the United States Air Force Academy was founded in 1954, it was based at Lowry Air force Base while the new Academy was being built near Colorado Springs. Since William R. Greenwood was head Budget Officer, Office of Comptroller at Lowry Air force Base, he was charged with developing the initial budget and scheduling the funding of all Academy projects. Bill assumed this huge responsibility in addition to his job of budgeting Lowry's millions of dollars. It was amazing how he handled both budgets efficiently!!!

In 1958, when the Air Force Academy moved to their permanent site near Colorado Springs, Bill spent several days at the new facility briefing the Colonel in Charge of Budget and training the budget Office Staff.

He was consistently recognized by the U.S.A.F. for his outstanding contributions. The following is a letter dated January 31, 1957, from the Department of the Air Force, Washington, D.C. This was sent to General Mussett, Commander of Lowry Air Force Base;

Dear General Mussett:

I wish to commend to you the excellent and efficient service Mr. William R. Greenwood, Budget Office, Office of the Comptroller at Lowry Air Force Base, has rendered to the U.S.A.F. School for Civilian Personnel Administration.

Mr. Greenwood and his staff have been most courteous and effective in keeping the school director informed of the funding necessary for school operation. He has worked closely with Mr. Brown and his staff for five and a half years in budgeting for school operations.

It is requested that a copy of this letter be placed in Mr. Greenwood's personnel file.

Sincerely,

John E. Ehrmantraut

Chief, Career Development Division

Directorate of Civilian Personnel

On October 3, 1963, William Greenwood, Lowry A.F. B., Budget Officer, was voted unanimously as President of the American Society of Military Comptrollers, a highly professional organization of top military men and high ranking civilians in the federal service.

It was noted that William Greenwood's financial accomplishments read like a text book as a Budget Officer:

1) Developed the budget for Lowry A.F.B.

2) Trained personnel for the Budget Office of the Air Force Academy

3) Developed the budget for the Air Force Academy

4) Developed the initial budget for the Titan I Missile site

5) Received a Certificate of Achievement for fiscal year 1969 at Lowry Technical Training Center AFB from Major D.O. Montieth, USAF Commander

He was credited with establishing an education Financial Management system and listed many of the budget officers from foreign countries whom he had trained.

Although Bill was Civil Service, his job was that of a Colonel, so he had to be accommodated as an officer of that rank attending any military base. He had a few interesting experiences in the South, but they had no choice!!!

When the Air Force Accounting Finance Center was organized on York Street, they were having so many problems that Bill was sent there to help them get their financial system in order. At first, he was resented for coming in to show them how to run their new Center. Bill discovered that the military and civilian staff knew very little about finances. It took quite a while to train and organize them into a working accounting office. When he left, they were working so well that they thanked him for his help.

The Air Force Accounting and Finance Center kept in touch with Bill even after it was moved to it permanent headquarters near Lowry

Air force Base.

While Bill was doing all of his work with the Air Force, in 1957 he was appointed to the Denver Citizens Capitol Improvements Budget Committee by Mayor William F. Nicholson. He was re-appointed by every succeeding Mayor.

One year, the city was faced with closing or selling their mountain parks. Bill devised a financial system that kept the parks open and cared for.

Another time the Denver Public Library's budget was so low that they were planning to cut their schedule to half day on Saturday and closed on Sunday. Bill met with the Library officials and presented a financial plan that made it possible to maintain their regular schedule at lower cost.

These were only two of the examples why Mayors kept him on the budget Committee for his financial expertise.

My husband was a devoted Prince Hall Mason. The old lodge hall at East 28th Avenue and Downing Street was a mess. A long flight of stairs led up to a dim hallway before entering the big room in which were splintering chairs donated from the old Roxy Theater. Metal and wooden single lockers were scattered about belonging to various Masonic and Eastern Star Chapters. The moth-eaten camel of the Shrine was a disgraceful eye-sore. It was unbearably hot in the summer and cold in the winter with all the heat in the high ceiling.

When Bill became Master of Rocky Mountain Lodge, he proceeded to remodel the Lodge Hall into a respectable meeting place. (I finally refused to attend affairs there and sit on those splintery chairs.) He had to fight with his lodge brothers every step of the way for money to make the improvements. He had determination and managed to achieve his goal.

He had a wall of individual lockers built so each organization had its own neat, storage on which to place their own locks. There was a special enclosed space to store the camel out of sight. A small entry room was partitioned off so late comers, especially the ladies, would not have to stand in the dimly lit hall. We donated our extra furniture and lamps to make a pleasant waiting room. He installed an inside ladies room so they would not have to go out into the dark hall to use the only other rest room.

He had the ceiling lowered to transparent plexi-glass with florescent lights for even, pleasant lighting, instead of the few dim light bulbs. It kept the heat near the floor so the Lodge Hall was warmer. Air conditioners were installed in some of the windows to cool the hall in summer.

He had a bigger fight on his hands when it came to replacing the seats. (I could not see why those men wanted to hang on to those old seats. They had not sat on those splinters, or had been scratched and snagged their hosiery as I had!) Bill took me with him to purchase adequate, stackable, plastic chairs from a warehouse that he had checked out. He had someone haul away the old seating, and billed the lodge for everything.

With the Lodge Hall comfortable, pleasant and a place in which to proudly have meetings and invite visitors, his Masonic brothers and ladies of the Eastern Stars and Daughters of Isis were happy.

One of Bill's greatest disappointments was that he was never permitted to become Grand Master. Every time his name was submitted at Grand Lodge, someone else was chosen. With all of his dedication to Masonry, he was constantly passed over. Some of his faithful brothers said it was, unfortunately, many of the members who were jealous of Bill's knowledge and achievements who continued to block his promotion.

He was an active member of Mountain and Plains Consistory #33. This is the benevolent and religious house of Masonry's 32° (degree).

When he joined the Shrine at his initiation, someone pulled a shocker that almost killed him. They knew he had a bad heart. His member Shriners brought him home, and it took days for him to recover. My respect for this Masonic house hit bottom! Over the years, I attended dances and parties of this House of Joy with Bill, but I never got over the resentment of their treatment of my husband at his initiation.

When Bill asked me with which Masonic House he should concentrate on working, I let him know exactly how I felt about the Shrine. To me, the Consistory seemed to offer more satisfying and spiritual benefit than the Shrine. However, he had to make the choice of which way he really wanted to go. He chose to concentrate on working in Mountain and Plains Consistory #33 and just enjoy the Shrine. This choice led him to the top of Masonry.

At the United Supreme Council (Prince Hall Affiliation) Northern Jurisdiction, in Cincinnati, Ohio, on May 11, 1964, William Rivers Greenwood was crowned a 33° degree Mason, the highest Masonic degree!

The United Supreme Council is the ruling body of Prince Hall masonry. Each year it is hosted in a different city. However, every third year it meets in Philadelphia where the Cathedral and headquarters are located, and election of national officers is held. In 1968, it was there that Bill was coronated a Sovereign Grand Inspector General, making him an active member of United Supreme Council. The following year he was appointed Deputy of Colorado, Wyoming and Utah. There were Consistories in Denver, Colorado Springs, Salt Lake City and Ogden, Utah, with a small one in Cheyenne, Wyoming. That is a wide spread of territory to cover!

He always took me to Supreme Council, but in the early days there was nothing planned for the ladies. There were only a few visiting wives, and it was quite boring for me since I did not know anyone. Bill talked to the men about bringing their wives and having the local ladies plan a get together for the visitors. This small start was the beginning of planning a bit of entertainment for the few ladies who came with their husbands. As time progressed, more and more wives came with their husbands. Year after year it grew from just luncheons to bus loads of ladies taken to points of interest, and on all day tours. Attending Supreme Council became a real joy. Each year I anticipated seeing the friends I had made.

Eventually, Bill told me he wanted to organize a Golden Circle assembly here in Denver. This is the women's auxiliary of the Consistory. Of course, he wanted me to be one of the charter members. I did not want to disappoint him, but I had to ask, "Is there a lot of ritual? You know, with all my respect for the Eastern Stars, I never joined because I am not a ritualistic person. Whatever I join, I actively participate in that activity, but a lot of ritual turns me off."

"Oh, the Golden Circle does not have a lot of ritual like the Eastern Stars," he assured me.

I was still a little uncertain, but I told him that I would take part in the organization, for him.

After he organized the Mountain and Plains Assembly in Denver, he organized the Pikes Peak Assembly in Colorado Springs and the Sego Lily Assembly in Ogden, Utah (which also included membership from Salt Lake City). With three Assemblies, he organized us into a State Assembly, which meets each October at the same time as the Consistory's Council of Deliberation. When the men tried to take over financial control of the State assembly, as Deputy, Bill let his members know that the ladies were independent and would abide by their own laws. He always protected the Loyal Ladies of the Golden Circle. I was secretary of the State Assembly for several years, then finally moved up to State Grand Loyal Ruler. I really enjoyed participating in the Golden Circle. Our Mountain and Plains Assembly meets only four times a year, so I had plenty of "breathing room" in between

Bill, Sr. as 33rd Degree Deputy of Colorado, Wyoming & Utah; Marie as State Grand Loyal Lady Ruler of the Golden Circle Denver Mountain & Plains Assembly Number 49

Often, Bill was sent to some of the largest state Councils of Deliberation as representative of Sovereign Grand Commander. I would participate in their State assemblies. We attended the Pennsylvania

Council in Philadelphia so often that they made Bill an Honorary Member of the Pennsylvania Council of Deliberation! I became an Honorary Member of their State Assembly.

When the Southern Jurisdiction had their Supreme Council meeting in Monrovia, Liberia in 1972, Bill was sent as a representative from the Northern Jurisdiction. They had a full charter plane flying out of the brand new Dulles Airport near Washington, D.C. We joined Bill's friend, Sovereign Grand Commander Northern Jurisdiction, Russell Gideon and his wife, Lillian, who introduced us to United Air Line's Red Carpet Club. They took us to a comfortable room to wait for boarding time. We were impressed and later secured membership in Red Carpet, which we used in our travels from then on.

After a long wait, we finally boarded our plane and took off for another exciting adventure – the other side of the world, Africa!!! The plane was full of happy, celebrating Southern Jurisdiction members and their families. It was a long flight, and gradually everyone settled down to quietly rest. Across the aisle from us was a couple, a dark brown man and a white-skin blond wife, whom I became aware of because she was complaining and being very fussy. She had brought her own pillow, but could not get comfortable in the small space of her seat. Her husband was trying to pacify her, to no avail. I thought, "I'll sure stay away from her."

After midnight, we landed in the Canary Islands to refuel. Soon thereafter another flight from South Africa landed. – all white. It was interesting to see the amazed expressions on their faces when they encountered this plane load of African-American people in the same airport with them. A few had enlightening conversations with some of our group.

The next morning we landed in Monrovia. It was hot and humid, the end of October. The first of November is the beginning of summer near the equator!

There was a mix-up on our housing reservation. Instead of the President's palace where we were originally scheduled, we were finally assigned to the residences of a most interesting couple.

Our gracious hosts were Dr. Togba and his vivacious wife. By the time we reached their home I was completely exhausted from jet-lag and lack of sleep from the all night flight, along with the intense heat and humidity we encountered while waiting for our housing accommodation to be settled. Bill was quite concerned because I was beginning to feel ill. Mrs. Togba understood and I was bedded down immediately. I slept for so long, I don't remember whether it was day or night when I woke up!

I took a shower and was frustrated when I couldn't get completely dry. As I towelled, I continued to perspire and the heavy humidity prevented the perspiration from evaporating. While I was in Africa, I learned to live with my clothes clinging to my damp body.

When I finally emerged to greet my hostess, I learned that another couple had been placed with the Togbas. To my surprise, it was the pair who were seated across the aisle from us on the plane! I was headed for another enlightening experience.

The men had gone to the lodge hall so there were just us three women. The one whom I had observed on the plane was Sylvia Allen, a highly respected attorney who was running for a government office in Fayetteville, North Carolina. Her husband was G. Wesley Allen, a successful physician in Fayetteville. They dearly loved each other and worked together in Civil rights and community activities. He was the official physician for the Southern Supreme Council.

Sylvia and I became buddies during the few days we were in Monrovia. We talked about our families, our children, our various activities, our communities and discovered we were Alpha Kappa Alpha Sorority sisters. We went shopping together by getting into the stores as quickly as possible, out of the heat. We both had a problem tolerating the intense heat and humidity, however, she was better acclimated than I.

I bought shirts for our sons, Bill and me, and something feminine for Louise. (I don't remember what it was.) One shop was special where beautiful African embroidered dresses were made. The dresses were cut out, but the parts were not sewn together. The embroidery was done on these flat sections of cloth by young men using sewing machines. For a half hour I watched in awe as they speedily created intricate designs on

231

ordinary Singer sewing machines! When the embroidery was complete, the parts were put together into a finished garment. I bought two beautiful dresses.

Eventually, I bought gold Africa-shaped earrings from the President's jeweler for $1.00 (marked down from $2.00). Everything I bought cost only a fraction of what I would have paid in the U.S.A.

All of the merchants were foreigners – Indian, Jewish, Italian and others. There were no purely Liberian business owners – except the mortician!!!

Mrs. Togba told us there would be a *Soiree*. (That's French for a special evening party.) Thank goodness it would be outdoors at night when it was relatively cooler than during the day. She was so excited about this special dress-up affair, that I knew it must be a real party highlight. We met Monrovia's Mayor and their wealthy mortician, both of whom were women! It was a joyful time of lights, good food, music, happy people and fighting off insects!!!

One day when Sylvia and I were returning from one of our excursions, we passed a school. There were three small children on the outside, one standing by the window and two by the entrance. I wondered what they had done to be put outside in the heat; they were so young. I told Mrs. Togba about my observation.

"Oh, they're listening to see what they can learn," was her shocking reply. "Their parents can't afford to pay for them to go to school. Many times students will come out and tell them some information. They are so eager to learn, but there are no free schools."

That was unbelievable! We have free education in the United States and have to make some children go to school, while children here were begging to go to school!!!

One afternoon Dr. Togba took Bill and me to lunch at their lovely hotel. He told us about the history of some of the Liberian tribes. He was a descendant of one of the most peaceful tribes. He was greatly concerned about the fact that Liberia had no middle class. There were only the wealthy and the very poor. He had acquired his higher education in the United States, where he met his wife, many years ago.

232

She is American, but has happily assumed the African way of life over the years. They sent their sons to the United States where they received their advanced degrees. Dr. Togba returned to Liberia and settled in Monrovia with his wife to help raise the level of education. He was a professor in the struggling college in Monrovia. He took Bill and me on a tour of the area to show us the highs and the lows of his country.

When we arrived home, Mrs. Togba was yelling at the servant in the kitchen. He had found some ground beef, boiled it and fed it to the dogs. She had planned to prepare the ground beef for dinner - a treat for us. She paid $1.50 a pound for it. (We were paying 79 cents a pound in 1972.) The young man had no idea what that ground meat was and was too poor to know how special it was. I was amazed at how expensive that meat was in Monrovia, since it was our cheapest at that time. (My, how times have changed!)

The final event was the Supreme Council banquet at the President's palace. I wore one of my new dresses and my African earrings. There was a huge reception in the great entry with hundreds of men and women visiting and being served drinks and delicious *hors-d'oeuvres*.

The banquet was set up in the massive ballroom. All of the vast number of members and visiting men of the Supreme Council were seated in one section of the ballroom. The women were seated separately. I was assigned to a special VIP table for a few outstanding ladies. I felt honored to be included with the Mayor, the millionaire Mortician, the wife of the Southern Grand Commander, my hostess, Mrs. Gideon, and a few other special ladies.

There was a formal menu with so much food listed, I thought it was by choice. However, after salad, each course was served in its entirety – chicken, beef, lamb, etc. I lost track! I could eat only parts of each course and felt guilty wasting food when there were so many poor people in need. I was miserably stuffed, and there was still dessert to come.

I happened to look up and discovered the ceiling was completely mirrored, and I could see all the men. I looked for Bill, and there he was looking at me in the mirror! We grinned and waved to each other, and continued to glance at each other off and on throughout the rest of the evening. Later, Bill said he had been watching me visiting with the ladies for some time before I looked up and saw him. It was just pure fun after that.

The next morning at breakfast, Bill was lamenting the fact that he had been so busy with the interesting Supreme Council meeting that he had not had a chance to get one of the comfortable leisure suits that he had seen some of the men wearing.

"You're not leaving until later today. Go on to the tailor now, and your suit will be ready this afternoon," Mrs. Togba told him.

Bill couldn't believe he could have a tailored suit in just a few hours, but away he went. This was about ten o'clock in the morning. By four o'clock, he had his comfortable, perfectly fitted, grey leisure suit in plenty of time before we were scheduled to leave. A few of us were taking an extra tour. The Allens were not going.

It was a short flight from Monrovia to Abidjan, Ivory Coast. We arrived at our hotel early that evening. French is the language of the "*Cote D'Ivoire*," but the *concierges* at the hotel spoke English, also. I exhumed my limited French, which I had not used in years, and had fun talking with them. They had a great sense of humor! The next day we were free to relax, and explore the city.

On Sunday, we were taken on an all day trip by bus to the back country. Somewhere along the way, our bus broke down! The bus driver had no idea what to do. We were on a dirt road in the woods. Off among the trees we could hear singing. Out of curiosity, some of us decided to find out what was going on out there in this wilderness. We arrived at a clearing to find what looked like a small, rugged outdoor chapel where a group of natives were sitting on the ground singing and worshipping. It was truly awesome that our bus had stopped at this particular spot, at this special time. We were all impressed with the lesson we learned: God can be worshipped any time, by anyone, anywhere! It set the tone of our trip for the rest of the day.

Miraculously, somehow the driver got our bus started. We sent up our prayers of thanks for what the Lord had revealed to us that day. It must have been a Divine Plan!!!

We had one more day in Abidjan, then on to Accra, Ghana. It was hot and dusty. All I remember about Ghana was visiting the place where slaves had been held before being shipped to America, and being taken to the grave of W.E.B. DuBois. He did so much for Ghana that Ghanaians actually worship him.

Our trip to Lagos, Nigeria, was cancelled because of the fighting and unsettled situation. We were scheduled to fly back to the United States, but there was a problem with one of the plane's engines, so we flew to Lisbon, Portugal, the nearest place where there was a facility to make repairs. We were placed in a Sheraton Hotel over night and had all of the following day free. Bill and I did some exploring. I bought some jewelry, and a lovely crocheted shawl.

It was late afternoon when our plane was finally repaired and we returned safely home. This was the end of only one of the many adventures with my amazing husband!

CHAPTER 13
More Amazing Experiences

This chapter is a miscellaneous assortment of other events and activities that occurred in our lives over the years. They are not in any chronological order. They are only as I happen to remember them.

When the children were growing up, they were active in Sunday School, YPD, Youth Choir and many programs at Shorter A.M.E. Church. I sang in the choir, helped Mrs. Slack with YPD, and served wherever necessary. Bill was at Shorter with us and our activities so often that he decided to join our church since we were not visiting Holy Redeemer very often. Shorter was his grandmother's church and he was well known here. He became a trustee and chairman of the Housing Committee.

Bill was faithful to his church. He had a "run-in" with only two ministers. At one trustee meeting he questioned Rev. Odom as to why the trustees nor the congregation had not been given a financial report. When Rev. Odom informed Bill that he alone handled the finances, Bill followed him to the office where they apparently had quite a "warm session"! Bill came home furious because not one trustee said one word! Of course, he got no report from Rev. Odom.

When the rest of the block of vacant property adjacent to the church was for sale, Bill tried to get the trustees to purchase it for future expansion. They would not. When Bean Apartments were built, Shorter was enclosed!

His other encounter with a minister was many years later when we were faced with selling the church and moving to where we would have more space, especially for parking. Rev. Carter was pushing to buy a church in Southeast Denver that had been recommended by a member who lived in that area, far from the center of our Northeast community. Rev. Carter and his followers had become so overbearingly persistent in pressuring for this move, that many members were leaving the church.

At a special evening meeting, Rev. Carter and his committee made it clear that this was the way to go and they wanted no objections.

Then Bill got up. He advised the members to investigate the condition of the proposed church, the cost and the far away location. While he was talking, Rev. Carter started singing to drown out Bill's voice. Bill spoke louder, and Rev. Carter sang louder. A few of his "henchmen" joined him in singing. When Bill kept talking, they finally walked out of the meeting – a blatant insult to my husband!!!

I was furious. I had been a member of Shorter since 1927. I had seen good, bad and indifferent leaders in our church, but this was the most degrading, insulting activity I had ever witnessed by a so called "Man of God." What little respect I had for Rev. Carter as a minister hit bottom!!!

Bill was hurt and disgusted, so he went back to Holy Redeemer. However, after a few weeks there, he told me he was coming back to Shorter. Redeemer had as many problems as Shorter had.

With the sudden death of Rev. Carter, as he attended a meeting in California, we were left with the unfinished decision of where we would move.

Omar Blair, member of the Denver Public School Board of Education solved our problem. He let Shorter officials know that the School Board had some vacant property at Martin Luther King Blvd. and Jackson St. that would be an ideal location and plenty of space to build a church and have needed parking. This time his words were heeded, so the property was purchased.

In 1978, when we were informed that our new minister would be a young man, Jesse Langston Boyd (who had served in Africa), Bill said he would do all he could to help this young minister through the problems, turmoil and uncertainties he would be facing at Shorter.

After Rev. Boyd and his young wife arrived in Denver, Bill invited them out to dinner. We told our friends, Chester and Myra Harris, and took them with us to meet the Boyds. We had a delightful evening of good food and cheerful companionship with this young couple. Bill let Rev. Boyd know that he would support him in every way, and to let him

238

know whatever he needed.

In 1973, Bill retired from Lowry Air Force Base after serving as the budget Director for 23 years. He was the youngest civilian Air Force retiree then, at 54 years old. He had been in Civil Service at Lowry for 33 years.

With all the training, planning and financial development that Bill did for the Air Force, he was never promoted past GS-13. He saw Budget Directors that he trained become GS-15 and GS-16, but every time his name came up for promotion, nothing happened! Was that subtle discrimination?

As Budget Director, he had made it possible for Colorado National Bank to open a successful branch at Lowry. When he retired, he was immediately employed by the bank for his financial expertise!

One year later, 1974, he became an officer of Colorado National Bank in Personal Finance, which he enjoyed. He, also, became a member of the International Bankers Association and attended the annual meetings of the National branch of the Association as a representative of Colorado National Bank. He met bankers from all over the world and learned so much about finances.

He frequently took me with him when something was scheduled for the wives. When we were at a meeting in Anaheim, California, Bill came back from a session and announced , "Honey, I don't want to be a millionaire. Those guys have so much stress and so many worries trying to keep their millions, they can't relax and enjoy life. We'll just live like millionaires with what we have and be happy!" He then grinned.

Eventually, when the branch bank at Lowry was losing so much business that the director was transferred, Bill was sent to his old familiar territory to take charge.

It was completely disorganized! There were only women employees. Most of the time there was no drive-up service because the women were visiting, eating or just ignoring it. There was no schedule. Everyone did whatever they chose to do. They were in for a shocking revelation! Bill laid down rules of conduct, dress and responsibilities. When some of the women resented being told what to do, they were given the choice of conforming or leaving. Two employees quit and the rest settled into unhappy compliance. Since most of the business lost had been due to the lack of service at the Drive-up window, Bill made sure that someone was always there.

One young woman was so happy to finally have specific directions and a sense of security, that he trained her as his assistant. Business began to increase and the employees became efficient, pleased and cooperative.

I do not remember how many years Bill was at Colorado National Bank, but when he resigned, the Lowry Branch was one of the top three producing facilities!

One day Bill stopped by Shorter to see how Rev. Boyd was getting along with the plans for building the new church. Rev. Boyd told him he had checked with every bank in Denver and all of them had refused to lend him any money. He did not know what to do next. My husband came home very concerned, and announced that he was going to see what he could do to help.

This is the story that Rev. Boyd told many times: "Bill Greenwood came knocking on my door one morning. When I let him in, he handed me a proposal and said he would make an appointment for me at one of the banks for a loan. I didn't expect any results, but I went to the bank anyway since he had been concerned enough to write the proposal. When I arrived, I found my appointment was with the bank president, not a loan officer. I was greeted pleasantly, and he led me into his office. I handed the proposal to him. The president was reading it, then stopped and asked who wrote the proposal. When I told him that Bill Greenwood wrote it, he just closed it up and said, 'If Bill Greenwood wrote this proposal, I know it is all right! How much money do you need?' "

Rev. Boyd walked out with the loan to construct our first building of the new Shorter. The cornerstone was laid in 1981. Bill was among the Masons who performed the ceremony. Rev. Boyd was instrumental in having Shorter's block of Jackson St. renamed "Richard Allen Court."

When Rev. Boyd had problems with the loan for building our sanctuary years later, I wished my husband had still been around to help him.

Bill was surprised when Ret. Col. Neil Wynkoop contacted him to tell him about a financial venture he was working on, and felt that Bill could help him. Col. Wynkoop was stationed at Lowry when Bill was Budget Director and he knew of Bill's financial expertise and success at Colorado National Bank. He was president of a company called "Dynamic Growth" that had built apartments on the Western Slope. They had bought a three-acre site from Denver's exclusive former Polo Grounds, and planned to build a 21-story luxury condominium apartment – Polo Club, Inc. – the first in Denver.

The East coast and the West coast had condominiums, but the concept had not reached Denver, so the banks refused to lend millions to Dynamic Growth for such an unheard of project. Neil Wynkoop actually asked Bill to join the company! The condos would sell for $22,400 to $70,900. That was in the 1970's.

As a member of Dynamic Growth, Bill learned that the company was stable and financially sound. The plans for the apartment were fantastic, and Bill told me about them enthusiastically. Since there was no money from Denver banks, he said to me, "I am going to New York to see what I can do, Honey. I am not going to tell anyone because it may not work out."

Through his experience at Colorado National Bank and the International Bankers Association, he had met financiers from all over the world. He was gone for several days. When he returned, he had a construction loan to build Polo Club from Chase Manhattan in New York City!!!

Bill was voted Vice President of the company. He was constantly checking on the construction of Polo Club. He was so excited about the unique arrangement of the apartments being built around an atrium. Since I had no idea of what an atrium was, he took me out to show me this unusual plan.

I was amazed at the huge open space in the center of the building, extending from the ground up through the entire 21-story structure. Every apartment would have a balcony overlooking this landscape and decorated transparent-roofed court.

One day, Bill called me excitedly from Polo Club and asked me if I would like a new kitchen stove.

"What do you mean?" I asked.

"They were finishing the kitchens in one of the apartments, but they sent the wrong color. Now they don't know what to do with it," was his reply. "It's brown."

"Why don't they send it back?" I wanted to know.

Bill had told me that General Electric had a brand new P-7 countertop cooker with new self-cleaning double side-ovens fresh off the drawing board, and Polo Club was the first to install them in the kitchens. They had not been put on the market yet. He said all they had to do was order the correct color for the apartment and this brown set was available at no cost. That was fine, so I said O.K.

I could visualize this lovely electric appliance in my kitchen, replacing our little gas range – just like Polo Club!

We had the heavy duty 220-Watt electric line run in. Our carpenter, Mr. Benns, removed our old stove, capped the gas, remodeled our cabinets, then installed the electric counter-top burners and the big double side-ovens. It is still in use in our family home on West 6th Avenue!

The condos sold - many before the building was completed. As time went on, Bill became concerned about inaccurate reports that Dynamic Growth was getting from Col. Wynkoop in regard to Polo Club, Inc. Bill tried to talk to him about the finances, but all he got was evasive answers.

Some of the remarks Wynkoop began making during meetings were so strange that Bill began to wonder about his mental balance. Even though other members were aware of the situation, they did not want Bill to become president, although they knew he would give them straight answers.

Finally, Col. Wynkoop became so mentally unbalanced that his wife had to commit him to a mental home. Then Bill became president of Dynamic Growth.

From the few records he salvaged, Bill discovered that the fortune received from the sale of Polo Club, Inc. condos was being spent on all kinds of personal luxury items and investments by Col. Wynkoop and the secretary. The members of Dynamic Growth could have, and should have, received small fortunes from this investment. However, there was so little to salvage from what was left, Bill divided the funds equally and paid everyone a few hundred dollars. Since membership had become so scattered, and disinterested, Bill closed Dynamic Growth.

While still at the bank, he became a member of Denver Symphony Association (now Colorado Symphony). We both love music and frequently attended symphony concerts. We had season tickets.

Rabbi Laderman was a member of the Association and frequently his wife came with him. She found out that I was a retired teacher, so she told Bill that she would like for me to join the Symphony Guild. It was the Women's auxiliary of the Symphony that raised money for the orchestra. I had never heard of it and was not interested. After several meetings with Mrs. Laderman insisting that I join, Bill said it would be a good idea for me to check into it.

The first meeting that I attended at an exclusive condominium near Cheeseman Park, I felt like an outsider with all those wealthy society women. I was the only brown face present. The various interest groups reported their activities and the amount of money they raised for the orchestra. There was not a single activity that interested me, but Mrs. Laderman welcomed me.

For Bill's sake, I attended a second meeting. This time there was a report from the Symphony Guild Tour Guides. Their activities caught my attention because they were doing what I had been happily doing for years – taking friends and visitors sight-seeing, especially to Colorado Springs and to the mountains. After the meeting, I told Mrs. Laderman that I would be interested in joining the Tour Guides. She said she would have someone from the group call me. This was early 1976.

I was surprised when I received a call from someone inviting me to attend a meeting of the Tour Guides one morning at the Eugene Field Library on South Colorado Blvd.

I arrived on time and I could see that the ladies were surprised to see that I was African-American. Louise Hamer was the instructor in charge. She greeted me casually, but I could see that she was not sure of what to do with this brown face as a tour guide. The first day went well with a few of the ladies talking to me. I discovered that there was information about each tour that needed to be memorized: tours of the city, various mountain trips, Air Force Academy, etc.

Fortunately, I was familiar with almost all of them, but there was much detailed information to be learned about each area. I was given a script for the Denver City Tour to be prepared for the next meeting. I think we met every other week.

Louise Hamer was very dramatic in her instructions to us guides in how to present information to a tour group. She had been an actress. After watching other guides perform, I learned what was expected. My presentation went off well. Louise Hamer complimented me, but said I needed to put a little more dramatic motion into my speaking.

During the next few meetings I became acquainted with most of the ladies. I could talk with them on almost any topic because I had been there, or knew something about everywhere they had travelled. My husband being a member of the Denver Symphony Association gave me an added boost!

My first beginner's observation bus tour was with an experienced guide who was taking a group to Georgetown. We were told how to dress so I bought a navy blue pants suit to wear as my guide uniform. The trip to Georgetown was an enlightening experience as I listened to her and observed her actions. Evidently, the report of my conduct on this initial trip was good because at the next meeting my name was given to the member in charge of scheduling tours to be placed on the active list. I was now a full-fledged Tour Guide, but I doubted that I would get any assignment soon.

To my surprise, on the next scheduled City Tour I was called to lead a bus load of tourists all on my own! It was from mid-morning to mid-afternoon with lunch at Spaghetti House. I was a bit nervous, but it went off well.

Over the years, I was assigned to many tours – sometimes alone on one bus, sometimes with several tour guided buses. One of our biggest tours was a convention with five full buses to the Air Force Academy! My favorite trips were to the mountains – Estes Park, Trail Ridge, Peak to Peak Highway, Black Hawk and Central City. I knew these areas well.

My greatest compliments were several times when it was reported at our meetings that there had been repeated requests for me to guide tours of groups that I had led before!

When the unusual Boettcher Concert Hall was built, the Symphony Guild Tour Guides were scheduled to lead tours through the unique building before it officially opened. It was fascinating pointing out the "tuning discs" in the ceiling that could reflect the sound evenly throughout the hall, even to the farthest balcony, and explaining their operation.

One all day tour turned out to be especially interesting and a bit exciting. I was scheduled to take a group to Estes Park, over Trail Ridge road, down to Grand Lake and back to Denver by five o'clock. We were to leave Denver at nine thirty a.m. This mature adult group arrived at our bus pick-up at ten o'clock, so by the time we got loaded on the bus it was after ten and we were due in Estes Park for lunch at noon.

We got to Estes Park a little late, but lunch went fine. I decided to shorten our time in Estes Park because we had a long trip ahead of us. At lunch I had noticed a few people staring at me, but they said nothing. While I was waiting at the bus for everyone to come out of the restaurant, one man said to me, "Who are you?'

"What do you mean?" I inquired.

"What's your race?" he wanted to know.

"Oh, I am African-American," was my reply. "I am a mixture like all Americans. I have African blood with drops of Indian, French, Spanish, and Lord knows what else. I am a true African-American."

He had a puzzled expression on his face. "But you don't talk or look Black."

I smiled and said, "Well, you know, we are all different individuals."

We continued on our trip to Trail Ridge, the highest continually paved road in the country, which is over 12,000 feet high. That's above timberline with very thin air. Before leaving Denver I had advised them to breathe deep so their bodies and brains would get as much oxygen as possible. In "Mile High" Denver air contains only 70% of the oxygen as the air at sea level. Up this high in the mountains there is even less oxygen, so I told them again to move slowly and breathe deeply.

All went well until we were getting on the bus to head down to Grand Lake. An elderly white-haired man was having trouble breathing. I got off the bus fast, found the Park Ranger who checked the old man on the bus. The report was that he needed to get to a lower altitude and out of the Trail Ridge thin air.

I told the Ranger that I was headed down to Grand Lake, and on to Denver without stopping. The Ranger assured me that would take care of my passenger's problem. He should be all right. What a relief! We had a wonderful bus driver.

We arrived in Denver on time. The elderly man had recovered, and I was complimented on conducting a safe and pleasant trip. Several of them thanked me for explaining about our thin air and deep breathing. No one had ever explained about our rarified air before. This was the first time some of them had not been dizzy or had headaches in our high altitude.

My generous tip was added to the money for the Symphony. This was purely enjoyable volunteering for all of us Tour Guides!

246

For many years, the Symphony Guild offered tours to areas that were almost exclusively ours, so we were kept busy. However, in the early 80's when AAA, Greyhound and some independent tour businesses expanded their tour selections into some of our special areas for discounted costs, we lost many of our regular customers.

In 1983, the Tour Guide officers decided to close this Symphony Guild interest group since the competition had become too great. I had been elected secretary during our last year. At our final meeting, I wrote the closing minutes and was told that I had supplied the most complete minutes they ever had. This closed out seven years of one of the most fascinating experiences of my life! Thanks to the Grace of God.

In May of 1976, Supreme Council was scheduled to meet in Denver for the first time. As Deputy for Colorado, Wyoming and Utah, Bill had been preparing for this event for two years. Since I had become active with the Symphony Tour Guides, he asked me to take charge of the ladies' Monday event which would be a trip to Black Hawk and Central City. (This was years before gambling.) Supreme Council was meeting at the Regency Hotel.

We had taken visitors and friends to the lovely Black Forest Inn in Black Hawk many times. Bill knew the owner, so he asked him if he could accommodate the ladies' tour. The restaurant was closed on Mondays, but he told Bill that he would be glad to open it just for this event.

I told Bill that I would conduct the tour, but I was going to organize it so there would not be the rude pushing and shoving of all those wild women trying to get on the first bus. We thought we would need at least three buses. I planned to color-code the buses, so I asked Bill if I could have just enough different colored tickets to match the seating capacity of each bus.

He said, "Honey, you can have anything you want."

I selected several of my golden Circle ladies far enough ahead of time so we had several meetings on responsibilities of being in charge of a bus load of women.

The Saturday morning of the opening of Supreme Council, I had a table for ladies' registration for the tour.

I had informed the members helping me that we would issue tickets of only one color first until they were gone before moving to another color. I had red, blue and yellow tickets. Bill had added a few white tickets in case we needed more. I planned to place a sheet of matching color construction paper of the three colors in the window of the buses.

We started with the red tickets. We kept a list of names as they paid for their tickets. When all the reds were gone, we went to the blue. A woman stopped to register and said her friend came in earlier and she would like to be on the bus with her. We checked the list and the friend had purchased a red ticket. I told her we had no more red tickets so she would have a blue one. She was not happy. I told her that she might find someone who would exchange tickets with her, but we could not give her the same color ticket as her friend; they were all gone! She took her ticket and left steaming mad.

All of the red and blue tickets were sold and most of the yellow. We knew then that there would be three bus loads of ladies on Monday. I met with the ladies who would be in charge of the red and yellow buses. I was guiding the blue bus. I made it clear that they were to admit to board <u>only</u> the ticket holders of their color buses.

Monday morning I place the colored paper on the windshields of the buses. Red was first, blue second and yellow lined up third. When the women came out there was a mad rush to the first bus. Three came to my bus with blue tickets. No one went to the yellow bus. I could see something was wrong, so I went to the red bus, and the member in charge was just standing by the door and letting everyone get on without checking tickets.

I stopped everyone in line, checked their tickets and told them they had to board the bus that matched their tickets. I got on the bus and told those ladies the same. Some did not want to leave the bus, but I made it very clear that we were not going anywhere until everyone was on the right bus.

I explained that this color-coding made it easy for everyone to find her bus and know she had a seat, instead of some of the scrambles we had often endured on other tours. We finally got on our way.

As we drove up Clear Creek Canyon, I gave my Tour Guide spiel of the history, the panning for gold, the natural beauty of the canyon and a bit of history of Black Hawk. To our surprise, when we arrived at the restaurant, the tables were set up beautifully in two rooms. There was a surprising special treat. While we were eating, a violinist went through the rooms serenading us. The food was absolutely delicious. We were all impressed!

After lunch we drove into Central City with a little time to explore. There was no parking lot big enough for all three buses, so one parked somewhere else. Later the ladies thanked me for my color-coded system. They said they didn't have to worry about their buses, because they were so easy to find and they had their seats. We returned to Denver by five o'clock in time to prepare for the seven o'clock banquet.

Over the years, at Supreme Council I have had ladies tell me they remember how much they enjoyed their first trip to Colorado in 1976.

When Highland Cemetery opened, we bought four plots for $100 each. Bill's grandmother was buried in one. When our cleaning lady, Mrs. Pink, lost her mother, we gave her one plot. She had become like one of our family. When Mrs. Pink died we gave her family the one next to her mother. With only one plot left, we bought six more in the comparatively new cemetery, so there would be enough for the two of us and other family members.

Bill had his own accounting business, which he never advertised. By word of mouth from satisfied customers he was kept busy at income tax time, because he was honest and thorough. He was also a financial advisor and helped many small businesses.

One woman in Lakewood came to him with problems when her small real estate business was failing. She followed his advice and the business began to grow. She could not pay him, so she deeded over the cabin on South Beaver Creek that became our "Lazy G" summer retreat.

We acquired five lots of beautiful property at Mountain View Lakes off of Highway 285 (just forty-five minutes drive from our Denver home), when Bill helped a couple get their floundering mountain business going successfully. Our carpenter, Mr. Benns, did all the work we needed at no charge. We just paid for materials. In exchange, Bill did his taxes, and gave him financial advice.

We profited by these exchanges of services, and others paid him his fee. However, when anyone had a need, Bill was the first to give a helping hand. One of his greatest disappointments was the refusal of "our people" to let him help them with his financial expertise.

My husband's basic philosophy was: "Remember the people you passed on your way up the ladder to success. If you slip, you are going to meet those same people on the way down, so reach back and help those who are still struggling."

Shortly after my daughter married in 1970, her husband, Ray Weathersby was sent to Korea. He was a Lieutenant in the Army, but spouses were not included even though the war was over. However, my enterprising daughter found a way to fly over to Korea to be with her husband! She was housed in Seoul, outside the base. Louise wrote to me about the primitive living conditions to which she was not accustomed. Somehow, she eventually managed to get housing on the base and enjoy the activities with her husband and other officers.

When they returned to the USA in 1971, Ray left the Army and had a teaching job in a college in West Virginia for a while. They finally moved to Chicago where Ray became a Certified Public Accountant (C.P.A.).

Bill and I had just planned our first Caribbean cruise, when Louise called to tell us that there would be a big banquet for those receiving the C.P.A. degree. She was so proud of Ray that she wanted us to be there to celebrate with her. It would be at the same time we were to leave on our two-week cruise.

We checked to see about rescheduling our cruise. We were told there was a choice, other than the entire two weeks. Some passengers took the first week, got off the ship at the Dutch island of *Curaçao,* and flew back to Miami. Those for the second week were flown from Miami to *Curaçao* and boarded in their places for the rest of the cruise. This worked out perfectly for us, so we reserved the second week and was able to attend the C.P.A. banquet to make our daughter happy.

We were flown to *Curaçao* the day before boarding for our cruise. We spent the night at a luxury hotel. The ship was due to arrive early afternoon, so that morning after breakfast Bill and I were sitting in the pretty courtyard near the pool relaxing. Two young men came out running, laughing and splashing in the pool. In a snide voice I had never heard before, Bill said something about those two being "queer."

"What are you talking about?" I asked.

I do not remember what he said, but the tone of his voice and the expression on his face delivered the message of his intolerance of homosexuals. I was surprised because this did not sound like my husband. As far as I was concerned they were just two young fellows enjoying themselves.

The ship was late arriving so we crossed the short distance and had a little time to explore the island of Aruba. We were all relieved when the big cruise ship finally docked. The first week passengers disembarked, and we "second-week" cruisers were able to board.

Ironically, the two young men we had seen earlier had a cabin just down the hall from ours. We would be leaving, often at the same time, and Bill would just bristle. My philosophy is "live and let live." As far as I was concerned, they were two young fellows happy in their life-style, not bothering anybody and breaking no laws.

Bill and I enjoyed relaxing in the luxury of the ship, the delicious food, the entertainment and the interesting people we met. One day, I had quite an audience watching me skeet-shooting. I missed only three out of several rounds, and they applauded!

One evening after a formal dinner and entertainment, Bill and I went out on the moonlit deck alone. In a few minutes we heard voices, and soon there appeared these two well dressed young men. They spoke to us, and much to my amazement Bill said, "Hello."

Out of curiosity, my husband seemed to relax and began talking to them. We found out they were two wealthy fellows from well-known families in New York. They were on this cruise as a vacation. The shorter one was dominant and did all the talking. The taller one was quiet, reserved and said very little. They wore beautiful, expensive jewelry. Bill became interested in knowing more about them and their professions, and learned their names. They talked for about twenty minutes. They were two happy, intelligent, educated, professional young men. As they were leaving, the smaller fellow thanked us for talking to them. He said no one else had said one word to them. We were the first!

We were shocked at that statement. Bill's whole attitude had changed. He saw that they were two human beings like everyone else, in spite of their life style. He made it a point to talk to them whenever he saw them, especially when there were other people around.

On the last night of our cruise, as we arrived for the final elaborate celebration, the smaller fellow was waiting at the door. When he saw us he broke into a big grin and said, "I've been waiting for you. I want to thank you for what you did for us. After seeing you talking to us, other people began to talk to us and made our trip more enjoyable. Thank you so much!" We shook hands and that was the last we saw of them.

I will always remember this as an eye-opener for my husband. He had never shown any deep-seated prejudice before. This incident is an example of why we should get to know people before we pass judgment on them, just because they are different!

We thoroughly enjoyed this cruise. We spent part of a day in *Caracas, Venezuela*, and had many exciting experiences as we stopped on several Caribbean islands.

On the river of a Caribbean Island

Louise and Ray bought a home in Park Forest near Chicago. In 1975, our first grandchild was born, Ray William Weathersby. Louise had to have an emergency C-section and I was there soon after, to be with her when she went home. The following week Bill came to see his new grandson. We were both thrilled to finally become grandparents!

Shortly after Bill arrived, Louise and I were showing off this little two-week-old baby whom we called Billy in honor of his grandpa. For some unknown reason, little Billy began to cry and kick uncontrollably. Neither Louise nor I could calm him down. Bill was sitting on the couch watching us. Finally, he said, "Let me have him." We handed the

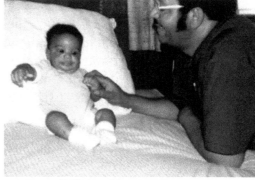

Ray (Billy) William, 1st grandson

screaming infant to his grandpa as though to say, "Here, good luck!"

Louise and I stood in the doorway with our mouths open in awe, as we witnessed what happened next. As soon as his grandpa took him, little Billy stopped crying, nestled into his grandpa's arms and looked at him. While Bill was talking to him, this baby relaxed and fell asleep. Right then, little Billy made an amazing life-time bond with his grandpa, whom he called "paw-paw"!!!

In January of 1977, Louise had a miscarriage. Of course, Bill and I were there immediately.

Billy got sick, so the doctor put him in the hospital in Park Forest. He was an unhappy little boy. Louise went into the hospital in Chicago. Bill and I were kept busy taking turns going to see our grandson and driving into Chicago to see Louise.

Billy was so rambunctious you could hear him screaming as soon as you got off the elevator. One day when I arrived in the children's hospital room, Billy's bed had a screen over the top so he was caged in. When I asked the nurse why he was the only child so enclosed, she said they had found him climbing up the side of the bed (over three feet), so they had to put the net on for his protection.

We were glad when we could take both Louise and Billy home. Bill went back to Denver, and I stayed to help Louise with Billy.

Louise was pregnant with our second grandchild by spring of 1977. I went to get two-year-old Billy to bring him to Denver to visit with us for a while. I had to teach him to call me "grandma" because he called me "paw-paw," too. He was so anxious to see his "paw-paw" that he ran into the plane and I had to call him back to tell his teary-eyed mother goodbye. His "paw-paw" has always been special!

Since this second child was due in late November, Louise hoped to schedule her C-section on my birthday, November 24th. However, my birthday would be on Thanksgiving that year, so Christina Marie (Chrissy), was born the following Tuesday, November 29th. Bill and I were there before Thanksgiving, so we were there to welcome our cute granddaughter.

Louise organized "Caesarian Way," a C-section group in Park Forest, Illinois to help other mothers. It started with 50 women and grew to 300-400 members.

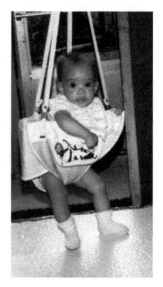

Back in Chapter 8 I mentioned that our son Jim had met JoEllen Seymour one summer while he was a lifeguard. This developed into a serious romance.

After receiving her B.A. degree in dance from Boston Conservatory of Music, and her masters in Dance Therapy at Hunter College (in New York City), JoEllen became the Dance Instructor at the Bronx School for the Deaf and the aquatic Director at the Recreation Center in Brooklyn, New York. She eventually received her Bachelor of Science degree from Howard University in Physical Therapy, which is now her successful profession.

Christina (Chrissy) Marie, 1st granddaughter

When Jim went to New York from Wisconsin University, he worked at several jobs: Paramount Pictures internship in management; American Management Association as Multimedia Director in charge of corporate training for directing film and video; finally, Panasonic where he worked his way up to developing and directing a department of security equipment.

Since he specialized in Panasonic government security equipment, he worked closely with the U.S. defense and the CIA. He was constantly travelling all over the country to set up displays, and give lectures at workshops, exhibits and conventions, so the salesman could move in.

In 1978, when Jim and JoEllen were home in Denver for Christmas, they announced their engagement and possible plans for a wedding in June 1979. This was the good news for which we had all been waiting. However, there was one problem. The three sisters who would be bridesmaids were pregnant!

JoEllen's sisters, Patricia and Ida, and Jim's sister, Louise, were all expecting to give birth about the same time at the end of summer 1979. My daughter's facetious remarks that they could save money if the bridesmaids wore maternity dresses was met with dead silence – not funny.

The wedding was postponed until June 21, 1980, the first day of summer. It was a beautiful wedding at Montview Presbyterian Church. The sisters had given birth to daughters, each two weeks apart in August and September, and were beautiful attendants in the wedding.

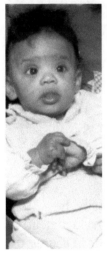

In August of 1979, I was in Park Forest, Illinois with Louise to take care of our two little grandchildren, Billy and Chrissy, while she would be in the hospital. On August 24th, Louise began having warnings of the impending birth of her baby. Amazingly, she drove herself to the hospital in Chicago where Ray met her from his work. Pretty little Lori Ann was born with a head full of thick black hair, the opposite of her cute, active sister who arrived with almost no hair. These three grandchildren proved to be the light of our lives!

In 1979, we attended Richard's wedding to his second wife in Minneapolis, Minnesota. Our second grandson was born April 10, 1980 – Ricardo Pierre Greenwood (Ricky).

Lori Ann, 2nd granddaughter

Our last two grandchildren did not arrive until Jim was transferred to Washington, D.C. as director of Panasonic's Office of Government Security Equipment. Joshua James was born on November 21, 1987. Jenna Marie arrived July 15, 1991 – her grandfather's birthday! There will be more on the achievements of these two lovable, bright late-comers when I write about the remarkable achievements of all my grandchildren.

Ricardo (Ricky) Pierre, 2nd grandson

Jenna Marie, 3rd granddaughter

Joshua James, 3rd grandson

While Bill was still at the bank, he heard about a new Time-Share condo vacation exchange system that was being offered in Vail, so way we went to check on it! For a small fee one could buy into the use of a condo in Vail with the privilege of reserving an exchange use of a vacation condo anywhere in the country for a week at any time, no set schedule of use. It fit our travel plans, so we signed up for a condo in Vail.

We had been to *Hawaii* on an "Island-hopping" tour to see what the islands were like. We spent several days on *Oahu* in *Honolulu*. We went out to Pearl Harbor, rented a car and drove around the island, visited a pineapple farm and spent some time just relaxing.

A limo was provided and we ferried over to *Kauai* where we stayed at a luxury hotel and witnessed a fabulous night program of music and fire torch dancing.

We flew from *Kauai* to *Kona* on the Big Island of *Hawaii*. We stayed in a brand new Sheraton Hotel, only seven stories high. We were told that the cities on these other islands did not want to become big metropolises with skyscrapers like *Honolulu*, so they were limiting their hotels to only seven stories.

We didn't want to eat dinner at the hotel. Someone told us there was a McDonald's a few blocks away. Just as we left the hotel, there was sudden lightning and thunder, then a downpour of rain and all the lights went out. We had our flashlight. As we approached McDonald's, we saw lights. We discovered that they had auxiliary power and were open for business. When we returned to the hotel, there was only candle light, no dinner and no elevators running. We were glad that we had only to walk up to the third floor. We found two candles in a drawer, so we happily ate our fast food by candle light out on our lanai (balcony)!

During the night the power came on. After breakfast, we were taken by limo on a scenic tour of the island on our way to *Hilo*. The exciting stop was at the volcano Kilauea in Volcanoes National Park. We were permitted to go only a short distance up the side. The Ranger said there had been some rumblings so they had cancelled the usual hike up farther. They weren't sure what was going on. (Shortly after we returned home this volcano erupted!)

We spent a day and a night in Hilo. The rain returned and it was so bad that our scheduled flight to *Honolulu* airport was delayed an hour. When we finally arrived, we were so late our reservation had been given to a tour group. We were upset! We would miss our connecting flight to Denver. However, an understanding airline attendant told us that he would see what he could do to help us. In a short time he returned to tell us there were two seats available in first class that we could have at no extra charge. Bill thanked him and gave him a tip. We flew back from *Hawaii* first class to Seattle and met our flight home to Denver. Again, the Lord provided!

For the next two trips to *Hawaii*, we used our vacation condo exchange. Since we had spent only that one rainy night in *Kona*, we decided to go back there to really see it. The apartment we reserved had two bedrooms, so we called Bill's cousin Sue Bowden in California, to see if she and her husband Melvin would like to join us for that week. They were delighted! We met them at the airport in Los Angeles, flew to *Honolulu* and took the little local plane to *Kona*. Our condo was lovely with a patio that faced the ocean and a papaya tree just outside one window. I had my first taste of delicious tree-ripened papaya! I do not remember what year it was, but it was a welcome break for all of us, so we did a lot of relaxing and enjoying our beautiful surroundings. We explored the immediate neighborhood, rented a car and drove around that portion of the island.

On our last day we drove to the National Historical Park. We were thrilled as we walked through the Royal Grounds of *Kona*'s early royalty. We felt the devastation of the Place of Refuge, separated from the world by a great wall built in 1550.

We had heard so much about the beauty of *Maui*, that two years later we reserved a vacation condo on this island. Again, we called Bill's adventurous cousin Sue; she was so much fun! Melvin wasn't interested, but Sue was ready to go again. This well-equipped condo had a convenient small apartment-sized washer and drier which we appreciated using. We were all so tired that we just enjoyed relaxing in the beauty of our surroundings, spending time on the near-by beach (where I swam in the serene ocean).

Our final exciting experience was a day's drive on the Road to *Hana*. Some called it "the Ribbon of Death"! We rented a car, fixed ourselves some lunch and away we went. The view was magnificent and the driving normal until we reached a stretch of miles of unbelievably sharp, hairpin curves on a narrow highway. At one point the road became a single lane with a small bridge. What would you do if you met an approaching car?! The forest was on one side, and the ocean was on the other side. We found a small park where we pulled off for a while to relax before continuing on.

We finally reached Heavenly *Hana*, a beautiful little coastal village. We enjoyed walking around and talking to people. We learned that Charles Lindbergh settled in *Hana*, died there and is buried just outside the little town.

Sue and I usually talk a lot, but we were mostly silent as Bill drove back on that hair-raising highway. We were all happy but mentally and physically exhausted when we finally returned to our condo that evening. This was a once-in-a-lifetime experience to remember!!! The Grace of God was with us all the way.

CHAPTER 14
Impressive Memories

For many years we had season tickets to the Broadway shows at the Denver Auditorium Theater. We saw the fabulous musical, *Fiddler on the Roof*, with famous Zero Mostel. We saw *Hello Dolly* twice: one year with Ginger Rogers and another season with Carol Channing. Our first seats were in the balcony, then the mezzanine. Finally, we could afford main floor seats – fifth row on the isle, so Bill could stretch his long legs.

When we saw that *Hello Dolly* with Pearl Bailey and Cab Calloway would be playing in New York, Bill sent for reservations so we could go on our way to Philadelphia (to Supreme Council). We received confirmation and arrived in New York the day before. When we got to the theater the next day, our reservation could not be found and our seats had been sold. I was disappointed and Bill was upset! The person in charge told us to wait, because they often had cancellations or "no-shows." What seemed like an eternity, just before show time, she finally told us that there were two "no-show" seats available that we could have. To our surprise, they were main floor, third row just off center-perfect! Our tickets had been for the balcony. Pearl Bailey was one fabulous "Dolly"! After her last curtain call when people began to leave, she called out "Just sit down. It ain't over yet!" She put on another twenty minutes performance of her own!!!

Of all the shows we saw in New York at various times, Danny Kaye in *Something Funny Happened on the Way to the Forum* was one of the most hilarious. He broke his leg during the second performance, missed one show and returned to perform for the rest of the season in a wheelchair. He adlibbed many of his line to fit being wheelchair bound. Danny Kaye was one of the funniest comedians I have ever known. I laughed until I had a headache. His humor was always just <u>good</u>, <u>clean</u> fun and to the point!

We took a short trip to Mexico City in the summer of 1967. It was a small tour group of five or six people. As we passed the officials at Mexico City Airport, I was the only one they stopped and questioned my citizenship. I could understand questioning on my <u>leaving</u> Mexico back in the 50's, but on <u>entering</u>?! I proved that I was an American citizen and moved on with the group. Bill kidded me again about almost losing me in Mexico!

We spent a few days in Mexico City, then moved on by limousine, stopping at a few picturesque tourist-stop villages on our way to Acapulco.

At one stop there were pyramids, one of which we were permitted to climb. I made it half way up and had to stop. Bill went to the top. I just enjoyed the view and waited for him to come down.

At the big, outdoor feast in Acapulco, on our arrival as usual, I was careful to eat only prepared food (which was absolutely delicious), and to drink only bottled water or juice. I love shrimp, and the big prawns were fabulous.

In Acapulco catching a Sailfish

About midnight I was awakened and spent the rest of the night in the bathroom. I could not remember eating anything uncooked. Finally, it dawned on me that the shrimp I ate had been lying on a bed of lettuce!

Bill had made reservation for us to go deep-sea fishing that morning. I felt terrible and did not want to disappoint him. He was so excited about going, but was worried about my looking so ill and did not want to leave me. I decided I would go and find a quiet place to sit on the boat. When we explained to the boatmen how I was feeling, they made a comfortable seat for me in the sheltered part of the boat, out of the sun, where I could watch the fishermen. There was one other fellow fishing with Bill as they sat in the two chairs at the stern of the boat.

8 feet, 9 inches long!

I don't know how we lost sight of all land. Suddenly, Bill's reel began to spin. The men helped Bill in his struggle to reel in this big catch. It was a shark and the men said they did not keep sharks, so it was released to swim away. They wanted him to continue fishing, but he was so exhausted that he said, "No," and just sat in the chair and watched the other man fish. This fellow finally caught a nine-foot Sailfish which was hauled in and he was ready to quit. Sailfish are a type of Marlin.

The seats were empty and the two fishermen were resting and gushing over their exciting experiences. One boatman turned to me and said, "Would you like to sit up there?"

I was feeling much better, but replied, "No, I didn't plan to fish."

"Oh, just sit there and see how it feels. You don't have to fish," he coaxed.

I thought, "Why not?", so I climbed onto the seat with my short legs wedged against the stern of the boat to keep me from sliding off the chair. I was enjoying the fresh sea breeze and the magnificent view of the vast expanse of Pacific Ocean, when the reel on the pole by me began to spin. The boatmen rushed over and cried, "You've got a catch!"

I didn't know what to do. I expected them to reel it in. They handed me the pole and helped me lower it as I reeled, then pulled up. This

263

Sailfish caught in Mexico

Certificate of the "catch"

went on for what seemed like an eternity as they gradually released their hold and left me to bring that fish in alone.

Just as it reached the boat, before the men could pull it onboard, it dove and away it went, line and all! With the reel spinning, I had to bring that fish back, and this time they were holding the catch securely to the boat. They asked me if I wanted to keep it. I was so completely exhausted that I ached, so I said, "No, you can just leave that fish in the ocean!" My only wish was that Bill had caught it.

"Oh, no, we have to keep that!" I heard Bill exclaim. It was a Sailfish with a beautiful, huge blue fin. This fish was 8 feet 9 inches long! When we reached shore my picture was taken beside my big, hanging trophy. That huge Sailfish is now mounted with my picture beside it, on the wall of our family room in our home on West 6th Ave. where my son Bill, Jr. still lives.

I became a good cook, only because of necessity. It was not the joy of my life. Bill wanted to learn to cook, so I taught him the basics and he took it from there. He loved to cook the turkey at Thanksgiving with unbelievable dressing. He developed a barbeque sauce for chicken, ribs and cook-outs that no commercial sauce could match. When he cooked a leg of lamb, I do not know how he seasoned it, but it was delicious!

He enjoyed having friends, family and visitors over for dinner or a party. I prepared salad and vegetables easily. Dessert was usually something we could buy like ice cream, cake, pie, etc. Unfortunately, Bill could use more pots and pans than was necessary. I didn't mind cleaning up the kitchen, but I finally insisted that he clean up the pots and pans that he used.

We invited our friends Adele and Gilbert Alexander over for dinner when Bill was going to cook a leg of lamb. When I told Adele what we were serving, she said, "Oh, Gilbert doesn't eat lamb."

"Just don't tell him," I said. "I bet he will like Bill's lamb."

When Gilbert was eating his <u>second</u> helping, Bill asked him how he liked his lamb. Gilbert could not believe the delicious meat he was eating was lamb!

One day in early March, my mother called to tell me that my father fell, hit his head and was taken to the hospital. When we got to the hospital, the doctor said it appeared he had a slight stroke. My dad was awake and coherent, but very weak. After several days, we were told that they had done all they could for him, but he needed constant care. They were not sure how much longer he would live - probably a few days or maybe a few weeks. This was in 1973.

A small, well-recommended nursing home was in our neighborhood at West First Avenue and Sheridan Blvd. He was accepted. My father was 94 years old, and my mother could not care for him at home. I went to see him frequently, did his laundry and took my mother to visit, occasionally.

My mother was 82. Bill, Jr. moved in with her to help his grandma with her needs – shopping, cleaning, heavy work. I took her to appointments or to visit friends. She could no longer attend church, because the steps were too steep at Shorter. With our son there with her, Bill and I knew she would be cared for when we were away.

Amazingly, my father got stronger. When he wanted, he would go to the dining room, with help, to have a meal. Twice he was dressed and went on nursing home bus trips that he told me about, excitedly!

A little Mexican man was admitted who spoke very little English. The nurses did not speak Spanish, so my father acted as his interpreter. They became Spanish speaking friends.

I began to notice that he was in bed more often and seemed to be getting weaker. One day when I arrived, he had little to say and as he turned I noticed his left hand and part of his arm was blue-black. I said nothing to him. I went to get a nurse immediately! Why hadn't anyone noticed this? The nurse took one look and went to phone the doctor. She told me my father was to be taken to the hospital right away! As they prepared to take him to St. Anthony's Hospital, I went to tell my mother what had happened.

When I arrived at the hospital, they were checking him out. I waited until he was placed in Intensive Care, and was told that a blood clot had developed in his shoulder which blocked circulation to his arm. There was no way to stimulate the blood flow. He was sedated and did not seem to be in pain. The suggested solution was possible amputation. In his weakened condition, at 94 years old, I said, "No." This was the middle of May. He had lived three months longer than expected earlier.

It was time for Bill and me to go to Supreme Council in Philadelphia. I told the doctor that I did not know what to do. He advised me to go since there was nothing I could do to prolong my dad's life. Since he had lived this long, the length of his life was uncertain. It was a tough decision to make, but I went on to Supreme Council. The morning of the day we were to return, our son called to tell us that his Grandpa had died.

Uncle J.C. Talamon and his wife, Ruth, came to my father's funeral. I asked Uncle J.C. why our last name was <u>Anderson</u>, but he, Uncle Dave and my grandma had the name Eliza <u>Talamon</u>? I had asked my father once, when I was in high school. He became very upset, but gave me no answer.

Uncle J.C. said he did not know since my father was so much older than he. (Of eleven children, my father, Joseph, was number three and J.C. was number ten!)

Later, when Ruth and I were alone, she said she did not know why J.C. did not tell me the real story, but she felt that I should know what happened. This is what she told me:

As a young man (born in Charenton, Louisiana, in 1879), Joseph Talamon worked in a restaurant. One night a drunken customer began berating my father and calling him names. Joe held his temper as long as he could, but the customer continued

Marie's grandmother, Eliza Talamon

his tirade, so my father threw a mug at him, hitting the man on the head. In those days, in the South, a man of color's retaliation to a white man was deadly!

For his own life's safety, Joe left Louisiana and fled to Mexico. He changed his name from Talamon to Anderson to shield his identity. He lived in Mexico for five years before returning to the United State as Joseph August Anderson.

My father never returned to Louisiana, but he kept in touch with his mother and several siblings. For his protection, they all accepted him as Anderson. A fire in the family home in Charenton, destroyed the Bible with the birth records, so Joseph Talamon could never be identified. Therefore, we were always legally Anderson.

I learned much of my independent thinking, decision making and believing in my own abilities as well as adequate use of tools from my father. He is buried in one of our family plots in Highlands Cemetery, next to Bill's mother and stepfather. I had a double headstone made, reserving a space for my mother next to my father. I thank the Grace of God for having had him in my life.

Bill was appointed to serve on the Career Service Authority for the city of Denver, the only African-American. They dealt with the hiring, firing and problems of city employees.

When Elvin Caldwell became Manager of Safety, he asked Bill to move to the Civil Service Commission, in charge of the police and firefighters departments. This group had never been integrated to help solve problems of Blacks in these departments. Bill accepted, but made sure that his place on the Career Service continued the integration. On his recommendation, Alfred Woods was appointed to serve on the Career Service.

Bill spent the first few meetings quietly observing the actions of the Commission members and how the decisions were made. One member, Ted who had been there for years, ran the meetings and seemed to have intimidated everyone else against opposing him. Bill began to speak up and slowly discovered that others had unspoken opinions. Some of the meetings developed into antagonizing issues between Ted and Bill in solving obvious problems.

When Bill discovered there had been few promotions of Black police and no promotions of firemen, he decided to find out why. He checked with the Fire Chief and was told they passed the physical but could not pass the written test. In talking to the Black firemen, Bill found out they were intelligent men who did not know how to take a test.

Bill organized a class to teach firemen the system of taking test, not the test itself. To have an unbiased instructor, he invited a fire chief from New Jersey for the first class. This was specifically for Black firemen, but was open to all firemen. The second class was led by a Black chief from Detroit. The third time it was a Hispanic chief from New Mexico. The firemen began passing the written test. Charles McMillan became the first Black fireman to receive a promotion.

Bill received two awards for his outstanding work on the Civil Service Commission – a certificate honoring him as an Honorary Fire Chief, and a badge as an Honorary Chief of Police which opened many doors for us, and solved a number of problems for Bill! He always carried it. The Executive Secretary had charge of the office in which records, reports, decisions and supplies for the Commission were filed. This was a salaried position with no voice in the Commission. The office could be locked to secure all confidential information. Eventually, the office became so disorganized that the Commission could not

Bill, Sr. receives award for "Honorary Fire Chief"

get material when needed. The Executive Secretary was fired. Bill was asked to accept the position.

This was a kind of "double-edged sword." They knew about his needed organizing ability, but it would also relieve some Commission members of Bill's active influence on the Civil Service Commission. Bill accepted the salaried position, but he recommended Ozwald Abernethy to take his place, so the Black representative door would remain open on the Commission. As usual my husband got the office running smoothly. In 1981, Bill resigned as Executive Secretary of the Civil Service Commission.

In 1979, we built a home on our Mountain View Lakes property – the "Lazy G, II." A company that specialized in pre-fabricated mountain homes was recommended, so we checked to see what they were like. The construction of these houses was great. I found a floor plan that I liked with a large living room, kitchen, two bedrooms and bath, but as usual I made some adjustments. Our property was on a slope, so I revised the one story plan to include a lower level with a drive-in garage, two extra rooms, laundry and second bathroom.

The kitchen came complete with stove, refrigerator, dishwasher, and a garbage disposal. We had a circulation fireplace installed. Fans on each side could be turned on to circulate the heat from the fireplace. This helped to reduce our electric heating bill in the winter, as we enjoyed the open fire.

This was a home with all the conveniences of our family home in Denver. We moved in!

In 1981, Louise and her family moved to Mesa, Arizona, where Ray was hired as a professor to teach Business at Arizona State University. When I attended the church Annual Conference in Tucson, they came down to spend the day and took me sightseeing along with a visit to "Old Tucson" where Western movies are made. It was great being with my three little grandchildren!

Once when Bill and I were visiting them in Mesa, it was unbearably hot – over 110 degrees F! Bill took off one day without telling us where he was going. He was gone so long we became worried. Finally, he returned, ill from the intense heat. He had driven out in the desert to an Indian Reservation to buy a pair of earrings to match the beautiful Indian necklace he had given me at Christmas. This was to surprise me! Since they had no matching earrings when he bought the necklace in Denver, they told him where he might find some when we visited in Arizona. His heat exhaustion was so severe that I drove most of the next day when we left for home. I would not let him drive until he felt better. That priceless jewelry emphasizes our love for each other every time I wear it!

In 1982, Ray was dismissed from Arizona University and they planned to return to Denver. I flew down to help them. It was decided that Louise and I would drive to Denver with the children. Ray would rent a U-Haul van to drive back with their furniture. Since Bill and I were living in the mountain home, they could stay in the family home on West 6th Ave. Bill and I reserved a bedroom and the bathroom downstairs for when we would come to Denver.

With Ray's business background, Bill prevailed on Colorado National Bank to hire him. Within a short time, because of Bill's plea,

Ray was offered a beginning position at the bank. He refused it saying he was worth more than that. Bill was hurt and embarrassed after all his efforts to help Ray get a job. Soon after, Ray left for Texas to be with his brother and his family leaving Louise with three small children and no financial help. She worked and she survived.

Looking back on other miscellaneous happy memories:

We were driving to Chicago to spend Christmas with Louise and her family in Park Forest, before they moved to Arizona, when we ran into a blizzard in Illinois. Visibility was only a few feet and we could barely keep the windshield clear, so we stayed behind a semi and followed the tail lights. Driving became so precarious and scary that we turned off the highway at Peoria, Illinois, where we saw a lighted motel. We lucked out by checking into the last available room with a television. We sent up our prayers of thanks. We were safe and comfortable and just in time to see the last episode of Alex Haley's <u>Roots.</u> Louise was relieved to get our call letting her know we were all right. We were cared for once more <u>by the Grace of God</u>!

When Supreme Council met on Paradise Island in the Bahamas late in the 1970's, the deputy, Basil Sands, offered us the use of their condo since he and his wife would be staying in the hotel where the meeting was held. (When the Sands were in Denver, one year, for the Shrine convention, they were tired and needed to rest, so we let them relax a few days at our "Lazy G II" mountain home.) We called Jim and JoEllen to share the condo with us. They had a great time on their own while Bill and I attended Supreme Council. We had them attend the banquet.

After the session, several of us from Colorado decided to spend some time in Nassau. Basil Sands and his family live in Nassau. His son was manager of a luxury hotel. We were assigned to the penthouse with a stocked bar and other amenities. Jim and JoEllen had an adjoining room. Bill wanted to share our luxury so we had a party for the Colorado delegation that stayed over!

Eventually Bill was assigned to the Supreme Council Finance Committee and became the Director of United Supreme Council Benevolent Fund. He came home furious. With all the hundreds of thousands of Prince of Hall Masons, the benevolent fund that was meant to help charitable organizations, educational institutions and the needy, had only $1500 in it!

Bill wrote a plan whereby every Masonic member would be required to contribute a specific amount to the Benevolent Fund as part of his dues, and contributions could be received from outside organizations. He presented this plan to the Finance Committee in 1983.

Supreme Council was scheduled to meet in Denver, again, in 1984. Bill started making plans in 1982. The hotel was reserved for our dates with specified rooms for all meetings. Specific rooms were reserved for Sovereign Grand Commander and other officials. Cost of accommodations, menus for banquet and special luncheons were set. He made sure there would be representative Black servant help. I was to lead the ladies tour, this time to the Air Force Academy.

Occasionally, we would go to Las Vegas for a few days. We loved the shows and witnessed the entertaining performances of stars such as: Lena Horne, Sarah Vaughn, Barbra Streisand, spectacular Liberace, Aretha Franklin, Harry Belafonte, The Mills Brothers, B.B. King, Dinah Shore and many others.

I am a very poor gambler. I hate to lose money. I had to figure some way of having fun playing the "One Arm Bandits." When we took trips or vacations, I enjoyed spending money on souvenirs and special activities. Why not reserve that same amount to spend in Las Vegas? My problem was solved! I would allot myself a specific amount of money to use playing the slot machines. If I won, I kept playing. If I lost my allotment, I quit, but I had fun while I played.

Bill was a cautious gambler. He knew when to quit. His favorite games were Roulette, Blackjack and 21. Occasionally, he would stop and find me. If I had won a bit, he would cash it in for me before I played it all back. Once I had any cashed-in winnings, that money went home with me. Unfortunately, that did not happen very often, but I had fun!

Frequently, when we left Las Vegas we would drive on to California to visit Bill's relatives and our friends, Noel and Eleanor Daniels. Once, when we were in Tahoe, there was snow in the mountains and "Heavenly Mountain Ski Area" was open. Bill suggested that I try this area since I had only skied in Colorado. (I had returned to skiing and took lessons and bought new equipment in the late sixties or early seventies.) This was a hazardous decision since I was unfamiliar with the area, but adventurous me took off!

When I finally got off the lift and started down the run, it was a narrow trail winding among the trees that finally led to a broad open-area. I was relieved! I had never skied on snow that was fine, icy grains that scraped the bottom of my skis. Now I know why people come to Colorado to ski on our smooth white powder!

Back at the hotel in Tahoe I met some skiers who had come from San Francisco. When they found out I was from Colorado, they wanted to know why, on earth, was I skiing there instead of at home?!

In 1974, our Alpha Kappa Alpha Boulé was being held in Miami. I had never been to Florida before, except to change planes on my way elsewhere. A small delegation of Denver sorors was planning to go, and their enthusiasm spilled over on me. Bill agreed that it would be good for me to get away with my sorority sisters.

The Boulé was being held at the brand new, fabulous Fontainebleau Hotel. Evie Dennis was Basileus (President) of our Epsilon Nu Omega Chapter. She was scheduled to stay at this hotel with other officers. Upon arrival, her reservation could not be found, and all the rooms had been assigned. Evie is not a person who accepts, "No"! She planted herself in the lobby with her luggage, and made it very clear that she was going nowhere until they found accommodation for her.

Finally, she was assigned to the only special vacancy they had available, the Presidential Penthouse suite! This became Epsilon Nu Omega's palatial "Hang-Out." We chipped in to supply snacks for our frequent "get-togethers." Our Denver delegation was housed in a hotel just two doors from the Fontainebleau.

One day, Evie told us that Lou Rawls would be singing at a night club nearby and she could get tickets for us. I had heard the name, Lou Rawls, and knew he was a singer. That was all. I wondered why my sorors were so overjoyed and excited about this man. I was old enough to be the mother of most of our delegates, but they accepted me in all of their activities and guided me through those that were new to me. I felt honored that they were so considerate. Of course, I bought a ticket to the Lou Rawls concert and hoped I would make it through the program. Since all the early show tickets were gone, we would attend the late performance at 10:00 p.m.

Lou Rawls opened a new genre of music for me. His clear tones and the expression in his voice made one feel the message he delivered. I could see why my sorors were so excited. Although, the night club was hot, I enjoyed every minute of the program. I was tired but happy when we returned to the hotel in the early morning hours!

A few of our Denver group were planning to take the "after Boulé" cruise to the Bahamas. When I told Bill that we would be stopping in Nassau, he contacted his Masonic brother, Deputy of the Bahamas in 1974, to let him know when we would be there. Hopefully, he could do something special for us.

On the ship, my assigned roommate was Mable Cozart, who proved to be a perfect companion for this senior member. When I went to the bar with the group, I wasn't sure what to order, since Bill always ordered drinks for me. My sorors introduced me to *Pina Colada*, sweet and creamy. I loved it! It became my cruise cocktail. We all had a sense of humor, so there was always great fun and laughter.

We would spend a day in Nassau browsing, shopping and at the Casino. I called the Deputy and he told me he had plans to take us sightseeing. He picked us up in a limo, took us all over Nassau: the beautiful, elite areas where tourists are taken, and back into the district where the poorer Bahamian natives live. This was quite an "eye opener" for us. He took us to his home where we were served some delicious Bahamian food before returning us to the Casino. We thanked him for the enjoyable enlightening tour, the delicious meal and the information we had gained from his lectures. Later, I wrote him a special letter of appreciation.

CHAPTER 15
Adventurous European Trip

In 1976, our son Richard was still in Denmark. He wanted us to come over to visit him in Aarhus. This was an opportunity for another adventure, but it would be foolish to spend a week with Richard and return home. Since we would be in Europe, why not see more of it? I began listing some of the places I would like to visit. Bill was happy with the idea.

We checked with our travel agent who had helped us with other trips. With the long list I had, she suggested a month by eliminating some stops, so we could spend a few days enjoying each of the places we wanted most to visit. We would travel by Eurorail and she suggested that it would be wise to have "Hotel Passes" with set rates. Since hotel rates in Europe were not posted, Americans were often charged as high as possible. These passes came in three levels: first class (like Hilton, Sheraton, etc.), second class (guaranteed best of native accommodations), and third class (ok but not sure). Since we stayed in first class hotels here at home, why not experience the atmosphere of the various countries? We selected the second class hotels. Our pass had a set rate of $25.00 a night at any listed native hotel in Europe. Our Eurorail passes were good for a month. On a map, our travel agent helped us make a scheduled plan of our exciting trip, September 2 to October 4, 1976!

We let Richard know our plans, and called Louise in Park Forest to let her know we would be flying to Europe from O'Hare Airport in Chicago. Packing to live out of suitcases for a month took some very careful planning. I was taking my large suitcase and my vanity case. Bill packed his large case and a smaller one. This was before luggage with wheels. I wondered how we would carry our luggage. Bill said, "Oh, the porters can take it for us at the stations." OK!?

Thank goodness Louise met us at O'Hare and took us to the foreign section which we knew nothing about. We were flying to Amsterdam on

KLM. I had never heard of this big, Dutch airline and was thrilled when I saw it! Louise knew what to do from her days as a stewardess.

We spent a couple of days in Amsterdam sightseeing. A breakfast smorgasbord was included at our hotel. From the many selections of foods that I sampled I tried the uncooked oats with hot milk and fruit. I loved it; so now I do not cook my oatmeal. I just stir it into the hot milk.

A friend of ours was living in Amsterdam and took us to a restaurant that served spicy food of India. There was a belly dancer who targeted Bill. He turned red in the face as she danced in front of him. Later he said he didn't know where to look!

Our tour took us sightseeing on the canal. The guide pointed out a windmill, described its structure and explained the importance of its use. We were taken to a shoe factory and saw wooden shoes being made. We witnessed the making of cheese. I did not know there were so many different kinds of cheese!

On our way back to the hotel we got on a bus. There was standing room only. Bill stood by the exit door; I was nearby holding on to a pole. Soon two older teenage fellows boarded and moved over to hold on to the pole with me. My purse was strapped over my shoulder, across my body, hanging to the right. The young men were leaning against it. I changed it to the left side of my body near the rear. One guy slowly moved to my left rear.

We reached the stop where we were getting off. As the door opened, Bill went down the steps to the open door, and turned around to give me a hand. As I turned and let go of the pole, these fellows slid their hands down to block me. Thank the Lord for being short and agile. I ducked quickly under their arms and dashed down the steps to the door and Bill!

After getting off the bus, as we were walking to the hotel, I found the outer pocket on my purse was half unzipped. It was not open enough to remove anything and there was nothing of value in that outer section. They were two young pick-pockets! I learned a valuable lesson. From then on, I always had my big special travel purse hanging in front of me.

We had our first ride on Eurorail when we left Amsterdam. To our surprise, there were no porters to help with luggage or carts on which to wheel them. You carried your bags!!! Bill and I just helped each other as best we could.

Our train took us to Hamburg, Germany, on our way to Denmark. We changed trains in the huge station in Hamburg and were taken by train a short distance to the far north shore of Germany to be ferried across the Baltic Sea to Copenhagen.

It was early evening when we arrived in Copenhagen. We found a nearby hotel, only to find out in the Scandinavian countries, hotels were not members of the "Hotel Pass" chain. We were disappointed, but so tired that we were just glad to light. We were told that we had arrived on a special day when a great celebration was being held at Tivoli Gardens just two blocks from the hotel. The best time to go was 10:00p.m. or after. This gave us a few hours to rest before enjoying this special treat.

We arrived at Tivoli Gardens just before ten o'clock, in time to see folklore dancers, a jazz concert and fireworks in the big brilliantly lighted outdoor theater. We walked through the Gardens, marveled at the many little decorated shops. Bill bought me a special Danish pastry. (He did not care for this kind of food.) It was delicious, but so big and so rich that I could eat only part of it. I finished it the next day.

My back had been hurting me for several days from carrying my heavy luggage. Bill was concerned because he could give me so little help. The next morning we took the train for a short distance to board the ferry to Aarhus. My back hurt so badly that I told Bill we should find some little wheeled carriers that I had seen strapped to other traveler's luggage, to relieve our backs. We could check for some in Aarhus.

As we ferried up the channel I hoped we could find Richard. As we approached the dock we couldn't miss him. He was the only brown face right in front of the crowd! It was great being together again after several years!!!

Richard had reserved a room for us in a nice little inexpensive hotel. My back was hurting so much that walking and sitting was painful. When I went to bed that night, the pain was so intense that Bill questioned if we should continue our trip. I finally fell asleep about midnight. When I woke up the sun was shining, but I was afraid to move. Bill and Richard were up and asked how I felt when they saw I was awake. I rolled over carefully – no pain. I sat up in bed – no pain. I eased out of bed and stood up – no pain. I took a few steps – NO PAIN! Where did that unbearable pain go during the hours I was asleep? It was one of God's miracles for which I could only say, "Thank you Lord!" God's Grace had provided the ease that I needed.

The next morning we had breakfast of Danish pastry and coffee, where I had hot chocolate, at a little restaurant nearby. While Bill and Richard were so engrossed in catching up on years of unknown experiences, I stepped out of the coffee shop to view the surroundings and watch the people going by. It was a bright sunny morning, and it seemed to be a time when mothers were out with their babies in strollers. As they walked by, I was amazed at how much all of those little ones looked alike. They had chubby white faces with pink cheeks, blue eyes and blond hair. Mothers know their babies, but I thought it would be difficult to identify them if they got mixed up!

Richard and one of his band members, Prebin Erickson, became very good friends. Prebin took Richard to his home to meet his family – mother Karen, father Agnus, little brother Mogens and older sister. Karen liked Richard and welcomed him to their home. As time went on, he became a part of their family activities. He did not have to spend another lonely Christmas day like the first one, when he was the only person out on the bare streets of Aarhus. Danish Christmas day is strictly family time. Richard was included!

Karen spoke English, as well as her two oldest children. In Denmark, English is taught from fifth grade through high school, since it is considered the universal language. Karen had learned English in an adult English workshop. Agnus spoke only Danish. Mogens was entering fifth grade, so he would begin learning the second language.

Karen was anxious to meet Richard's parents, so she had us over for dinner. It was a pleasant, happy, warm welcome to their home that made us feel completely comfortable. Karen let us know that Richard was very special in their family. Richard communicated with them in English and in Danish. We felt that we had made new friends! We had rented a car to get around.

Another of our son's friends invited us over for dinner to meet his wife and family. They had two daughters, twelve and eight years old. They spoke English. As we sat at the table and chatted, we were learning more about Danish culture and how Richard fit into the activities. He seemed so well liked. Also, they were learning more about American culture. I don't

Richard & the Erickson's

remember how it came up, but as they looked at us they were curious to know why we were different colors as a family. Bill was almost as white as they were with blue eyes; Richard was brown, and I was a shade of tan between the two.

We proceeded to explain to them about the history of miscegenation in the early lives of slaves and Black people in America along with intermarriage. The result has been that African-Americans are multi-colored. We range in skin color from white to black and all shades of brown and tan in between. That's why <u>our</u> family members vary in color.

The next shocking remark came from the mother: "I wish our daughter was older. She could marry Richard and we would have some color in the family. All we see around here are white faces!" She did not smile. She was dead serious.

One afternoon Richard took us to see an American movie starring Robert Redford. I expected the dialogue to be in Danish, but it was in English with the Danish caption run below. That was a pleasant surprise. However, since most younger and many older Danes speak English, that made sense.

Richard told us the musical drama *Chicago* was playing at their nationally known theater in Aarhus. He wanted us to see it. We went early that evening to get good seats. The theater was small and it filled up fast. Curtain time came, but nothing happened. Fifteen minutes, twenty minutes passed. The curtain did not open. People became a bit restless. After half an hour there was an announcement for everyone to stay in their seats. No one was to leave or enter the theater. The Queen was arriving! (Richard translated this Danish announcement for us.) After the Queen and her three officials were seated in the regal box, the lights went out and the play began.

This was *Chicago* performed completely in Danish, which Richard thoroughly enjoyed. Bill and I could not understand one word of the dialogue or the lyrics, but it was amazing how the acting and the music held our attention. Music is truly a universal language!!

When it was over, the Queen stood up and waved to the crowd. No one was permitted to leave the theater until the Queen was gone.

Richard's band was preparing to play at a music festival. They had a rehearsal scheduled out in the country in a barn. We drove Richard out to this unusual place. He told us that we could visit a nearby castle while the band practiced. Off we went to find the Rosenholm Castle, one of Denmark's famous historic landmarks. As we drove along we passed a tiny shopping center. I told Bill I would like to stop there on our way back to check for wheeled luggage carriers, since we had not had time to shop in Aarhus.

The castle was interesting. We spent an hour or more browsing through. As we returned we stopped at the unique walk-in shopping center. It was small, u-shaped, about half a block long with little shops of all kinds – some no wider than their doors. Amazingly, the largest was a luggage store with a door and a display window.

I said, "Let's go in and see if they have carts. I doubt that they will know what we are talking about."

As we entered, a woman met us and greeted us in English. We told her what we wanted. She smiled, called to an assistant and spoke Danish. To our surprise the assistant brought out <u>three</u> different kinds of wheeled luggage carriers! We bought two with the smallest wheels. For the rest of our trip, our luggage problem was solved. Prayers are often answered in unusual places in unusual ways!

Since Richard would be busy rehearsing his band for the festival at the end of the week, we decided to take a couple days to go to Oslo,

Norway, and return in time for the festival. We would take a ship across an inlet of the North Sea to Goteborg, Sweden. A train would take us to Oslo. Our Eurorail ticket covered all the transportation. Unfortunately, rain and lightening delayed the boat from leaving on schedule. When the weather calmed down a bit we finally set sail. However, the storm returned. The wind and the huge waves in the sea slowed down the bouncing ship. We arrived in Goteborg an hour and a half late. We missed our train to Oslo and had to wait for the night train. Thank goodness, dinner had been served on the ship.

It was almost midnight when we wearily arrived in Oslo. We asked the station master for a hotel, and he recommended the best. We took a cab, checked in and went to bed. The next morning we discovered it was a big, beautiful hotel which had a breakfast smorgasbord with more food than I had ever seen all at one time.

We went out for a walk and could see the elaborate Palace a few blocks up the street. At the dock, we found all day boat tours that we could take for half price with our Eurorail tickets. The guide told us to be back in half an hour for boarding and to bring some rainwear. The hotel was near, so we got what we needed and returned for another exciting adventure.

On our small boat were individuals from several countries. I was amazed at our guide giving information in the language of each country represented – English, French, Japanese, German, etc. She had to talk fast! We made many stops. For me, the outstanding exhibit was the stop at the "Kon-Tiki Museum" where the actual raft on which Thor Heyerdahl sailed alone across the North Atlantic Ocean. Years ago I read his hair-raising story. After seeing the small log raft, it strains the imagination to realize how dangerous, stressful and historic that famous trip must have been!

There was a cool breeze. We had to wear jackets. Later in the day there was a blowing cold rain. The guide said she could never figure out why people came to visit Norway in September. Their summer ends the last of August. However, it was a fascinating tour. Thank goodness, I had my raincoat with me.

The next morning, after breakfast, we checked out of the hotel to find that our room cost $75.00 a night! That was expensive in 1976. As we walked to the train station, we marveled at the brilliant colored flowers that were still blooming. Our train ride to Goteborg was beautiful as we traveled along the seacoast. The ship had smooth, sunny sailing as we returned to Denmark.

The music at the festival in Aarhus was a bit loud and wild, but we enjoyed watching Richard's band perform. We spent the last enjoyable night with our son in Aarhus, and prepared to take the train the next morning to Switzerland.

There is a narrow strip of land that connects this island of Denmark to Germany so we could take a train from Aarhus to Hamburg and transfer to the Eurorail for Zurich, Switzerland. The European trains are different from our trains. On one side of the coach there is an aisle, off which are little enclosed compartments, usually with two comfortable double bench seats. You may ride alone or you may share with someone else. There are a few single compartments. Luggage is not checked. You carry it on with you. The Eurorail is <u>fast</u> and leaves <u>on time!</u>

As we checked our schedule and our maps, we saw the journey would be long from northern Hamburg to Switzerland (south of Germany). One of the many stops along the way was Mainz on the Rhine River. We decided to get off there to view this famous river. It was early evening when the train arrived in Mainz. At our hotel we found we could take a cruise up the Rhine the next day.

It was a bright, sunny day with many people on the huge tour boat. A large section of the deck had comfortable seating for scenic viewing. To our surprise, we met two women from Denver, whose company we enjoyed the entire cruise. We seemed to be the only Americans on board.

The scenic views were broadcast over a loud speaker. Many vineyards covered the hills. This was the source of fine German wine. The mystic tale of *Lorelei* was told as we passed the legendary rock from which it was believed a siren lured men to their doom.

The most scenic stretch of this long river is the mid-Rhine area from Mainz to Koblenz. We got off at Koblenz to return by train. We had dinner in this town, boarded our train and spent the night in Mainz. The next day we left for Switzerland. We were in Zurich only long enough to change trains to go to our destination, the alpine town of Lucerne. From what we saw of Zurich, it looked like any other city. We were anxious to get to an alpine setting!

Luzern was a quiet, peaceful little community sprawled along the edge of a beautiful big lake. Our room was comfortable, sunny and immaculate, with a big soft bed. We found the people friendly as we browsed through the town. The Alps were an impressive background, but much farther away than they appeared. Our Eurorail pass proved to be a ticket for a cruise on the lovely Lake Luzern.

We asked about the Alps and were told that a short distance by train would take us to a little alpine village. We rode the train through lovely mountain scenery to a peaceful little rural community. There were small farms like we had never seen before. In one green field stood two calm, brown cows with bells around their necks staring at us. We were standing at the base of one of the towering Alps!

We could see what appeared to be a narrow gauge railroad track going up the steep mountain. We saw someone and asked about that Alp and the track that disappeared in the clouds. We were told that was the track for two cog cars that took people to the top of the mountain. There was always one car on the ground and one car at the top. They passed each other half way. "How could they pass each other on a single rail?" I wondered.

We decided to ride up and see what was on top, above the clouds. There were only a few people going up. Half way along, the track split into two. The other car was coming down; they passed each other and we were back on a single track. The timing was perfect!

At the top we were above the clouds. It was sunny, but cold. To our amazement there was a few inches of snow and two eager skiers were having fun in that limited space on top of an Alp!

Another day, we were taken to an area near Luzern, where we had the thrill of hiking on an alpine trail. We got our exercise and the magnificent view of the scenery below! Thus ended our short visit in Switzerland. It was time to head for Venice, Italy.

Our train took us through spectacular Swiss Alps into northern Italy where the peaks gradually diminished in altitude. It was evening when we arrived in Venice. It took us a while to find our hotel, which was a complete opposite of our pleasant, comfortable Swiss lodging.

Our room was on the second floor with adequate furnishing and dim lighting. It was hot and humid here at sea level! We asked about a near-by restaurant and were told the hotel was just outside the famous *Piazza San Marco* (St. Mark's Square) where there were several nice little places to eat. We had some spicy Italian food and planned to explore *San Marco* the next day.

Our room had no air conditioning, so sleeping was a bit uncomfortable. The next morning when we went to *Piazza San Marco* we were anxious to see the *Campanile,* of which our Daniels and Fisher Tower in Denver is a copy. We were thrilled to see what an amazing duplicate we had at home. There was much to see and explore in the *Piazza*: St. Mark's ornate basilica, the Clock Tower, the *Doge*'s Palace and the dozens of little shops.

One night we took a romantic *gondola* ride on the Grand Canal with a serenading *gondolier.* Everywhere you went, you went by boat (like water taxi), and some of the canals were not so clean. One day we were eating at an outdoor café and relaxed just watching the people in *gondolas* and boats float by.

On our last day in Venice, after we made reservations to go to Rome, we decided to take the adventurous ride on the Grand Canal. We boarded the big crowded water bus that travels the length of the Canal. At every stop more people got on, until it was so crowded that we were jammed together like sardines as we stood. Behind Bill were some rowdy young fellows. We were excited to see the Rialto Bridge which we had heard so much about. It spans the canal in the heart of the city, so we got off to explore this part of Venice.

I don't remember how we got back to *San Marco*, but it was a relief to get out of the crowd and into less humid heat with a bit of a breeze.

That evening we were packing so we could catch our train to Rome the next morning. I noticed Bill was anxiously searching for something.

Finally he said, "Honey, have you seen my wallet?"

"No," I answered in surprise. "When did you have it last?"

The last time he used it was at the train station, before we got on the waterbus. Apparently, his pocket had been picked as we floated along the Grand Canal or in the crowd on the Rialto Bridge.

I had read about some of the precautions Americans should be aware of when traveling in Europe. Before we left home, I had told Bill about the danger of carrying his wallet in his back pocket because it made it so easy for pick-pockets to steal.

He replied that his wallet was safe because his pocket was always buttoned. Later, he had laughed when he saw some men in Venice carrying purses.

Early the next morning he went to the nearby police station to report the theft. In his wallet were all his IDs, except his police badge. He always kept that in a separate pocket. He said that the police showed very little concern when he first told them about what happened. He pulled out his badge and immediately they came to life! He was told that they could not help him replace his passport, credit card, Eurorail and hotel passes. They gave him the addresses and names of personnel to contact for everything in Rome. He was told they would pay for the Eurorail ticket to Rome and a reservation was made for us on the afternoon train. He was sent somewhere near to report his stolen traveler's checks (which were replaced).

Bill was gone so long, I was worried. It was a relief when he finally returned with the good news. Our only worry was finding the places we needed in unfamiliar Rome! I reminded him that I had warned him about his wallet in his back pocket.

Our reservation on the morning train was an express to Rome. The afternoon train was a local with a change of trains in Florence. The train leaving Venice was late, so we were worried about making our connection. We were late getting into Florence to find that train was late, also. In fact, we spent an hour and a half waiting for it. The result was, we arrived in Rome late that night. The only country we visited where Eurorail was late, was in Italy.

It was almost midnight when we finally reached our hotel. Bill had called to let them know why we would be late. The night clerk could not find our reservation. He said he had a friend who could accommodate us for the rest of the night. He made a call. We took a cab to the address given.

The manager took us through a dismal area, up a flight of stairs, out across the roof to a dimly lit room the size of a walk-in closet. The excuse for a bed was the size of a small couch. After the day we had we were exhausted and upset with this experience. Bill was so furious I was afraid he would have a heart attack! He insisted that I try to get some rest on the tiny bed. He slept a bit in the chair. By 7:00 a.m. we were out of there, after Bill gave the manager a good part of his mind!

When we arrived at our hotel the owner was at the desk. Before we could say anything, he was apologizing for the mix-up and said he had reserved their best room for us, which was not quite ready. Our luggage was right where we had left it last night when we were assured that it was safe. What a relief!

We explained to him the business that we had to take care of immediately. He told us how to get to the U.S Embassy and the office for replacing the Eurorail pass. He even marked a map for us, and said we could have dinner in the restaurant at no charge. Every place was within walking distance! We were truly thankful and had renewed faith in human kindness.

We went to the Eurorail office first. We met a pleasant, friendly old man who apologized for his limited English, but seemed eager to help us. When we told him what we needed, he said he could replace the Eurorail ticket but he had nothing to do with the hotel pass. When he found out Bill's name was William, he laughed and said, "We have the same name!" His name was *Giuseppe* (William in Italian). We had a most enjoyable visit with him. Since it would take an hour or more to get the ticket, we left for the U.S. Embassy office.

At the Embassy we were told cheerfully that they were replacing passports frequently. However, a passport picture was necessary. They gave us the address for an official photographer a few blocks away, so off we went.

The photographer was a pleasant, understanding fellow, but he was busy. He finally got to us, took the picture and we returned to the Embassy exhausted! As we walked in, with a grin on his face, the official told us, "We have your wallet." It had everything in it. We were amazed!! The Venice police had retrieved it and sent it on to the Embassy. Bill had to have the new passport, since the other one had been cancelled. We had our irreplaceable hotel pass. Everything else of importance had been voided and was replaced. We returned to see Giuseppe, and Bill had his Eurorail ticket.

Our luggage was missing from where we left it when we returned to the hotel. We were told, however, that it was safe and it had been taken up to our room on the second floor. It was a bright, pleasant, comfortable room with a view of the busy street below. We were so tired that we did very little the remainder of the day. After a delicious meal in the dining room, we looked forward to a restful night. So much for our first day in Rome!

The next day we explored this particular section of Rome. Bill wanted to find something in which he could carry his wallet safely, so we checked the interesting little shops in the area. To our surprise, he found a zippered pouch that had loops to fit on his belt, just the right size to hold his wallet and the other small necessary items. It would be worn in front.

"Now, I see why men here carry purses," he said with a grin. "I would not carry a purse, so this is perfect."

By the Grace of God we survived these experiences and could settle down to enjoy our days in Rome. We took a commercial guided bus tour of Rome. There was so much to see that I only remember a few highlights. The famous *Trevi* Fountain is where people toss coins and make wishes that are believed to come true. We tossed in a few. We walked through the ruins of the massive Colosseum while being told of gladiators fighting till death, and Christians or criminals facing lions while thousands of spectators and the Emperor clapped and cheered. The Catacombs where early Christians and saints were buried in underground cemeteries outside the city walls was eerie but interesting.

The big stop was at the Vatican. As we entered the circular *Piazza*

San Pietro, there was a massive obelisk soaring up in the center of this entrance to the Vatican grounds. The guide told us that this huge monolithic shaft was a gift to the Vatican from Egypt. It is so big and so heavy that it was shipped in sections to be erected here. In the Sistine Chapel, we viewed the awesome beauty of Michelangelo's brilliantly colored frescoed art on the walls and on the ceiling. We were told that he lay on his back on a specially designed scaffold to paint on the ceiling! Each of the overwhelming number of paintings depicts a scene from the Bible. This lecture and viewing leaves one in unforgettable awe!!! Our tour ended in the little souvenir shop. I was disappointed that we were not taken inside St. Peter's Basilica – only told some of the history of this massive cathedral.

One day we took the train to *Pisa* to see the Leaning Tower. Our first view of this structure, leaning at such a precarious angle from all other buildings was awesome! Climbing the stairs inside gave me a strange, unsteady feeling. By the time I got a little more than half way up, I felt unbalanced as I looked down on the upright structure below. I was a bit dizzy, so I told Bill to go on to the top, and I waited for him to come back down. I am still amazed at how that massive Leaning Tower remains at that angle and defies the pull of gravity!

On our last day in Rome, we took the train to *Pompeii*, the town that was buried in 20 feet of pumice and ash when Mount *Vesuvius* erupted in 79 A.D. After lengthy excavations in the 1700's, a city was revealed that had been petrified in time. We were amazed at the beautiful, often colorful paintings, sculptures and buildings that survived. There stood the huge, now inactive, volcano that caused it all, Mount *Vesuvius*!

We still had most of the afternoon, so we stopped in Naples on our way back to Rome. This was just a big busy, noisy, bustling city. As we were standing on a corner watching the hustling crowds go by, a funeral procession was approaching. It stopped at the intersection with people walking behind the hearse. Several members of the group began yelling, swearing and fighting with each other in what appeared to be a family feud. This went on for several minutes. Then they calmed down, reformed the procession and moved on. Bill and I watched in awe. This was my vivid memory of Naples!

We had a 10:00 a.m. reservation the next morning for the train to *Nice*, France. The hotel manager made a call for a taxi to pick us up at 8:00 a.m. No taxi had arrived by 8:30 a.m., so he had his son drive us to the station. I thought I had seen traffic congestion in some of our American cities, but the morning traffic in Rome was unbelievable. There seemed to be no rules; everybody drove as he chose. There appeared to be hundreds of cars blocking traffic and blowing horns. For over an hour we were either standing still or moving at a snail's pace. I kept hoping that the train would be late, as usual.

When we finally reached the station, Bill and I thanked the young man, grabbed our luggage and ran to find our train. Just as we reached that departure area the train was pulling out; the first time we had seen an Italian train leave on time! We would miss the all day scenic trip along the *Ligurian* Sea, a far north extension of the Mediterranean Sea.

The next train to *Nice* was over night. The exertion and stress was taking its toll on Bill. He was exhausted and breathing hard, worrying about getting our new reservations. I told him to relax; I would take care of it. (I had no idea of what to do, but I was not going to let him push any longer.)

I had to go down stairs to a small room with a line of people leading to a desk with an attendant. When I finally reached the desk, I explained that we missed our morning train and needed a reservation for the next train to *Nice*. He spoke very little English and I spoke no Italian. He let me know that my Eurorail pass was fine, but there was a fee for missing our original reservation. He would not accept my American money nor my travelers check, only Italian cash. Someone tapped me on the shoulder. It was a woman and a small child standing behind me. When she saw how confused and upset I was, by word, a big smile and gestures she let me know that she would pay the small fee. By gesturing some more, I told her that my husband, who was upstairs, had some lire and we would repay her. After I got our reservations, I waited for this pleasant lady, took her upstairs, explained what happened to Bill who repaid her with a little extra and thanked her. Again, the Lord provided unexpectedly in a time of need!

Since we would be in Rome all day, we took a bus to the Vatican to explore what we had not seen on the tour. We crossed the *Piazza San*

291

Pietro, marveled again at the massive obelisk and continued on up the broad steps of St. Peter's Basilica. We entered the cathedral not knowing what to expect or which way to go.

As we wandered about for a few minutes, a young man appeared dressed in sack-cloth, who seemed to be a novice. He asked if he could help us. When we told him we were visitors who wanted to see as much of St. Peter's Basilica as possible, he said he would be happy to guide us. He showed us much of the magnificent beauty in this massive structure and told of its history. We saw the famous sculpture of Michelangelo's *"Pieta"* (which is now enclosed in glass). The large room in which the Papal Altar stands is awe inspiring, with its huge ornate dome. He showed us a small door, at last, which he said led to a crypt where some Popes and a few special priests were entombed. He gave us permission to go down the steps for a few minutes. He was not allowed to go there. It was like a miniature catacomb; a few minutes were all we needed! When we came up, we told the young novice how much we appreciated his taking the time to show us around. He disappeared into the cathedral and we exited into the sunshine. Was he an Angel in disguise?! We saw no one else being guided. God's Grace was still with us.

It was late afternoon and I was tired. Bill wanted to go to the little shop that we had visited on the tour, so I just sat on the Vatican steps and watched nuns and priests go in and out, up and down the steps, while I waited for him.

We returned to the station, got something to eat, retrieved our luggage and settled down to wait for our night train to France.

It was a long, boring ride with little sleep. We arrived in *Nice* about seven o'clock that morning, found our beautiful hotel, ate a bit of breakfast and went to bed. It was mid-afternoon when we finally woke up and were once more mobile.

The Chief of Police in Denver had given Bill a letter of introduction to the Police Chief in *Nice*. (They had met at a convention, became friends and kept in touch with each other.) We made it to the nearby police station before five o'clock. The Police Chief read his friend's letter with a smile. After a warm welcome and a pleasant visit, this official said he would set up a tour for us for the next day. He spoke fluent English.

We forgot to ask what time to be at the station, so we leisurely took our time getting together that morning, and arrived just before noon. The Chief was expecting us to be there by mid-morning. He had an officer waiting to give us an all day tour. We apologized for not understanding about the plan, but assured him that half a day tour would be just fine.

The young officer asked us if there was anything special we wanted to see. We wanted to visit the world famous *Mont Carlo Casino*, otherwise we would be happy wherever he took us. It was quite a drive from *Nice* to *Monte Carlo*, so we had an interesting visit with this young man.

When we arrived at the casino, he told us to wait in the lobby while he went to get someone to show us around. He returned with an older man who was a Casino Official. This person greeted us pleasantly, shook our hands and said he would be pleased to show us around. The young officer told us that *Nice* had no authority in *Monte Carlo*, so he would have to leave us. He gave us a number to call him from the Monte Carlo police station and said he would come back for us when we were ready.

Our official guide informed us that since we were special guests he would show us the big casino room where they never took regular tourists. We thanked him for this surprisingly unusual privilege, and wondered what the young officer had told him about us.

It was a large room with various kinds of gaming tables. I was surprised to see a small alcove partitioned off with a few slot machines. It was afternoon, so there were only a few people there. A few were playing Roulette. Several men were at the Baccarat table making high bets. We watched in awe as our guide explained about the casino gambling. The busy time is night! We were asked if we would like to see other parts of the building with different kinds of entertainment, including a theater where they usually took tourist. We told the official how much we appreciated his making this visit a special treat for us, but it was late afternoon and we needed to call our young officer so we declined.

We found the nearby *Monte Carlo* police station where no one spoke English! With my limited French and many gestures they finally understood that we needed to call the *Nice* police. We gave them the number. The call was made and in a short time our police car arrived.

The officer apologized for not being able to take us to see more sights, since it was getting late, but he would like for us to see the Monaco Castle of the Grimaldis, where Prince Rainier and the American Princess Grace Kelly lived.

We arrived at the castle at five o'clock when the last of the tourists were leaving. The young man left us in the car and went to speak to the guard. He came back and told us to come with him. Although the castle was closed to visitors at five o'clock, the guard would take us through the tour. This was unbelievable!!!

We were told that Prince Rainier and Princess Grace were away. This was before they had children. By this time I was thrilled, but tired. I only remember going through ornate rooms with many beautiful valuable heirlooms. I was glad to get back to the police station where we thanked the Police Chief for setting up the great tour for us, and praised the young officer for being a wonderful guide.

Nice is part of the French Riviera. Our hotel was just two blocks from the beach. On the short walk back from the police station, we decided to take a look at the beach while the sun was still shining. What caught our eyes was a huge hotel with a big sign, "Deep River Boys – tonight." We absolutely had to see our Black American gospel singers here on the Riviera, so we went in and made reservations for the evening!

The program was in a small theater in the hotel. The Deep River Boys had been around for a long, long time. I was surprised to see how young they seemed to be, except for one who was much older. Listening to their harmonious spirituals made us feel like being at home in a foreign land!

After the program, we were nosing around the hotel and found a bar downstairs. As we entered, the oldest singer was sitting at a table alone. We walked over to tell him how much we enjoyed the program, and the pleasure of seeing some brown American faces. He looked up at us with sad eyes and asked us to join him.

We sat down, told him who we were and how pleased and surprised we were to see that The Deep River Boys, about whom we had known for years, were still performing. We did not know we were talking with a legend performer. He was so glad to have someone with whom to communicate that this is a small part of his life the he told us about: he was Jimmy Lundy, the last surviving member of the original group. He lived in Copenhagen, Denmark, since they performed mostly in Europe. His wife had died just two months before we met him, and he missed her. The other fellows in the group were younger than he, middle-aged, and liked to have fun and "let go" when not working. He was past that stage. His only connection with them was his love of singing in the group. Otherwise, he was always alone.

Jimmy was a college student in the 1940's at Hampton Institute (now Hampton University) when the singing group was organized by Dr. Frederick Douglas Hall, an outstanding Black music professor whom we knew. As time went on and they became professionally successful, they became known as The Deep River Boys. He did not remember when or how that became their name. Most of the music they sang was composed or arranged by Dr. Hall. One of their special numbers, "Dry Bones" was composed by Dr. Hall. He never copyrighted it. Jimmy was not too sure how much longer he would be singing with the group. With the loss of his wife, he was lonely and would like to return to his home in the United States.

Bill and I were excited when we heard the name of Dr. Fred D. Hall, who was head of the music department at Dillard University in New Orleans. He was married to Mildred Greenwood Hall (who was in charge of piano instruction at Dillard) - Bill's cousin! Her mother was the sister of Bill's paternal grandmother. She and Fred had visited us a couple times in Denver. Whenever we were in New Orleans we usually stayed with them. What a surprise! I do not remember how Bill and Mildred found each other, but we had some happy times together.

We visited for over an hour and he seemed to relax. We told him what a special treat it was meeting him and how much we had learned talking with him. We also told him that we understood his loneliness at losing his wife, but we knew the Lord would take care of him. It was after midnight when we left him. We praised God for sending us downstairs that night. What a way to end our short visit in *Nice*!!!

The next morning we left for Paris. We arrived in the "City of Lights" late afternoon or early evening. Our hotel was located in the far northern suburb of Paris, a long way from the center of the city. It was a brand new, small friendly hotel which we thoroughly enjoyed during our stay in Paris. There was a train stop a few steps in front, which provided transportation into the city with our Eurorail passes.

On our first trip into the city of Paris we discovered the fastest and easiest way to get around was by the Metro subway. As we stood in the station watching the actions of people, we noticed some would slip a small ticket into a slot of a metal box by the turnstiles to an escalator going down.

The ticket would emerge from another slot at the end of the box, the person would retrieve it, the turnstile would open and the person would go down the escalator. We went over to the window where tickets were sold and asked about the system. We were told that was the entrance to the Metro and we could purchase tickets for a day, a week or a month. As long as it was valid it would go through the machine, to be used until it was outdated, and then the machine would keep it. Since we planned to spend five days in Paris, we bought tickets for a week. The tickets were good for the Metro and the city train to our hotel.

The day that we went to the Eiffel Tower we could go only part way up. They were making repairs on the upper part. However, we had quite a view of Paris. The French engineer who built the 1,040 ft. tower for an exhibit in 1889, also designed and built the Statue of Liberty.

The *Louvre* Museum has one of the largest and greatest collections of masterpieces in the world. There are so many departments and wings that we could cover only a small portion. We saw the famous painting of the *Mona Lisa,* housed in glass in a special room. The *Venus de Milo* statue and other priceless works of art are housed in the *Louvre*.

We watched people and traffic hurrying by on the *Champs de Elysées*. We walked through the *Arc de Triomphe* and marveled at its architecture.

One day we took the train to *Versailles*, a few miles from Paris. This palace was built by King Louis XIV, the most opulent in the world. Aristocrats and nobles were entertained at banquets and balls in the most famous room of all, 233 ft. long, the Hall of Mirrors. We spent hours at *Versailles*, but saw only a small portion of the elaborate palace and walked through only a small area of the expansive, beautiful 247 acres of gardens.

We planned to attend the *Folies Bergère* that evening. We knew it would take some time to get back to Paris, so we headed for the little platform to wait for the train. It was a long wait! Finally, the train arrived. Bill got on and turned to help me. The train started to move just as I leaped for the door; Bill grabbed my jacket and pulled me in as the door slowly closed! I was terrified, as I realized what could have happened. I could have missed the leap to the door and fallen to the tracks. My feet could have slipped when I landed on the edge of the doorway, but Bill saved me. What a horrible death that could have been if I had missed that slowly moving train! I started shaking all over and was on the verge of tears. As we sat, Bill held me as I trembled and neither of us spoke for some time.

By the time we reached Paris I had calmed down, but I was weak as I talked about my close call. Bill did all he could to comfort me and made sure that I felt strong enough to continue our plans for the evening. Once more, the Lord had made it very clear that He was not ready for me yet!!

I needed a happy change, so we took the Metro to this famous theater. It was quite a walk from the Metro station to the *Folies Bergère*. Along the way we saw a street vender who was selling warm *crepes* the size of which I had never seen before. The thin pancake was as big as a dinner plate. There were several choices of flavors which he brushed onto the *crepe*, rolled it up and placed a covering on one end for holding. We watched people buying them, then walking away joyfully eating their treats. I wanted one, but we could not take any to the theater with us. I told Bill that I hoped the vender would still be there on our return to the Metro.

When we arrived at the *Folies Bergère*, we were surprised to find a special program was scheduled honoring Josephine Baker! She was an

African-American entertainer who left the United States in the 20's or 30's when her talent was not recognized. In France, she became famous. As a star performer at the *Folies Bergère,* she became the "Toast of Paris"! Bill and I thoroughly enjoyed this program of songs, dance and costumes performed as in the days of Josephine Baker.

On our way back to the Metro the vender was still there. Bill and I bought different flavored *crepes.* We enjoyed eating the delicious treat on our way back to our hotel. Next door to our hotel was a small shop. One morning we were in no hurry to go anywhere. We decided to check this little store for food. At the bakery counter I spotted some breakfast rolls. One looked so delicious. In French, I asked the woman what was that? She replied so fast I could not understand what she was saying, so I asked her, in French, to please speak slowly. She smiled, slowed down and I understand enough of what she said to buy the roll that proved to be as tasty as it looked.

One day we took a sight-seeing trip on the Seine River. As the boat passed where we could see *Notre Dame* Cathedral, we remembered that we had not visited that historic edifice. Later we spent a short time in the cathedral with gargoyles, on which Alexander Dumas' classic novel *The Hunchback of Notre Dame*, is based.

In France, wine is served with every meal. I enjoyed the wine, but I drank bottled water to quench my thirst. On our last day in Paris, we were eating lunch at a small restaurant. I asked for water to drink and the waiter looked at me in awe. He said, "Water is for washing." Since I insisted, he shook his head and eventually brought me a small bottle of water.

As we entered the restaurant, we noticed a tour business in the block advertising a nightclub tour, and we decided to check it out after lunch. It offered such a fabulous schedule of dinner and nightclubs including *"Le Moulin Rouge"* theater, we signed for that evening. We were to be at the tour office by five o'clock. Since it was early afternoon, we had plenty of time to go to our hotel to dress for the evening and we returned on time.

We were divided into two small groups in vans of seven or eight. One group would do nightclubs first ending with the first performance at *"Le Moulin Rouge,"* then have dinner. The second group would have dinner first, then nightclubs ending with the last performance. My prayers were answered when we were assigned to the second group. I definitely wanted early dinner. This was approximately seven o'clock.

At the restaurant, a special table was set for us. We had time to visit and get acquainted with each other. The food was delicious, and at each setting was a small pint-size bottle of wine. No water.

After leaving the restaurant, for the next several hours we were taken to two small, delightfully entertaining night clubs, before arriving at *"Le Moulin Rouge"* before the eleven o'clock performance. There had been a delay during the earlier performance, so that audience was late leaving. By the time we were admitted and seated, it was well past eleven o'clock when the curtain opened and the show began. It was a fabulous two hour presentation of singing, acting and choreography. They danced the *"Can-Can"* as depicted in *Toulouse Lautrec*'s famous painting of *"Le Moulin Rouge."* What a way to end our stay in Paris!

When the show was over, we were surprised when each person in our van was returned to their respective hotel. Since ours was the farthest away, we were the last, but happy that we did not have to ride the train at two 'clock in the morning.

Our flight reservation was for late afternoon, so we had time to rest for several hours before taking the train to the airport. Unlike the Eurorail, there were carts at the airport in which we could place our luggage.

The line for our flight was long. Bill had seen a liquor shop with a sale of wine a short distance from our line. I waited in the long line while he went to get the wine. Our luggage filled the cart. When he returned, he laid the wine on top of it.

I said, "I think we better carry the wine. It might fall off of all this luggage."

He was so excited that he said, "Oh, it will be all right."

As the line moved, we pushed the cart. The wine shifted a bit. It hung on until we were almost at the check-in counter. Bill gave the cart a push; the wine rolled off and shattered on the concrete floor! The aroma was so pleasantly potent that nearby people were sniffing and smiling. Bill was embarrassed and disappointed at losing his precious wine. I just looked at him and said nothing. Someone came to clean up the mess. Later, we laughed about this stupid mistake. We had a sense of humor that eased many traumatic experiences when we could see the funny side.

On October 4, 1976, we returned safely home with unforgettable memories of a once in a lifetime of European experiences. All <u>by the Grace of God</u>!!!

With help from my son Bill, we developed a 1 ½ hour visual slide presentation of our exciting adventure with an accompanying audio script which I wrote and recorded. I enjoyed showing these highlights of our trip to several enthusiastic groups.

CHAPTER 16
Closing an Era

Early in 1977, Richard came back to Denver and resumed his music profession and renewed old friendships.

Karen Erickson and I had kept corresponding with each other. In the summer of 1977 she wrote that they were planning to come to the United States in the fall. Would that be a convenient time for us? I wrote back that any time would be fine with us. They decided to come in late September or early October. After a flight connection problem in New York, they finally arrived in Denver.

We were delighted to see the Ericksons again. During the two weeks that they were with us, we developed a most unusual happy relationship. We spoke English to Karen who interpreted in Danish to Agnus. After his first year of English in school Mogens was not yet comfortable with the language, so he still spoke mostly Danish. Richard spoke both languages with them.

One day there was no one in the house but Agnus, Mogens and me. (I have no idea where everyone else had gone.) We were sitting around the kitchen table and I was wondering how I could possibly communicate with Agnus. Somehow, with my talking, gesturing, naming a few objects and Mogens interpretation with his limited knowledge of English, Agnus became interested and even repeated some of my English words in his Danish accent. I, in turn, said the Danish that he told me. It became a kind of game with the three of us. Agnus actually relaxed and smiled for the first time. I was elated! Later, Karen told me that Agnus was self-conscious about being different. Now his tension was finally relieved and he was beginning to enjoy being with us.

In October the Masonic Council of Deliberation and the State Golden Circle had their annual meetings. In 1977, they were meeting in Ogden, Utah. We took the Ericksons with us. The Consistory brothers and the Golden Circle ladies accepted them graciously. While Bill and

I were in meetings that Saturday, one of the men took the Ericksons to Salt Lake City for the day. When they returned, they were excited about what they saw, especially the Great Salt Lake! They were guests at our banquet.

Since Mogens wanted to see Disneyland, we planned a trip to California. They were amazed as we drove through our huge, spectacular mountains. Karen remarked about all the cars they had seen in Denver and on the highway.

"You don't have any poor people, do you?" she said. "Everybody seems to drive a car. We don't have many cars in Denmark; petrol is so expensive."

"Oh, yes, we have plenty of poor people," I replied.

"This is the first time we have ridden in a Cadillac!" she exclaimed. "There are only two Cadillacs in Denmark. The Queen has one and her assistant has the other one."

We had an interesting arrangement in the car. Bill and I were in the front seat speaking only English. The Ericksons were in the back seat speaking only Danish. Karen was the interpreter for all of us. Somehow we developed a comfortable, understanding, enjoyable relationship with each other.

We spent the night at a nice little motel in Utah where Bill and I frequently stopped on our way to Las Vegas. The next day we took them to Bryce Canyon. They were awe-inspired as they viewed the spectacular colorful formations. (Every time we have visited there, we are amazed!) We drove through Zion National Park and pointed out some of the scenic wonders, then on to Las Vegas. We spent the night in one of the big hotels, but since Mogens was only eleven years old, we spent only a short day there, drove to Hoover Dam, and then headed for California.

We arrived in Anaheim, found our hotel and settled down to rest in preparation for the next day's big adventure – Disneyland!

Bill called his cousin Sue in Pasadena and we planned to spend the day with them. We told the Ericksons we would take them to Disneyland when it opened, and they could have all day to enjoy it. We would pick them up late afternoon at whatever time they chose. Bill and I were not interested in spending another day in Disneyland. They understood and seemed to be happy to finally do something on their own.

We had our usual exciting visit with Sue and Melvin. We called Eleanor and Noel in Altadena. Since our time was limited, we would not get to see them.

As we headed back to pick up the Ericksons, we ran into the biggest traffic snarl on the freeway to Anaheim that we had ever encountered. Our friends had been anxiously waiting for us for some time. They had a good time, but they were tired. They learned that Disneyland had certain days, about which we did not know, when there were guides who led foreign speaking groups. The Ericksons missed the Danish group by one day.

We returned to Denver a few days before they left for home. They were amazed at how big the United States is, compared with the countries in Europe – especially tiny Denmark.

Karen sent me two beautiful glazed china doves. She wrote that she called the one with the tail up "Optimist," the one with the tail down "Pessimist." I treasure this gift and have those doves where I see them all the time. A few months later, Karen wrote to tell us that Agnus had died. For a long time we continued to write to each other, until finally months went by and she did not answer my letters. Eventually Prebin wrote to me to tell me that his mother died peacefully after months of painful cancer, about which she never complained and did not want me to know. Thus ended a very special friendship.

Bill and I were thankful that, <u>by the Grace of God</u>, we were able to make their trip to the United States an enjoyable one just a miniscule fraction of repayment for all their caring for our son while he lived in Denmark!

I woke up early one morning to find that Bill was not in bed. I presumed he had gone to the bathroom, so I rolled over and went back to sleep. When I woke up again, the sun was shining and still there was no Bill. I got up to look for him and found him sitting on the bed in Louise's old bedroom.

"Why are you in here?" I asked. "Are you all right?"

He looked at me and said, "I was having trouble breathing lying down. I didn't want to disturb you, so I came in here." He did not look good and his breathing was erratic.

As he went back to our bedroom, his walking was unsteady and as he sat on the bed he was gasping for breath.

I calmly said, "We need to get to the doctor. Can you get dressed?"

"Oh, I'll be all right if I just take it easy for a while," was his reply.

I could see that putting on clothes was too much, so my next emphatic remark was, "Put on your robe. I am taking you to the hospital!"

I got him in the car and away we went to St. Joseph Hospital. He was taken into Emergency and I was told to go to the nearby waiting room while they checked him out. They would let me know as soon as they determined what was happening.

I know so little about illnesses, but I knew this was serious and I was worried. A half hour passed - no word. An hour, and still no word. That did it! I went to the nurses' desk and asked why I had not been told what was going on with my husband. The nurse informed me that I would hear from the doctor eventually; he was busy.

That was too much and I let go. "If you do not get the doctor for me, I'll go into the Emergency room and find out for myself. I have waited long enough!"

She left and brought the doctor. I was upset and let him know what I thought of him and his delay in letting me know about my husband. He told me Bill was having a heart attack and they were entering him into the hospital as soon as the room was ready. I could go in to see him.

There was no apology or explanation for the delay in letting me know.

I stayed with my husband until he was settled in his room, and was so tired that all he wanted was to rest. I went home and let the children and my mother know what happened. Bill, Jr. was the only sibling in Denver, so he helped me as much as possible. Bill was in the hospital for three days before they got his heart beating normally. I was there every day and was so happy when I could take him home. He followed his doctor's orders, gradually regained his strength and eventually resumed his regular activities. I do not remember what year that happened, but I sent up my prayers of thanks to the Good Lord for saving my beloved husband!

Singing in Shorter's choir were four of us sopranos who became friendly as we always sat together – Adele Alexander, Vernease Clardy, Margaret Moore and me.

Adele was a musician who played the piano and lived and breathed music. Her son, Gregory, sang beautifully and was a friend with my children in Sunday School, Junior Choir and YPD. Adele and I developed a close friendship through our mutual love of music. I attended some of the national meetings of the Black musician's organization with her – Kansas City, Los Angeles, Detroit and New York. I was not a member of the organization, but each time I attended, I was permitted to sing in their big closing choir. I felt honored! I learned so much about music with Adele.

One day Bill made a surprising remark. "Honey, I am so glad you have a good friend. You need to have a woman friend." It wasn't until much later that I understood what he meant. He was my only close friend.

Margaret and I developed a closer friendship when we were roommates at our church Annual Conference in Phoenix, Arizona. (I believe it was 1982.) We sang in the Conference Choir and found plenty to laugh about with our mutual sense of humor. She was planning to retire and hoped to travel. I told her about *Ports of Call* and how we enjoyed this travel club, so she joined.

Vernease and I had a kind of natural friendship bond that developed into a special, much needed closeness as the years rolled by. Most of the time we actually saw each other only at church.

Bill and I were happy with the friendships I was making. However, I had no idea how valuable these relationships would be later on. By the Grace of God, these were my friends when I needed them the most of all.

After I began skiing again, I found an adult group that went to various ski areas where there was usually an hour of instruction before we were released to ski on our own. I learned to parallel ski and turn, using my snowplow and stem turn only when necessary. I actually improved from beginner to intermediate skier! They were surprised when I paid for a half price ticket, since I was past 65 – the oldest in the group and the only brown face.

In 1981, I went skiing with Jim and JoEllen at Keystone. We were spending the weekend at the Seymour's mountain house near Frisco. If we were skiing together, they had a safety routine for me as we came down the higher, faster runs. Jim would ski out ahead of me and JoEllen would ski a distance behind me.

This bright sunny day we had spent the morning skiing on our own. I enjoyed the fun of the easy runs, while they took off for the more advanced runs. We met for lunch, after which they planned to ski with me on an intermediate slope. That would be our final run together for the day. I was ready!

I could see Jim ahead of me and I knew JoEllen was behind me; I felt safe. I would "shoosh" down the gentle sections of the slope, but I would traverse the steeper areas to keep my comfortable control. In these quick reversals, you automatically transfer your weight to the downhill ski. You don't think about it, it just happens. As I made a downhill turn on my traverse, I looked for Jim. For some unknown reason, I did not automatically shift my weight to my downhill ski; it began slipping away. Immediately I tried to get my weight shifted, but with my short legs, my body was pulled over and down on the ski in such a way that I landed on the safety release, which prevented my ski from releasing from my boot. My knee twisted and I felt something give. I knew I was injured. I yelled to Jim, and JoEllen skied down fast. Again, the Lord provided. Jim had stopped just past a ski patrol emergency phone box, so he had no problem climbing back and calling for help. Jim and JoEllen removed my skis and kept me as comfortable as possible until the ski patrol arrived. I could not stand up.

They immobilized my left leg, strapped me onto a toboggan and away we went. For some reason, my toes ached and were so cold they felt frostbitten by the time we got to the first aid station. Otherwise, it was just a cold adventurous ride. The doctor x-rayed my knee and told me I had torn a ligament. They splinted my leg and said I was to keep my weight off of it. They could not believe I was 69 years old. I showed them my driver's license with my birth date on it to convince them. They gave me a written report.

Jim and JoEllen got me safely back to the house. Jim called his dad to tell him about my accident. I was not in pain; I just couldn't walk. They helped me as I hopped on my good right leg. Bill called the doctor and let us know I had an appointment for the next day. My children got me back to Denver on time.

The doctor read the report, checked my leg and placed a removable splint on it to immobilize my knee. I could remove the splint when I went to bed. I had crutches so I could navigate without putting any weight on my left leg.

Since it was my left leg I could drive, so I went wherever I wanted to go – just slower. I made every choir rehearsal, crutches and all!

I had been told it would take about six weeks for my knee to heal. When I returned to the doctor in two weeks, he was amazed at how fast it was healing. He said I could walk carefully with only one crutch. After three weeks, the splint was removed and I was told I could walk freely. My doctor said he had never seen this kind of injury heal so quickly. It must have been because of my good health. However, I still used the crutch for a week longer and let my knee continue to strengthen. I did not ski again for a few years.

     I am a neutral politician. I believe in voting for the candidate whom I feel is the best suited for office, regardless of party. My only political affiliation was in the 1950's with Mrs. Lucy Harris, who organized the Women's Republican Club. Mrs. Harris was one of my Mother's best friends, a dedicated member of Shorter A.M.E. Church, a strong influence in the community and highly respected in Denver's political circle. The one highlight I remember, as a member of this club of Black women, was their tea party at which I sat at the table as a hostess and served tea to the wife of the President of the United States, Mamie Eisenhower!!! She came with Mrs. Love (governor's wife) who was a friend of Mrs. Harris. Mrs. Harris had that kind of city and state political connections in Denver.

Marie (seated) serves tea to Mamie Eisenhower.
Standing left to right, Lt. Earl Mann, Mrs. Love (wife of
Gov. Love), Mrs. Lucy Harris, Mrs. Mamie Eisenhower.

Bill kept in touch with what was going on politically. Once he came back from a caucus meeting in our area to tell me, excitedly, that they wanted him to run for councilman in our far west Denver district. I knew he could be one of the best, but he would not be able to survive campaigning.

"Are you planning to run?" I asked.

"Oh, yes, I think it would be great," he replied.

"I know you would be a great councilman, but I don't think you should run," I answered. "With your bad heart, the stress and strain of the campaign would be too much. Even if you won there would be too much pressure."

"Well, I think I'm going to run," was his answer, determinately.

"Well, if you run, this will be a very strange and embarrassing situation. For the first time, your wife will not be with you. I will do everything within my power to prevent you from being elected. With your bad heart you would never make it," was my positive reply. "I love you, Bill, and I am proud of you, but I would rather be a <u>poor wife</u> any day, than a <u>rich widow</u>!"

A few days later Bill went to the doctor for his usual checkup. When he returned home, he was very quiet. As usual, I asked him what his physical report was. The way he looked at me I was afraid I would hear bad news.

"Honey, I hate to say this," he finally answered. "When I told the doctor I wanted to run for councilman, he told me the same thing that you said. With my bad heart I would not make it through the pressure of the campaign in good health. I am <u>not</u> going to run."

As I sent up my silent prayer of thanks to the Good Lord, all I could say was, "Honey, I am so glad that your doctor convinced you." This was the best news I could have heard!

In 1982, we had coupons for pictures to be taken at Olan Mills studio. We decided to use one coupon on our 39th anniversary, April 17th. Bill surprised me with a beautiful yellow-gold orchid corsage that matched the gold jewelry I was wearing. We had invited our friends, Eugene and Evelyn Cason to join us later to celebrate.

On the way to Olan Mills, I said to Bill, "You know, the 39th anniversary is an odd one to celebrate. We really should have our picture taken on our fortieth."

He didn't say anything.

I continued, "Oh, well, since we have these coupons, we might as well use them. Who knows, we may not be here next year." (Little did I know what an ominous prediction that was!) The pictures were beautiful. We gave them to our children as Christmas presents and had a large one made for us.

We took Evelyn and Eugene to dinner and enjoyed celebrating our anniversary with these old friends we had known for many years.

39th Wedding Anniversary

One year I had the pleasure of flying to New Orleans to celebrate the 100th birthday of my Aunt Sidonie, my father's oldest sister. It was amazing how alert she was and how well she moved around. She understood some English, but spoke only French. My cousins spoke English and acted as interpreters for me. Since my French was limited, my communication in the language was sporadic. We laughed and had fun speaking in the two languages. There were eleven children in my father's family, and Aunt Sidonie could name every one of them in order; my father was the oldest son, number three after two older sisters. It was a happy party with balloons, gifts, a letter from the President and all kinds of delicious Creole food. Aunt Sidonie died at 104 years old.

Our house on 6th Avenue was broken into twice. I came home one evening to find the back door partly open. When I entered the house, I found someone had gone through the drawers in the bedroom chests. As I checked I could not detect anything missing. When Bill arrived home and checked his drawers, his precious gold watch, which he inherited from his grandfather was gone. This was a beautifully engraved watch that opened up. Inside was inscribed, "To Joseph D.D. Rivers from Booker T Washington." Mr. Rivers was a student of Mr. Washington at Hampton Institute, where they became lifetime friends. Bill would proudly wear the watch with its gold chain fob on special formal occasions.

We reported the break in, describing the valuable watch. By the Grace of God, it was found and returned to us. I told Bill to put this watch in our big safe downstairs, since he wore it only occasionally.

Our next invasion occurred during the day. This time I arrived home one afternoon to find disruption all over the house. It was scary! I frantically called Bill at work. This time my small jewelry box was missing. It contained my many pairs of earrings which I had converted when I had my ears pierced. One set that meant so much to me was a beautiful old cameo set of a brooch and tiny matching earrings that Bill's grandmother gave me. Fortunately, I did not keep all my jewelry in one place. Again, the historic watch was gone. Bill did not put it in the safe; he said he forgot. This time the watch was gone for good! Later our son, Bill Jr., found that his saxophone had been stolen, also.

The robbers had jimmied our front door to enter. We could see the marks and the door was forced open. We had a loud burglar alarm installed after this scary episode. Our neighborhood had always been so safe, but times were changing.

In February of 1983, Bill and I were in Denver for separate meetings. Instead of waiting for each other to finish, we decided to drive back to the mountains separately, since our timing was uncertain. I had the Cadillac and he was driving the four-wheel-drive Subaru.

My meeting ended and I was back at the "Lazy G II" just past noon. Bill had not arrived. Hours went by and I had no call from him. I was worried because he said he would be coming home as soon as his meeting ended. By four o'clock, I was frantic and very upset. Where could he be all this time and no word? Shortly thereafter, the phone rang. It was from the Colorado Highway Patrol! There had been an accident and they wanted to know if I could come to get my husband.

"How is he?" I wanted to know.

"He is all right. We have him in our car," was the reply.

"Where are you?" I asked frantically.

"We are on 285 at the Tiny Town cut-off," I was told.

"Okay. I'll be there in about fifteen minutes!" My heart was pounding, and away I went.

It was dusk when I reached the accident. The patrolman told me he was not sure what happened, but it was a one-car accident and my husband was not at fault. The car was not badly damaged, but was not safe to drive. Bill had been badly jarred and was unsteady getting out of the patrol car. He really looked as though he should have been taken to emergency for a check-up. The patrolman said he would be all right with some rest.

On the way home I asked him what happened, but he couldn't tell me. That was unusual! When we got home I helped him into the house. As he sat on the couch he tried to talk, but his words were mumbled and erratic. From the expression on his face I realized he was in shock. I got him into a tub of warm water. He had a number of bruises. I talked to him continually and got him into bed. I told him how worried I had been, that I loved him and was so relieved to see that he was safe.

This happened the day before Valentine's Day, and he had stopped to buy a Valentine for me after his meeting. We found it in the car when it was towed to our mechanic. It was beautiful, with sentimental words

312

that told how much he loved me. I placed it on the mantle over the fireplace where I could see it every day.

Eventually he regained his strength and resumed his activities, but he was never sure about how the accident happened. We turned the car in after it was repaired, for a Subaru panel truck. We needed a four-wheel-drive vehicle in the mountains in the winter, and the truck would be good for hauling.

April 17, 1983 would be our fortieth anniversary, so we had planned to celebrate by taking a trip to Mexico which our *Ports of Call* travel club had scheduled at that time.

Ports of Call was an exclusive club that had its own terminal, hangar and plane, just south of Stapleton Airport (off Montview Blvd). They coordinated their flight schedule with the airport and actually flew out of Stapleton. They had their own guarded parking lot where we could leave our cars while on a trip. We enjoyed taking these completely planned, carefree vacations.

Somewhere along the way, Bill had helped someone who had become the manager of a hotel in Guadalajara, Mexico. He had invited us to come down to enjoy his beautiful tourist hotel as his special guests. Since that's where the *Ports of Call* trip was scheduled, we signed up for it. Bill wrote to his friend and let him know we would accept his invitation and stay at his hotel, instead of the club's accommodation.

We told Margaret of our plans and invited her to take her first *Ports of Call* trip with us. She would stay at the club's scheduled hotel. When requested, a roommate would be assigned for single travelers. This was fine with her, so she signed up for her first travel adventure. Bill's friend wrote back that he was looking forward to our first visit and planned to make our anniversary special.

The week before Easter we took our three grandchildren to the mountain house – Billy 7 (almost 8); Chrissy, 5, and Lori, 3 ½. We were driving the Subaru. The children enjoyed riding in the truck. They also had fun playing in the snow with their grandpa (paw-paw). By the middle of the week the sun was out, the snow began to melt and the roads were clear. Bill drove to Denver for his Maundy Thursday evening service with his Masonic Lodge. He came back the next morning, so I drove down to Denver that Friday to do some Easter shopping. When I returned late that afternoon, Bill and the children were dying Easter eggs and filling little baskets for their friends Jennifer, Stephanie and Nicole Daniel.

When I walked in, Bill said, "Honey, you won't believe this, but I have to go to Denver tomorrow morning. I got a call reminding me they are expecting me there by ten o'clock to audit the Eastern Star books."

"You didn't put it on the calendar," I replied in surprise. We had a calendar in the kitchen on which we recorded everything as a reminder.

"I forgot," he said. "I didn't think of it again until she called. I'm sorry, but I have to go down."

We had planned to take the children back to Denver on that Saturday afternoon to be there with our friends and Louise for Easter.

"Okay. I'll stay up tonight and get the children's clothes washed so we can go down with you in the morning," I told Bill.

We had our usual joyful evening with the children – planning for Easter fun, games and stories. After the children were in bed, Bill said, "Honey, you don't have to stay up tonight to do the washing. I'll go down in the morning and come back for you and the children. You can wash while I am gone."

"I hate for you to make two trips," was my reply, "but it will make it easier for me."

"Don't' worry, there will be plenty of time," he said with a grin.

The next morning April 2, 1983, after breakfast, Bill was ready to leave by nine o'clock. Billy wanted, desperately, to go with his grandpa. Bill took his grandson with him almost everywhere. He would be busy auditing the books and could not take Billy with him. For the first time, he said, "Not this time, Billy." Billy was disappointed and hurt. I was combing Chrissy's hair when Bill gave me a kiss and told me and the children goodbye, as he left through the kitchen and went downstairs to the garage. Five minutes later, to our surprise, Bill appeared again in the kitchen.

"What did you forget this time?" I asked. He was always forgetting something. He gave me the strangest answer.

"Oh, nothing. I just came back to look around again."

He went into the bedrooms, came back and started to go in the kitchen, turned around and came over to kiss me again. I wondered how I happen to rate two kisses this time!

I can still see him as he waved to me and the children when he left through the kitchen for the second time. He was wearing his grey leisure suit that he bought in Liberia, his old grey felt hat and he was growing a beard, since he now called himself "an old man of the mountains." He had recently been elected president of the Mountain Lakes homeowner's board.

I washed the children's clothes and had them in the dryer.

A little past noon, the phone rang. When I answered, it was a call from St. Anthony's Hospital. A nurse asked for Mrs. Greenwood, and I said, "I am Mrs. Greenwood." She went on to tel me that my husband had an accident and was there in the hospital. She apologized for not calling sooner. The only ID they could find on him with a telephone number was an appointment slip for Dr. Elliott, our chiropractor. They called him and he gave them our number.

"How is he?" I was shocked. "What happened?"

"He is very critical," she answered. "The car overturned and rolled over on him. We are doing all we can to help him. The doctor will call you later." He would not wear a seat belt.

"I'll be there as soon as I can get there," I gasped.

I called my neighbor, Donna, to see if she could take us down. She said she would be glad to take us, but it would be a half hour or more. Her three year old son, Damon, was asleep. I thanked her and told her that would be fine, because I still had to check the laundry to see if it was dry.

I told the children what happened. We got their Easter baskets packed and made sure everything was ready to go.

I had decided not to try to pack all their clothes, just get the washed jackets for them to wear. I went downstairs to check on the jackets, and the downstairs phone rang. It was a nurse from the hospital again.

"How is my husband?" I asked frantically.

"The doctor wants to talk to you," she said.

"Mrs. Greenwood, I want you to know that we have done all we possibly could," he assured me, "but your husband is dead."

"I don't believe it!" I exclaimed as I actually saw big capital letters <u>DEAD.</u> "I don't believe it!!!" I kept saying over and over.

The doctor replied, "We hate to have to call people like this, but it was the only way. Yes, your husband is dead! We did everything we could to try to save him."

Just as I hung up the phone, Donna was knocking on the back door. I called to Billy to let her in, as I retrieved the jackets from the dryer, in disbelief. Billy had a problem unlocking the door. As I came upstairs, I let her in and told her what had happened. She was shocked. I told the children that their paw-paw had died.

The shock left me completely helpless. I asked Donna if she would give me a little time to call my children before we went down to the hospital in Denver. She said she would go back home and return whenever I called her.

I tried to call Louise, but I couldn't get her, so I called her friend Ida Daniel. They always knew what each other was doing. Sure enough, Ida knew where Louise was. She was shocked when I told her Bill was dead and I would be at St. Anthony's Hospital. Ida called Louise. I tried to get Richard in St. Paul, Minnesota, but could not reach him. I called his wife and she got word to him. I got Jim, who was in Virginia with JoEllen to spend Easter with her sister, Pat and her family. He said he would be here as soon as he got JoEllen back home to Brooklyn. Louise called to tell me she would meet me at the hospital.

When I called my mother she seemed surprised, but not shocked. She told me that Bill had been to visit her the week before. All he talked about was his concern about my welfare if anything happened to him. He wanted to be sure that I would be taken care of financially. She said she had wondered why he had such concern. Now, she realized that he must have had some kind of premonition of his coming death. She and Bill had developed a strong mother-son relationship, so he felt free to talk to her about anything.

I called Myrene Waugh, part of our extended family who had known Bill from infancy. We were in close touch with her and her husband Harry. She was stunned. She called Bill, Jr. for me and the two of them spread the word by phone.

I called Donna and she drove me and the children to St. Anthony's Hospital in Denver. When we parked in the parking lot, I turned to tell the children to get out of the van. Donna spoke up and said she would take care of them; I should go on in. Donna was pregnant with her second child, and I had no idea how long I would be, but she assured me she would be fine.

I entered the hospital, found a seat and waited for Louise. For the first time in my life I felt completely helpless. When Louise arrived, I told her where the children were. She told me that she saw them and Donna planned to keep the children until we were through. What a blessed neighbor!

"For the first time in my life, I don't know what to do!" I blurted out to Louise. "I have always been able to help everyone else. Now, I don't know what I am going to do. I haven't tried to check on dad or anything." For some reason, I could not cry – only hurt inside and feel bewildered.

Louise replied, "Mom, you are not going to do anything. I will take over and check to find out everything."

We were escorted to a small private waiting room. To my surprise, Mrs. Slack was there with Adele and Gilbert. They had come as soon as they heard of Bill's death and were waiting for me. Louise took off to see what needed to be done. Soon Rev. Boyd arrived. It was consoling to have these friends and my minister responding so quickly, but I was numb from shock. I still could not shed a tear, although I ached inside and could only talk of my disbelief in suddenly losing my husband. Louise and I believed he had a heart attack.

My memory of the following events is a bit sketchy. We relieved Donna of the children and thanked her profusely. Louise took me home with her to 6th Avenue.

News travels fast! Soon after we reached home, our councilman called to render his sympathy, and tell me that he would see that Denver City Council honored Bill for all the good he had done for Denver. Frances Melrose, special reporter with the Rocky Mountain News, called to get information about Bill. She wrote an impressive column about him.

About five o'clock the phone rang. It was Richard!

"Hi, Mom, can you come and get me?"

"Richard, where are you?' I asked in amazement. I couldn't believe his answer.

"I'm at Stapleton. Please come and get me."

The Cadillac was in the garage, so I drove to Stapleton Airport, in dismay, to pick up my son. I asked him how, on earth, did he get the money for the airfare to come home immediately. He said as soon as he had the word about dad, he went to his credit union in Minneapolis and told them of his dire emergency. They gave him the money and he took the first flight he could get to Denver. I was relieved to have my oldest son here.

Easter Sunday, after church, Adele and Gilbert came to see me and brought Margaret. They assured me they would be there for me whenever I needed them.

On the Monday after Easter, Jim arrived. He and Richard assumed the responsibility of going through their dad's belongings to relieve me. Each of them called back to their jobs to let them know they would be on emergency leave.

There was to be an autopsy to determine the cause of death. By Wednesday, I had heard no word, so I called Caldwell-Kirk Mortuary to see if they had received the body. They told me the body had not been released when they checked earlier because the Coroner was waiting for the report from the Colorado Highway Patrol, so the death certificate could be filled out. I called the Coroner's office and was told they were still waiting, but should have it any day.

I called the Colorado Highway Patrol headquarters in Golden. I could get no satisfactory answer as to why there had been no report of my husband's accident. That did it! I drove out to the headquarters in Golden and found someone in charge. I told the person what the circumstances were. I was assured that the report would be sent in. That was not enough for me!

"I want a copy of the accident," I said. "I am not leaving here until I have it."

With my positive, determined look, the officer headed for an office and I followed him. On a desk were a pile of reports. As he thumbed through the papers, he found the report of Bill's accident buried in that mess!!!

"We will mail the report, right away," he told me.

"No," I was furious. "I will not wait any longer. Give me the report and I will take it in myself!" He complied and I had a copy..

By the time I found the Coroner's office, adjacent to the old Denver General Hospital, I gave them the report and returned home. I was physically, emotionally and mentally exhausted. I was so accustomed to handling responsibility myself, it never occurred to me to ask one of my sons to go with me. My adult children were flabbergasted when I told them what I had done.

The body was released to Caldwell-Kirk, and the service was set for Saturday, April 9, 1983 at 12:30 p.m. Shorter's little church building would be too small, so Rev. Liggins was asked if it would be possible to have Bill's funeral service at Zion Baptist Church. Rev. Liggins was more than happy to permit us to have these final rites at his church. Our friends, Eleanor and Noel, and Bill's cousins, Sue and Melvin, came from California.

When Bill's lodge brothers were told of his death, some of them asked, "How is Marie?"

They knew Bill and I were always together. They were relieved to know I was all right.

Sovereign Grand Commander Russell Gideon of the United Supreme Council came. I was surprised when he said he did not know what he was going to do without Bill. They had developed a close relationship on this highest Masonic level.

We were pleasantly surprised when we received the death certificate. No medical drugs and no signs of heart failure were found. Bill's accident was listed as <u>purely accidental</u>!

I was given his wallet, rings, Chief of Police badge and watch in which were a few tiny chips of dried blood caught between one or two of the links of the expandable band.

On Friday evening the Consistory had their final rites service at the mortuary.

Saturday, April 9, 1983, was a bright, sunny, cool day. As I sat in the limo in front of Zion Baptist Church waiting to be escorted into the service, people stopped by to tell me how much Bill would be missed. Many were people he had helped when they needed money or had no jobs. I did not know most of them, but was pleased to hear their expressions of appreciation for his help in times of need.

It was a dignified, impressive service that justified the unknown legacy that my husband had left in Denver. Richard spoke about what a great man his father was. Gregory Alexander sand the song that exemplified Bill's life, *If I Can Help Somebody.* He was accompanied by Richard playing his violin. Rev. Boyd told again about Bill's making it possible to build our new Shorter A.M.E. Church. I was deeply impressed, but I still could not cry.

As the family was led out of the church, I was amazed to see that Zion Church was completely full, even their balcony!

There was quite a long wait forming the procession to the cemetery. We were finally on our way. My four children were in the back of the limo and all I heard was laughter and talking about our many family trips and happy get-togethers they had with their dad – even when he lost his cool! The procession was so long we could not see the end of it.

At the Highland Cemetery, as we were walking over to the grave site, Noel came to me to tell me that Eleanor would remain in their car.

"She is having a problem breathing," he said. "Her doctor has warned her that she should not come back to this high altitude, but Eleanor was determined to be here for Bill's funeral.

I replied, "Tell her I understand. Just having the two of you here means so much – especially Eleanor."

Rocky Mountain Lodge #1 performed a beautiful Masonic last rites ritual. I was amazed at the huge crowd that had followed us to Bill's final resting place.

On our way back from the cemetery, our driver said the procession was so long that the two motorcycle police escorts had a problem protecting it. Thirteen blocks!!!

When we got home, my children congregated in my bedroom to talk over memories and comfort me. They gave me some pills and told me I needed to relax and get some sleep. I was blessed to have my loving children.

The following week I received a Resolution from Denver City Council complimenting Bill's achievements as Budget Director at Lowry, and his devotion to public service in Denver through his work with the Civil Service Commission, United Way and other civic organizations.

I did not know what adjustments I would have to make, or what life would be like, now, without Bill. Our marriage had definitely been a Divine Plan, considering our age differences. When Bill died he was 63 and I was 70. However, I had forty of the happiest years of my life. All by the Grace of God!!!

Bill, Sr. with his grandchildren

CHAPTER 17
Life After Bill

One day when Richard was driving me to the mountains to get something from the house, I was talking about his dad.

"I don't know why dad had to go, and not me. We were almost always together."

"Mom, it was dad's time to go, and not yours," was Richard's calm reply.

"I guess you are right. I hadn't thought of it that way," I finally answered. "And we would have had the grandchildren with us!"

This leveled me off enough to realize that since it was Bill's time to go, this had been another one of God's life saving plans for me and the children.

My recommended attorney specialized in wills and settling estates. Bill and I had made our wills in the mid-70's, giving everything to each other. We had talked about updating them, but never got around to doing it. When I presented our will to the attorney in 1983, I was told there had been several changes that could benefit me, but unfortunately my husband's Will would have to be probated according to the date it was made. She took care of all necessary notifications to insurances and to the government. She told me I should hear from them soon. Bill had two policies with New York Life; one was double indemnity. There was a federal insurance from his civil service work with the Air Force, and my Social Security. I had it through Bill's since DPS does not have Social Security.

A few weeks went by and I heard nothing. I called my attorney to let her know. She was surprised. When she contacted New York Life Insurance, she was told they were waiting for their attorney to check on the double indemnity, although the death certificate clearly stated <u>Accidental Death</u>. Checking with the government, she was told they were working on it.

More time passed, and my only income was my small DPS pension. We had an AA credit rating, but that didn't count when I could not pay the bills while I waited for the settlement of my estate and for my bank account to be re-opened. (All of our accounts were joint, so it took a while for me to re-open them only in my name.)

I decided to check the government holdup myself. I called Washington and was told to call one office after another until I finally ended up where I started! I couldn't believe the runaround.

I remembered when we visited Rep. Pat Shroeder in Washington, that she had told us to let her know if we ever needed anything. I called her Denver office to report my problem. I was surprised when Pat Shroeder called me the next day. When I told her about my delayed experience in dealing with the federal government, she was irate and said she would take care of it. I don't know what she did, but two days later I received a phone call from a federal office informing me that I would receive everything immediately, and all compensation was retroactive to the date of Bill's death. I wrote Pat Shroeder a profound note of thanks!

I still had heard nothing from New York Life, so I called my attorney again. She said that was enough; she had plenty of evidence to sue them! It must have worked, because soon thereafter both policies were paid. Finally I could pay my bills and settle down to organizing my new life on less income, but enough to be comfortable with careful planning.

Bill and I had made a reservation for a vacation exchange two bedroom condo in Pennsylvania for a week in the summer of 1983, so we had invited Jim and JoEllen to join us. I don't remember just where it was. At first, I thought I should cancel it. However, I realized that this would be good for me to get away from Denver for a while.

I flew into New York a couple of days early. We shopped for groceries and they took care of a few needs. We were late leaving that Saturday afternoon, so it was night when we arrived at our destination. Sunday we were so tired that we enjoyed taking it easy and exploring the immediate area. On Monday morning Jim said they had to get back to Brooklyn. He took me to get a rental car so I would have transportation. They would be back in two or three days.

This proved to be a very wise move. I had time to write thank you notes, go through material that I had brought and begin to adjust to living alone.

I drove to little communities in the area. I attended a play at the little local theater. I had a list of many activities, one of which was rafting on a nearby river. That was one exciting all day trip. I was the oldest in the group, but I did my part in helping to steer the raft through the rapids. We stopped half way, went ashore and had box lunches. We were wearing "wet suites" and by the end of the trip I was really soaking wet! However, as I drove back I was relaxed and happy.

I was glad when Jim and JoEllen returned, but I realized what a blessing it was for me to have spent that time alone. We enjoyed the last few days together.

My children were concerned about my welfare during my first Christmas without their dad. To relieve me of the anxiety of going through the busy preparation for the holidays, Richard had me come to St. Paul, Minnesota, a week or more before Christmas. We would return to Denver in time to celebrate with the family.

I asked Richard what kind of clothes I should bring. He said to bring the warmest clothes that I had. I told him that my warmest were my ski clothes with my thermal underwear. He assured me that was what I would need.

He was right! I lived in my ski clothes – cap, gloves and heavy boots. It was too cold to worry about how I looked. One sunny day, it warmed up from minus 20° degrees to zero and people were delighted!

Richard and his wife were separated, but shared responsibility for little Ricky. He was with Richard most of the time, so I enjoyed caring for my three-year-old grandson. Richard took us Christmas shopping, and one day he skied while Ricky and I enjoyed being in the lodge.

The afternoon of the day before Christmas Eve, we left St. Paul in a blizzard with the snow blowing parallel across the highway, so thick that visibility was only a few yards. The temperature had dropped to 50 ° degrees below zero with an unbelievable wind chill. I was scared, so as soon as we saw the lights of a motel, I insisted that we stop for the night.

The next morning the wind continued to blow, the sun was shining, but it was still bitter cold. We continued slowly driving south on Highway 35. About thirty miles down the road we came to a cross roads town where all traffic was stopped. The highway was closed in both directions due to the gale wind and the blizzard! It was Christmas Eve and traffic was heavy with no indication the road would be opened that day. The big Holiday Inn was already full, and people were milling around trying to find accommodation. How were we going to survive in this bitter cold? Richard decided to take a little-used side road to see what we might find. Surprisingly, there was a small motel. Another car drove up just as we parked. Richard got out of the car fast, entered the office just ahead of the other driver and registered for the last room available. By the Grace of God we had a room for the night! Richard went out and found some fast food for us. There were very few businesses open in the intense cold. We sent up our prayers of thanks to the Good Lord for taking care of Richard, Ricky and me.

The highway was not opened until mid-afternoon the next day – Christmas! There were abandoned cars strewn all along the highway. With the bad weather and the late start, we had to stop again for the night, so we did not arrive in Denver until the day after Christmas! Of course, we had kept Louise informed of our problems and delays. We had a safe and happy after Christmas celebration!

Although I was living alone in the mountains, I went to choir rehearsal on Thursdays and stayed in Denver until after church services on Sunday. I had contributed as much as possible to my church, even when my funds were low. When all was settled, I began to tithe – pay first Sunday for the entire month. The Lord has blessed me, and I send up my prayers of thanks every day!

To have a winter supply of firewood for my fireplace, I bought a small electric chain saw and a 25 foot heavy duty cord which I could plug into the garage outlet. I had my ax sharpened. I would drag dead timber (Aspen or pine trees), up to the garage apron and saw them into fireplace lengths. When I ordered a cord of fireplace wood, the cut logs were thick, so I used my ax to split them. One day when I was splitting away, a neighbor stopped by and to my surprise he said he had a log splitter and would be glad to bring it over to split my fireplace wood. I appreciated his offer. Although, I am strong, splitting fireplace wood with an ax is not easy. I just had to stack the wood after he finished. I thanked him profusely and offered to pay him, but he would take no compensation. He said he was glad to make it easier for me. <u>By the Grace of God</u> he was sent just when I needed some help!

I talked about Bill to everybody, but I still had not been able to shed a tear. I began to think there was something wrong with me. One day in mid-July, over three months after his death, I took the valentine off the mantel and began to read the beautiful words of love. It finally hit me, and I began to cry. I was all alone and wept for the longest time. It took several days and nights for me to stop sobbing intermittently, whenever I thought of Bill and how much I missed him. When I finally calmed down, I realized that at last, I had released the pressure of shock that I had been carrying all those months, and I relaxed!

It was getting to be difficult to take care of both the home in the mountains and the one on 6th Avenue. I did not want to rent or sell the Denver home, although, I actually lived in the mountains. Bill, Jr. was living in his own home on Spruce Street, which his dad had helped him buy. I decided to ask him if he would like to move back to 6th Ave. <u>By the Grace of God</u>, the day that I planned to ask him, he beat me to it.

"Mom, would you mind if I moved back here?" he asked as we stood in the family home kitchen.

I laughed and said, "That's what I was going to ask you!"

My son still lives in the house in which our family grew up – The Greenwood home that we built in 1950!

My grandson, Billy, received a full scholarship to *Colorado*

Academy in Lakewood when he entered fourth grade. At the same time Louise had a contract to teach again in Colorado Springs. She wanted her son to take advantage of this education opportunity. She desperately needed the job in the Springs. What could she do? I was telling her brother Bill about her dilemma. Immediately, he said, "Billy can stay with me. I will be glad to see that he gets to *Colorado Academy*. I'll enjoy having him."

This proved to be a perfect solution. Billy would be picked up on the *Colorado Academy* bus route at West 5th Ave. and Sheridan Blvd., only a few blocks from our home. Bill would take him there by 8:30 a.m. and meet him about 4:00 p.m. When I came down to Denver, I would schedule my arrivals so that I could meet his school bus and take him home.

One day, Bill called me ahead of time to let me know that Billy was not to watch any television when I brought him home. He did not do his homework and had failed to fulfill some other request. When I met Billy at the bus stop, I was surprised when he told me why he was not to watch television and that it was his own fault. He was to do his homework and catch up on reading in his room for a week. Billy and his uncle had a great time going places and doing things together, but Bill made it clear to his nephew that he must abide by the rules.

I would help Billy with his homework. When he was having a problem with multiplication, I taught him what it meant to multiply and how to remember multiplication facts. It was different from what he was taught in school, but he let me know that it worked for him, and thanked me for my help.

Occasionally, Louise would drive to Denver with the girls to spend weekends with her son. Otherwise, I would put him on the bus to Colorado Springs (if he and his uncle didn't have other plans), to spend weekends, school breaks and holidays with his mom and his sisters. At nine years old, Billy became a happy, well-behaved little traveler of whom we were proud.

Once when I had the girls in Denver, I put them on the bus with Billy. Louise called to tell me that on arrival in Colorado Springs the bus driver got off the bus to let her know how loud and disruptive Lori and

Chrissy had been all the way. Billy was embarrassed and Louise was furious. She must have "lowered the boom" on those little girls. The next time they came to Denver on the bus, the same driver got off the bus to let me know how proud he was of Lori and Chrissy. They were so well behaved all the way, just like their brother.

Louise missed her son and wanted to have him back with her. After she married Harold Phipps, she had a family with a father for the children. Billy was in fifth grade at Colorado Academy. At the end of the first semester Louise took him home to Colorado Springs. Bill and I wanted him to finish fifth grade at the Academy, but Louise had been long enough without her son.

During the year and a half that Billy was with his Uncle Bill, they developed a close "father and son" type of understanding relationship. Billy learned some valuable lessons from a male perspective when he really needed it. He still keeps in touch with his Uncle Bill.

Richard and his second wife were divorced in 1984. Their four-year-old son's custody was given to the mother, according to Minnesota law which eventually proved to be a mistake. Richard had visiting privileges. Richard returned to Denver from St. Paul. I don't know how he met Chinn, a Korean, but they soon married. She was a fabulous artist. I have two of her unusual pictures made with fine silk threads.

Ricky came to visit his dad and we got acquainted with him. My little grandson met his cousins in Colorado Springs and Louise took him under her wing like a mother. He was so tiny to be traveling alone.

When he was five years old, Ricky came to spend the summer with Richard. He loved being with his cousins, Billy, Chrissy and Lori. His dad bought him a bicycle so he could ride with them when I took him to Colorado Springs. One day, when Louise was reprimanding the children for something they did, Ricky took off on his bike and we were upset when we could not find him. Billy got on his bike, took off and finally brought Ricky back. Those two developed a lifetime brotherly bond. Ricky learned to "face the music" just like his cousins when necessary.

Richard said Ricky did not want to go back to Minneapolis. He cried and wanted to stay with his dad. I asked him why he didn't keep him, since life with his mother was not going well. My son said if he did not send him back, he would lose all privileges to see his son.

I frequently took my three grandchildren up to the "Lazy G II," which they called "The Mountain House." Sometimes Louise would bring them to Denver, and away we would go. Otherwise, I would drive to Colorado Springs and we would take the long scenic route through the mountains: Cascade, Woodland Park, Deckers, Buffalo Creek, Pine to nearby Pine Junction on Highway 285, then home to the Mountain House. Whenever, Ricky was here to visit, I would take all four grandchildren for several days.

The "Lazy G II"

I set up, in the kitchen, the little table and four chairs that my children used when they were young. I made four scrapbooks out of paper sacks and wrapping paper with their names on them. They could cut out pictures from old magazines and catalogues and paste them in the books. I bought four scissors – three "lefties" for Lori, Chrissy and

Ricky. I tied a small red thread on the right hand one so Billy would know that was his scissor. I arranged a small, open shelf area with everything in it, including crayons, colored pencils, coloring books, easy reading books and puzzles. They had fun, but learned to clean up any mess and put things back where they belonged.

Chrissy, Ricky, Billy & Lori

We hiked among the trees. I had several board games, of which Monopoly was our favorite. We watched game shows on television. I read stories to them, usually before bedtime. I loved having my grandchildren.

Louise and I often laugh about this one "scary" incident. The children discovered a tree house that someone had built in one of the near-by pine trees. Of course, they wanted to climb up to it. I wanted to be sure it was safe, so I told them I would climb up to the tree house to check it out. I weighed more than they did collectively, so if it held me, it would hold them. If I fell, there was a lower limb I could catch on the way down as I visualized my experience at ten years old. It never occurred to me, at past seventy years old, I might not be as agile as I was a t ten. I managed to climb up the tree, and just as I reached the tree house, I heard the phone ring. I called to nine-year-old Billy to answer the phone. It was his mother calling to see how things were going. She was at a workshop in Vail.

"Where is grandma?" she asked.

"Oh, she's up in the tree house," was his answer.

"What's grandma doing up in a tree house?" gasped Louise.

"Oh, she's checking it out to be sure it will be safe for us kids," he replied. "She said if it will hold her, then she knows it will hold us."

Louise told me, later, that she could see her mother falling out of the tree. What could those three little children do to help way up there

The tree house

in the mountains?! She panicked, and had everyone at the workshop upset, as they wondered what, on earth, was an over seventy year old grandmother doing up in a tree?!

The tree house was strong with protective siding, and it held me securely. Louise was relieved when she called later and I answered the phone, all safe and sound. The children spent many happy days in that tree house.

Some of my greatest joy was during the years that I spent with my grandchildren as a loving, disciplinary, positive, understanding and happy grandmother, receiving their love and respect in return.

In 1984, when Supreme Council met in Denver, I conducted the ladies tour to the Air Force Academy as Bill and I had planned. My heart wasn't in it, but I fulfilled my commitment. At the banquet the Supreme Council Finance Committee announced that Bill's financial plan for developing the Supreme Council Benevolent Fund was accepted and would be put into effect immediately. Bill's plan is still in use. Now the Benevolent Foundation is over $85,000. Each year, at Supreme council, charities and educational institutions receive over a thousand dollars each from the Foundation.

At this Supreme Council in 1984, the first Double-Headed Eagle Award to inductees into the Scottish Rite Hall of Fame was presented. I accepted Bill's posthumous award. Every year, thereafter, I was one of the honored widows at Supreme Council – all expenses paid wherever Supreme Council met. I enjoyed meeting each year with these former wives of national Masonic officers from all over the Northern Jurisdiction and one from the South. Three of us widows, eventually developed a special friendship: Rosanna Ford from Rhode Island, Mary Williams from Indiana, Marie Greenwood from Colorado. Rosanna's husband had been Grand Minister of State, Mary's husband, Deputy of Indiana and my husband Deputy of Colorado, Wyoming and Utah. I called us "The Three Musketeers." The entire group looked after each other, but the three of us had a special close bond. Sovereign Grand Commander Brogdan called the group his "Golden Girls." His daughter, Lenore, handled plans for us and made sure we were taken care of at Supreme Council.

As the years went by, our group became fewer and fewer, until in 2000 Rosanna and I were the only two "Golden Girls" left. Mary had died of a sudden heart attack. After we memorialized Rosanna a few years later, I attended only a few more times. The Supreme Council administration had changed with a new Sovereign Grand Commander, and travel was not as easy, at my age with all the security measures, so by 2008 I lost interest and stopped attending Supreme Council. I have the wonderful memories of the friendships I made and being treated so special in honor of my husband's contribution to Masonry.

When Supreme Council met in Denver in 2000, the new class of 33° degree Masons was named the <u>William R. Greenwood, Sr. class!</u> Periodically, they have kept in touch with me.

Since Bill's death happened in 1983 approximately two weeks

before we were to celebrate our fortieth anniversary in Mexico, I called *Ports of Call* to cancel our reservation. I was told there would be no problem. My reservation would be held until I wished to use it to go anywhere I desired. Margaret took her reservation for the trip to Mexico, had a friendly roommate, and enjoyed it.

Margaret & Marie

Margaret became my traveling companion. When I felt ready to travel again, we took a pleasant trip with *Ports of Call* and became happy travel buddies. I do not remember where we went.

Our second trip was a long, for fun adventure in Europe. After hours of delay from Denver, because of strong winds and heavy rain, we finally flew to Boston. From there we flew to the tiny grand duchy of Luxembourg. After a day and a night, we went by bus to Cologne, Germany, for two days. Next was an all day trip down the Rhine River to Mainz. From there we were scheduled to go by bus into France. We had a cheerful young driver with a great sense of humor, who got lost trying to leave Germany. We finally got into France, spent a pleasant day and a night somewhere, and then drove to Paris. We stayed at the big International Hotel. We were on our own for several days, to explore the city. When we flew back home, we had had one exciting experience. Soon, thereafter, *Ports of Call* began having financial problems and the travel club closed.

Margaret and I joined another adult travel club, Specialty Tours, that planned trips especially for seniors. We took two trips within the state to make sure it was what we wanted. They were great, so we took longer tours: Boston, colorful fall New England, Hawaii, Alaska and others.

When I had my cataract surgery in 1986 and 1987, Bill, Jr. and Margaret were with me. For several days she stayed with me each time until my eyes healed. In 1990, when I realized I needed to give up living in the mountains, and move back to Denver, Margaret wanted to

334

move from where she lived, so we rented a nice apartment at Crestmoor Downs and became roommates.

While I was still living in the mountains, Richard divorced his third wife and moved in with me. He set up his quarters in the down stairs area, and was a great help to me. I told him he certainly had a problem choosing wives. He remained in the mountain house after I moved back to Denver. He became active in the little St. Laurence Episcopal Church near Conifer, was their music director, met and married his fourth wife, Judy. I deeded the house over to him to relieve me of responsibility.

Bill, Jr. wanted to know why I didn't move back to the 6th Ave. home with him, or buy a condo. I wanted no more responsibility for property; we had always owned our houses. I wanted to be free of replacements, repairs and general upkeep, so I chose to rent an apartment. Margaret and I shared expenses.

Adele and I were still close friends, and enjoyed our musical get-togethers, but gradually she began to change. She had some strange, unfounded ideas of things that were happening in her life; she became easily upset; she quit singing in the choir because of what someone said or did. She depended on me to hear what she had to say and I was always there for her, although I had no idea what was happening. (I learned years later that it was dementia.)

One day her son, Gregory, called to tell me that he found his mother dead that morning. She died in her sleep. I sang in the choir at her service. I had lost a sincere friend.

My mother needed more and more help. She still lived in her home on Lowell Blvd. and did her own cooking. Bill, Jr. no longer lived with her, but still helped as needed. I did her laundry, her shopping and took her to doctor's appointments or to visit friends. She missed going to church after she could no longer make it up the steps. However, she was always talking on the phone with friends who kept her posted on what was happening at church and in the community. She kept me up to date on all that was going on!

I had a helper come every day to help her bathe, dress, clean house and prepare meals for her. I was concerned about her being alone at night, as she began to need more and more help. I spent three nights with her. I had very little sleep, because she would call me several times to help her to the bathroom or to get something she thought of. By the end of the third night, I realized that my mother needed constant care that I was unable to give her. I was completely exhausted and would be able to help no one if I did not get some rest.

I told her doctor about my experience. He said he wondered how much longer she could remain at home. She had done so well. He recommended a small nursing home near where we lived. My mother was determined to stay home. She refused to consider a live-in assistant, even though she realized she needed help. We finally convinced her that the nursing home would be temporary help for her to get her strength back so she could return home. She was 95 years old.

Every week, when I came down from the mountains, my first stop was to check on my mother. I would bring her laundry or anything else she wanted. If she had a complaint, they heard from me loud and clear in the office. They invited me to have lunch to approve of their service. She was determined to go home, but physically she was getting weaker. She was confined to a wheelchair. However, her mind was clear and she knew everything that was going on!

In 1987, I planned to spend Thanksgiving with a friend, Camilla Jenkins, in South Carolina. Bill, Jr. would keep check on his grandma. On November 21, my grandson, Joshua James, was born. I could not get to Springfield, Va., to help Jim and JoEllen with their new baby until after Thanksgiving. JoEllen's mother, Lolita Seymour, was with them until I arrived.

I enjoyed taking care of little Josh, and helping Jim and JoEllen (Jo) to adjust to their new life as parents. They became happily dedicated to caring for their active baby son.

I had been there approximately two weeks, when son Bill called in early December to tell me that his grandma had been taken to the hospital. He had to go to work, so he called Richard to check on my mother at the hospital. (This was before Richard divorced Chinn, and was still living in Boulder.) Richard called to tell me that he arrived at the hospital just after his grandma died. He told me not to worry; he would take care of everything.

I told Jim I had to get back home, but my reservation was for weeks away. Immediately, Jim said he would take care of it; in fact, he would get a ticket to go home with me. He did not want me going alone. During the next several days, Richard kept me informed. One day Elvin Caldwell, from the mortuary, called to assure me that all was going well. Jim got the tickets. A friend would help Jo with the baby, so we returned to Denver.

I was relieved to find all plans were completed, and my mother's funeral service was scheduled for less than two weeks before Christmas at Shorter, the church that she dearly loved. Rev. Boyd had visited with her many times at the nursing home. Richard told of his wonderful spiritual visits with his grandmother, as she actually spoke with God. At 96 years old, my mother was buried next to my father at Highland Cemetery.

As I look back over the years, I can see what a strong role model my mother was in my life. I am now aware of the many lessons I learned from her that have helped to make me the person that I am today: the value of true friendships (be a friend through thick and thin); importance of discipline in one's life; the joy of being a woman, wife, mother and grandmother; do good, do not harm anyone; being honest; knowing right from wrong; most of all, a strong, everlasting faith in God!

Sarah & Joseph Anderson, parents

Louise took me to her home in Colorado Springs to spend 1987

Christmas holidays with her and her family.

80th birthday celebration

In 1992, Richard planned a special family celebration for my 80th birthday. He knew I loved seafood, so he made a reservation for the party at *Fresh Fish Factory*. He said someone would come to get Margaret and me.

On the evening of November 22nd (two days before my birthday), we were ready when we received word that our pick-up was here. We went downstairs and out the door looking for a car. To our surprise, there was a limo waiting for us! Judy's mother and dad, the Stolls, greeted us when we entered the limo, so the four of us arrived at the celebration in high style!

It was a happy, relaxed, family get-together. There were my children, grandchildren, extended families of Seymours and Stolls. The only one whom I wished could have been there was my son Jim.

Soon, in walked my missing son! My children had planned Jim's arrival as a complete surprise for me. I was elated!!!

When the wait staff brought in my birthday cake, they could not believe I was 80 years old – a real compliment! We enjoyed the food. We visited. We took pictures. We laughed and were happy. I will always remember my 80th birthday celebration as one of the highlights of my life!!!

Margaret, Vernease and I continued to sing in the choir, whenever and wherever it went. The three of us were among the regular helpers serving dinner after funerals. Mrs. Kinney was in charge of our kitchen at Shorter and had everything well organized. We would arrive early to set the tables and follow whatever plans Mrs. Kinney had for us. Margaret took charge of punch and coffee. I became the hot table server and Vernease helped everywhere. We stayed afterward to clean up.

Margaret and I continued our travels, but she was beginning to show a slow change. She gradually stopped communicating with me and seemed to resent me. I had to remind her to pay a bill, or of scheduled activities at church or elsewhere. Since I had no idea of what was happening, I attributed it to change in old age, although I was much older than she.

Fortunately, her daughter, Joy, returned to Denver, saw the change in her mother and had her medically checked. The resulting analysis was the beginning of dementia. I had no idea what that was, until Joy explained to me that it was a mental condition that precedes the development of Alzheimers disease. Now I understand what was happening, and what had happened to Adele. This was a new learning experience for me. When my parents died their minds were perfectly clear; their bodies just wore out.

Margaret had to be placed in a care facility. Whenever Joy took me to see her, her face would light up when she heard my name, then she would forget and ask who I was.

In January 2006, she turned 90. Her daughter, granddaughter, great grandson and I had a little party at the nursing home for her. She enjoyed it with us, but she did not remember that it was <u>her</u> birthday. Margaret died on Christmas day 2007. I lost another good friend.

Vernease and I continued to sing in the choir and serve wherever needed. Our friendship grew stronger as we did things together.

I had three other funerals to attend in California. When Eleanor's husband, Noel, died, I was there as soon as possible to be with her and her family, just as she had been for me.

In January 1993, Eleanor had just passed away. She missed her 81st birthday by one week. I got a ticket and reservation immediately, and flew into Burbank. (I managed to avoid LAX!) Bill's cousin Sue met me and I stayed with her in Pasadena. Eleanor's home was in nearby Altadena. All three of us were friends and AKA's. Eleanor and I had been friends for 67 years. She was the one person whom I loved as a real sister!

In December, 2000, I received a call from Emerson Williams telling me my friend, Fannie Williams had died in Washington, D.C. the loss of Jeannie and Fannie left me as the last of our <u>Triangle</u>. I shall always cherish the memories of that unique friendship we had long ago.

I don't remember what year it was when I received a call from Sue's niece telling me of the sudden death of Sue. When she did not arrive for her volunteering schedule at Meals-on-Wheels, her sister checked to find her sitting at her breakfast table, dead of a possible heart attack! Again, I flew off to Burbank to be with the family of Bill's cousin, with whom I had developed such a close relationship.

On February 28, 2002 we attended a great celebration in Colorado Springs. William Seymour, the first Black Juror in El Paso County was honored – the grandfather of Winfred Seymour.

In 1843, William Seymour was born into slavery in Kentucky. In the late 1890's he and his wife, Elizabeth and their children moved west and established a prosperous farm and dairy north of Colorado Springs.

The family moved into town after Mr. Seymour retired. He was the first person of color to serve on a jury in the new El Paso Courthouse in 1903. It now houses the Colorado Springs Pioneer Museum, in which there is a fabulous picture of the William Seymour family.

In 2002, we attended the dedication of the life-size, bronze statue of William Seymour standing on the Northwest corner of the Museum property. Since my two youngest grandchildren, Josh and Jenna, are both Seymours and Greenwoods they are the descendents of two honored achieving Colorado pioneers. Their great, great-grandfathers are William Seymour and Joseph D.D. Rivers.

Jenna & Josh at the Seymour statue dedication

By the Grace of God, my life has continued on in the most satisfying and unexpected way. I have continued my church activities. (I gave up singing in the choir when my voice became "iffy" after seventy years!) I kept on traveling and volunteering. However, one of my most satisfying and happy activities were the years I spent helping with my grandchildren, from birth through high school and college. My next chapter tells why I am so proud of them.

BY THE GRACE OF GOD

CHAPTER 18
Grand Achievers

Ray William Weathersby (Billy), my oldest grandson, was deathly afraid of the water as a young child. When he was three months old Louise took him to a "Mom and Tots" swim class, but he screamed and wanted no part of it. His mother could not get him to put a foot in a pool even when he was older. (Taking a bath was no problem.) When he was six years old, he finally consented to take swimming lessons, so he could play with his friends who had pools in their yards. Louise was taking no chances of her son drowning. They had moved to Mesa, Arizona.

To everyone's surprise, this little six year old became such a strong, fast swimmer that he began to swim in competition. After they returned to Denver, I saw him, at nine years old, compete against ten and eleven year old boys and win! He continued swimming competitively until sixth grade, when he became interested in playing football.

That summer he attended the Broncos' Football Camp in Greeley as a wide receiver. He was smaller than most of the boys, but amazingly, at the end of camp he was awarded "Most Valuable Player"!

In high school Billy invented an <u>Automatic Toilet Seat Put-Downer</u> with a hydraulic lever to lower the seat. It won third place in the National Duracell Invention Competition! (This was an inspiration from complaints from his mother and two sisters about leaving the toilet seat up.)

In 1992, he was an honored Beau in an early Jack and Jill Beautilion here in Denver. He graduated from Coronado High School in Colorado Springs in 1993. Academically he qualified to enter the Air Force Academy. His grades were great! Instead, he entered the Air Force Academy Prep School on a football scholarship for a year in preparation for playing football in the Academy

In 1994, Ray William Weathersby became a cadet in the United

Lieutenant Ray
Weathersby with his
mother, Louise & father,
Ray, Sr. at the Air Force
Academy graduation

States Air Force Academy. He was wide receiver #84 on the football team. They won the Commander in Chief Trophy every year. He flew gliders and received his "jump wings," for jumping out of a plane five times.

In 1996, his squadron #32 was chosen as representative of the Air Force to march in the Presidential Inauguration Day parade.

His senior year in 1998, he met President Clinton in the Oval office. His picture was taken as he accepted the Commander in Chief Trophy for Football. His mother cherishes the photograph of her son receiving this "Seniors Only" award from President Clinton!

Upon graduation in 1998, he was assigned to Langley Air Force Base in Virginia as a Communication Officer. To my grandson, graduating from the Air Force Academy was a special tribute honoring his grandfather, William R. Greenwood, for his pioneering work as its first Budget Director in helping to establish this military institution.

In 2001, he was transferred to Scott Air Force Base in Illinois as part of the Engineering Flight of the Air Force Communication Agency. He became a Captain. He was sent to Air Force bases all over the world to work with communications (Europe, Japan, Africa, etc.)

He was honorably separated from the Air Force in 2004. He started an outreach ministry called With Jesus Christ's Spiritual Blessing. Billy was beginning to lose his eye sight. He thought of his "paw-paw" telling him how he led his grandfather, Mr. Rivers, when he became blind. Billy was fortunate enough to have a cornea transplant that restored his sight. His spiritual belief paid off!

He has developed a successful company called <u>ANOINT – Information Technologies, Corp</u>. His contracts are with the government – Army, Air Force and Navy. It is growing!

He bought a large, roomy, beautiful house in O'Fallon, Illinois across the Mississippi River from St. Louis, Missouri.

In 2005, Billy and Tracee Jackson, whom I liked from the day I met her in 2001, were married in a beautiful ceremony uniting another warm family to ours.

Tracee and Ray (Billy)   Lauren and Michael

They developed a happy home with his business office right there. I now have two loveable great grandchildren – Lauren Marie born in May 2006, and Michael Ray born in December 2007. Tracee was a physical education teacher. She is now a dedicated stay-at-home mom and a "down to earth" partner for Billy. They are wonderful parents.

They moved to Greensboro, North Carolina to be near Tracee's parents. This was a blessing when Tracee's father died suddenly. They are there to help her mother and grandmother – all <u>by the Grace of God</u>!

I am proud of this young, intelligent, successful business man that everyone knows as Ray William Weathersby; but to me, he will always be my beloved grandson, <u>Billy</u>.

Christina Marie Weathersby (Chrissy) was a tiny little child with a mind of her own and was not afraid of anything. She learned to walk early, and after approximately ten months old, her mother took her to the "Moms and Tots" swim class. Unlike her brother, she scared me and Louise by suddenly jumping into the pool. Fortunately, her mother was there and rescued her!

Chrissy, dressed for "The Nutcracker," 1988

At fifteen months old, Chrissy wanted to go to pre-school with her brother. One day she was playing in the yard with a little friend while the mothers visited in the kitchen and would occasionally check on them. The child came in alone and said Chrissy was gone. Louise panicked when she saw the yard was really empty. Chrissy had climbed over the special high fence that enclosed their yard! Louise drove frantically block after block. No one she asked had seen the child. Finally, she drove near Billy's pre-school and there was little Chrissy just arriving. She had crossed several streets safely. How she knew the way to get to her brother's pre-school is still a mystery to Louise!

Little did we realize that this young child's fearless independence was an indication of her potential for future achievement.

When Chrissy was ten years old she was enrolled in a gymnastics class that met once a week during the summer. She not only finished that class, but she completed all the classes given in that gymnastics course that summer! Six years later she was a Level 10 Junior Olympics National Champion, winning the silver medal on the uneven bars. I saw her compete with skill and determination.

She was an Owl Club Debutante here in Denver in 1996, when she graduated from high school in Colorado Springs.

Chrissy had twelve scholarship offers. She accepted the full athletic scholarship in gymnastics at Michigan State University. I saw her compete in Michigan State Big Ten Gymnastics her freshman and sophomore years.

In 1998, she had injuries. She was wearing a knee support and a bandaged ankle in competition. However, on her uneven bars performance, she made a grade of 9.75 for which she won the Bronze! Her dismount was perfect! I was so proud of my granddaughter. She became a member of the All Conference Gymnastics Team.

It was after this competition that she took me to see the movie *Titanic* – a special treat just for the two of us!

Chrissy graduated from Michigan State in 2000 with a major in Psychology. She was invited to audition in Las Vegas for Disney World. Her performance was tops! She was offered a job as one of the two female star aerialists in the Tarzan Rocks Show in the Animal Kingdom. It included rollerblading between acts.

Since Christmas holidays are busy times at Disney World, Chrissy had to perform. We spent three Christmas' in Orlando – 2000, 2001 and 2002. The first two times we rented apartments for

Chrissy's college graduation

the family. Chrissy had bought a house in 2002, so we spent the happy holidays at her home. It was a thrill watching Chrissy perform, and a joy visiting the exciting activities in the area.

Discrimination at Disney World became evident as other top level performers were promoted, but Chrissy was not. She had had a bit of filmmaking experience in Miami. Under these circumstances, Chrissy felt ready to make a transition to the film industry.

In 2003, Louise, the grandchildren and I were planning to attend a family reunion with Bill's cousins in California at the same time that Chrissy had made her move. She knew no one and really needed a helping hand. We were having a wonderful time getting acquainted and happily telling of our varied family experiences. When Sue's daughter,

Evangeline Lewis (Vange), heard Chrissy tell of her new move to California without knowing anyone, immediately, Vange said, "You can stay with me. I will be glad to have you."

During the time that Chrissy spent under the protective care of Vange, they developed a life-long friendship. This was obviously another one of the Lord's Plan! It was the first time my grandchildren had met any of these cousins.

Chrissy slowly began to develop her stunt career. She became so efficient, trustworthy and reliable that she was in constant demand for stunt work.

Chrissy has performed in over seventy feature films and TV shows. She has won two Screen Actors' Guild Awards for best stunt ensembles for feature films, *Inception* and *Star Trek*_(2009).

She has received many nominations for other stunt work in feature films. One was the World Stunt Awards.

One of her latest feature films was *X-Men*. She performed all of the stunts for the female star. In the flight scene, that was Chrissy strapped to the underside of a helicopter! In the film there is no helicopter. Only the character is seen flying through the air. She recently told me that she is in the new *Batman* film that will be released this summer (2012).

Eddie & Chrissy Ball

In July 2010 Eddie Ball (a graduate of University of Tennessee and also an executive in a major corporation in southern California), and Chrissy were married in Cincinnati, Ohio, with his wonderful family. It was one of the merriest weddings I have ever attended! They still live in California. Christina Marie Ball is now taking yoga lessons to become an instructor. However, she will always be known and loved as <u>Chrissy</u>!

Lori Ann Weathersby was "mama's little girl." Unlike her older dare-devil sister Chrissy, Lori would cry if she fell on the lawn and came up with a grass stain.

One day she was watching the Olympics and was fascinated with the performance of a Black girl figure skating. Lori was excited and told her mother that's what she wanted to do. Louise could not visualize her daughter out on that cold hard ice falling down. However, as days went on, Lori's enthusiastic determination to be an ice skater grew.

Finally, Louise checked the *Broadmoor World Arena* in Colorado Springs and found that membership in the *Broadmoor Skating Club* was only $20 per month. She enrolled both Chrissy and Lori and rented skates. This was in 1988. Lori was only nine years old and loved every minute of her lessons. She would fall on the hard cold ice, get up and keep going. Louise was amazed. Within two months she had gone through every level of instruction. Chrissy did not like skating so she quit and entered gymnastics.

After observing Lori, three coaches asked to coach her. Louise had to think about possible competition interfering with school. She accepted a coach, but told her that the special coaching would be on Saturdays in the summer when school was out. That summer Lori learned all the jumps and turns and loved every minute of it. Louise finally bought skates, on sale, as she recognized her daughter's figure skating talent.

Lori continued regular skating lessons at the Broadmoor. Louise laughs when she tells of the little white dress with red polka dots and a full skirt that Lori insisted on wearing to rehearsals, while the other girls were in jeans. She wore it every time until she outgrew the dress. Louise was at all rehearsals.

Lori had been skating for less than a year when I saw her in her first competition here in Denver. She performed beautifully. I was so proud of her as she stood on the podium in <u>second place</u>! She was so tiny.

Lori as 1st Place
Champion
of the 1991
Southwestern
Regionals

As a representative of the *Broadmoor Skating Club*, Lori was the regional figure skating champion of the *Southwestern Regional Championship* for three years – 1991, 1992 and 1993! I attended all of her performances here in Denver and at the Broadmoor.

Lori performed in all of the shows at the Broadmoor. The last one that I saw was *Christmas Pops on Ice* with the Colorado Springs Symphony. The Olympic champion, Scott Hamilton, was fabulous, and my granddaughter soloed beautifully!

Chrissy and Lori were asked to appear on *Tonight* and other shows, since they were two Black girls who were champions in their related sports. However, Louise was very protective of her children and did not want them exposed to the glamour and pressure of publicity so young. Chrissy and Lori were permitted to appear on only one talk show. That was the end of that!

Louise wrote a curriculum for the classroom about world junior figure skating champions to present to school children. It starred Scott Hamilton and Lori. It was filmed by Fox Network.

The last *International Figure Skating Competition* was held at the old *World Broadmoor Arena* in 1994. The building was closed and demolished to make room for the expansion of the Broadmoor Hotel. Louise found another ice skating class for Lori, but she no longer had the friends, coaches and enthusiastic competition that made Broadmoor skaters a close-knit family. Her interest waned and she stopped skating. Thus ended a great experience to remember!

Lori graduated from high school in 1997 and was an honored debutante in Colorado Springs.

She entered Hampton University in Virginia from which her father,

Ray Weathersby, and her great, great grandfather, Joseph D.D. Rivers, had graduated. Lori was near her brother who was still at Langley Air Force Base, and he looked after his little sister.

In the spring of 2000, Louise and I were at Hampton to witness and participate in Lori's initiation into Alpha Kappa Alpha Sorority under my Legacy Provision as our third generation Soror. In 2001, Lori graduated from this historic institution with a major in English and Mass Media.

She became a cheerleader with the Miami Dolphins immediately and worked as an instructor in a real estate company in Miami. Lori left the Dolphins after one season and moved to Orlando to be with Chrissy in her new home. (These sisters have an inseparable bond.) Lori had a skin problem from the time she was a teenager, so she was fortunate enough to find employment in a cosmetic skin care company. She learned so much about skin products and thoroughly enjoyed the work.

Lori graduates from Hampton University

In 2003, Lori had the opportunity to go to Japan. She was the assistant to the Dean of Academic Affairs at the *University of Maryland Asian Division*. Along with her many educational activities, she taught English to some Japanese executives in a national corporation, and learned a bit of Japanese herself. Lori became a model on the cover of a Japanese magazine! She sent me a portrait of her that was used for this exciting experience.

After flying the long distance so many times for family events, Lori decided to return home to the United States. She found a job with a major skin care company and became a top executive trainer.

She met Eddie Moore, a graduate of the University of Tennessee who was a Miami Dolphins football player. This romance blossomed and in March 2007 Eddie and Lori were married at a private country

Eddie & Lori Moore

351

club in Boca Raton, Florida. It was a beautiful, sacred wedding.

At the end of 2006-2007 football season, Eddie was traded to the Denver Broncos. What a great surprise to have the newly-weds here in Denver!

Lori was a tremendous help when it was my turn to host Coterie. She planned and prepared the menu, and served as a delightful hostess at our meeting. She met Alpha Kappa Alpha Sorority sisters and transferred to Epsilon Nu Omega chapter, but did not have the opportunity to participate.

Unfortunately, Lori's planned activities here in Denver came to an abrupt end. Within a short time with the Broncos Eddie had a severe knee injury and decided to retire from football. They moved to Tennessee near his family.

Lori Ann Moore is the traveling consultant for a major make-up company. She consults and trains the staff at stores – even one assignment at *Sack's Fifth Avenue*! Her territory now covers Southeast Atlantic states. She and Eddie are developing a company of their own, *Skin, Hair, Beauty, Inc.*, which they hope will eventually become a beauty store.

Eddie is a Branch Manager and Assistant Vice President of a bank in Chattanooga. <u>By the Grace of God</u>, Eddie fully recovered from his knee injury.

I am blessed to have lived long enough to see my three oldest grandchildren successful in their careers and happily married to loving companions.

Louise was a devoted mother who actually put her life "on hold" until her children were in college. While Billy was at the Air Force Academy she opened her doors to cadets as a "home away from home" for them. With Lori's skating activities and Chrissy's gymnastic competitions, she was always there no matter what it cost or where it was held. Whenever Louise was gone, I would be with the children who were at home.

Louise finally went back to her dancing – ballet!

She entered the Masters program at the University of Northern Colorado. After completing her Masters Degree in Communications, she was unable to attend her own graduation because it was scheduled for May 6, 2000, the same day as Chrissy's graduation at Michigan State University. Of course, we were all in East Lansing, Michigan with Chrissy!

Louise dancing at AKA Founder's Day - 2002

My grandchildren can give their mother credit for being the powerful force that has helped them to become the successful achievers in their professions. My greatest reward is when they call to tell me how much they love me and that I am their role model.

My grandson, Ricardo Pierre Greenwood (Ricky), had a stressful, confusing childhood when his parents divorced and custody was given to his mother. Ricky was always happy when he came to visit his dad, Richard, and spent time with us. He bonded with his three cousins. Ricky was eleven years old before Richard was able to legally prove that his son was living in an abusive, unstable environment in Minnesota with his mother. He gained custody of Ricky. By this time the boy had developed frustrated, insecure, confused attitudes. Richard sent him to St. John's Military School in Kansas. I was there for his graduation and saw a much calmer, happier boy. He participated in several parts of the graduation program. His singing of the SJM school Alma Mater was beautiful!

Ricky & Marie, at his
graduation

Richard, Marie & Ricky

Ricky has had problems as he has matured. He lives in Kansas. He now has two young sons, Trace and Conner, whom he dearly loves and is trying to be the kind of parent to them that he never had. I saw Trace when he was a baby. I have not seen Conner. I hear from him only occasionally, but he keeps in close touch with his cousin Billy, who is like a big brother to him. I keep Ricky in my prayers constantly. I love my grandson and hope to see those great grandchildren. I just received word that I have a second great granddaughter, Alexis Marie.

Trace, Connor & Alexis
Marie Greenwood, great-
grandchildren

Jim and Jo moved back to Denver from Springfield, Virginia, in early 1994 with their two children, Joshua (Josh) six years old and Jenna, two and a half. Josh became a first grader at the Stanley British Primary School (BPS) and Jenna was in the Child Care Center at Park Hill Methodist Church. It was great having my two youngest grandchildren here.

JoEllen, James, Jenna & Josh

Josh

Jenna

My greatest joy was reading to them. About once a week we had story time together. Since Josh was in first grade and learning to read, I not only read to him, but I had easy stories for him to read to me. This way, I taught him to read smoothly and with expression. As time went on, I had him imagine what the characters were like and read the dialogue in voices that fit. We had fun!

Josh was an energetic little fellow who had started doing gymnastics when he was three or four years old in Springfield, Virginia.

He continued gymnastic classes here in Denver and won many awards in competition.

Josh's enthusiasm and skill won him the opportunity to be invited to an international gymnastics competition in London, England, July 25, 1999, where there would be teams from England, France, Belgium and Italy. His dad went with him. He was eleven years old.

Josh was housed with a host family in London. The meet was held at Hillingdon School of Gymnastics and the United States team won second place. He had a wonderful time seeing the highlights of London and meeting interesting people from other teams. JoEllen and Jenna flew over later so the family had a few days to explore London together.

By the time he was in fifth grade I was no longer reading with him. He was busy with school, soccer, gymnastics and other activities. However, one day when I was reading with Jenna, Josh came in excitedly and exclaimed, "Grandma, I have something I want to read to you!" It was a story with various characters to whom he gave individual voices of expressions as he read. With his enthusiastic presentation, you could almost see each one. This was probably the first indication of his talent for acting! Josh could sing! He was in the Rocky Mountain Children's Choir for several years.

BPS only went through fifth grade, at that time, so Josh entered middle school at Graland Country Day School. He was an excellent student and performed in many of their programs. He remained at Graland through ninth grade instead of going to high school as a freshman. He had made many friends at this school with whom he was developing the joy of performing.

When Josh entered East Denver High School some of his Graland friends enrolled there also. His first year at East he was given a part to play in *Androcles and the Lion*. There was very little speaking, but Josh certainly played the part. We were proud of him in his first theatrical role!

While at East High School Josh had star roles in *The Wiz*, *Oklahoma* and *Fiddler on the Roof*. He sang, danced and performed in character. He sang in the *Chambers Choir* of choral music and in

356

the *Angelaires Vocal Jazz Group*. Josh was involved in many school activities, physically and academically.

In 2004, Josh was one of the honorees of the *Links Tribute to Black Youth*. He was a Jack and Jill Beautillion Beau in 2005.

At his graduation from East High School in 2006, Josh sang with the Angelaires and sang a solo with the Honor Choir.

Kappa Alpha Psi Fraternity honored him with the Winifred Coker Memorial Scholarship.

The highest of Denver's society is Denver Ballet Guild's *Le Bal de Ballet* presenting Debutantes and Young Men of Distinction. Mr. Joshua James Seymour Greenwood, son of Mr. and Mrs. James Lee Greenwood, Denver, was one of two

Josh & Marie at the LINKS Tribute to Youth Awards

young men of color who were honored among the forty male honorees presented! Josh was a leader and received many honors while in high school.

A month after entering the University of Colorado at Boulder, Josh performed in the play, *All that I Have Lost* that focused on language and expression. He was the only freshman in this cast of characters that was admitted to the *Department of Theatre and Dance* to pursue a Bachelor of Fine Arts in Performance degree!

I saw Josh perform in many plays. He was always in character, whether it was comedy, drama or mystery.

In 2009, his theater professor recommended him to a friend in New York who conducted a summer theater workshop. Josh spent that summer learning more about theater and exploring New York City. He loved it!

We were in Boulder on May 8, 2010, when Josh graduated with

357

a degree in Bachelor of Fine Arts in Performance. Friends with whom Josh had gone through East High School and C.U. together had formed a comedy group, so off they went to Scotland to perform in the *Edinburgh Fringe Festival*. They were the highlight of the event! They spent some time traveling in Europe before returning to the United States.

Some of his friends settled in New York and Josh returned to Denver in preparation to joining them in the Big City. He spent about six months working, saving his money and preparing to move to New York.

Now, he is happily enjoying that busy metropolis life. He has a job with the Gibbon Company. He is the demonstrator for their *Slack Line*, a bouncy tight rope. (It is actually made in Boulder.) His balance and agility are amazing! I saw him perform on the Slack Line one morning on a television show.

He is also checking on auditioning and working in theater and film. With his charming personality and positive goals, Josh is well on his way to success.

Most of all, he keeps in close touch with his family and comes home as often as possible.

Jenna, my youngest grandchild, entered BPS kindergarten at five years old. She joined a soccer team of five-year-olds and became the leading scorer! She continued playing soccer on through high school, becoming an outstanding goalie on her team – even asked to play guest goalie on other teams.

About third grade Jenna wanted to play in the band at BPS. She learned to play the clarinet so quickly that within weeks she was playing in the band. However, for some unknown reason, she became interested in playing the drums like her dad. He taught her the basics; her rhythm was perfect and she became an enthusiastic, skilled drummer.

For several years Jenna sang in the Rocky Mountain Children's Choir and later was a guest drummer with the choir.

358

BPS expanded from fifth grade to eighth grade, so Jenna remained there through middle school. I attended the annual Grandparents' Days while my grandchildren were at BPS.

In 2005, Jenna Marie Seymour Greenwood graduated from Stanley British Primary School and entered East Denver High School as a freshman.

During her four years at East High School she played drums in the band and sang in the Seraphim Choir. At her graduation in 2009, Jenna was the special drummer in the band.

In 2008, Jenna was a recipient of the *Links Tribute to Black Youth Award*. That summer she had the privilege of traveling to South Africa with the *Seeking Common Ground*, a group of young people learning about other cultures. She played drums with various bands there, resulting in her acquiring some African drums.

The summer of 2009 Jenna traveled with this same group to Israel to study cultural issues and conflicts in the Middle East. She enrolled in Colorado University at Boulder in the same year that Josh was a senior. Her brother was a help in easing her adjustment to freshman college life. She continued to play soccer during her freshman and sophomore years at C.U. until she became actively involved in other activities. Sometimes she referees soccer games with her dad.

James, Marie, JoEllen, Josh & Jenna at her LINKS Tribute to Youth Award ceremony

Jenna is finishing her junior year at Colorado University. She is now chairperson of the Culture Events Board, which is part of student government that sponsors cultural events. President Obama was their recent outstanding presentation! They have a budget of half a million dollars.

Jenna is looking forward to graduation in 2013, with a major in Sociology and a minor in Religious Studies. She plans to continue graduate studies at the University of Northern Colorado in *Higher Education and Student Affairs Leadership*. Jenna could be the third generation of our family to attend U.N.C. The future will tell.

By the Grace of God I have lived long enough to be an active part in my grandchildren's lives and to see them succeed. I love them dearly and I am proud of all of them!!

CHAPTER 19

Happy "Highs" and One Final "Low"

After I moved back into Denver in May of 1990, I had more free time and needed to keep busy with volunteer activities. For years I had wanted to record for the blind, since I love to read and have a clear voice. When I finally managed to get the information I needed, the place and recording schedule would be difficult for me. In the mean time, I had become involved in the <u>Dr. Justina Ford Community Project</u>, since I was one of the few people left who had known her.

I don't remember how I became involved in a Buddy Reading program in the fall of 1990. (I think that's what it was called.) I was assigned to a first grade at Park Hill Elementary School. I was paired with a little boy who was non-communicative, seldom talked and was showing very little signs of learning. The teacher was unable to get any response from him.

The only quiet place where we could go was in a corner of the library with comfortable seating and a small table, at a time when no classes were there. Fortunately, this fit my schedule.

It took days of patiently working with him to get him to gradually open up and talk to me. We worked on beginning reading with books that I brought and used some of my former first grade materials. We did simple math. He began to show some interest. He finally became an animated little boy and began learning. He had a strong average mind! We had fun.

One morning when I arrived, the teacher met me with the news that my little "Buddy" was gone. She said he had come to life, was reading, talking and actively participating in class activities. She was amazed at how I brought him out, and she thanked me for what I had done. I did my best, but it was really just another one of God's little miracles!

I called Volunteers of America and found they had a Retired Senior Volunteer Program (RSVP). They told me about the Denver Public Library Read Aloud program. I applied and was given a date and time to meet personnel at the Main Library. I requested to read in Northeast Denver. I was accepted and assigned to read to the Clayton Center Pre-school children.

There were two pre-schools. I was reading to "Head Start." Soon there was a request for me to read to "Family Futures," also. Each week I would receive one bag of books from, and return my previous bag of books to Park Hill Library. The Clayton Center is just across the street (Martin Luther King Blvd.) from my church. Since Shorter had a daycare program, (Sarah Allen Pre-school), with young children in the 1990's, I checked with the director to see if they would like to have me read to them. They were delighted! So every Tuesday when I finished reading at Clayton, I went over to Shorter and read to two groups – 2 ½ and 3 year olds, then 4 and 5 year olds.

One day a little five-year-old surprised me with a cheerful grin and said, "Mrs. Greenwood, I like your stories. I feel like I am really in the story!"

I got Sarah Allen Pre-school scheduled into the regular Read Aloud Program. When I would go to Park Hill Library, I would see many beautiful, exciting books that I would like to read to the children. I began checking out books on my library card, in addition to the books in my bag. Soon, I did not need my card. I was put on the computer!

Eventually, I accepted an additional assignment to read at Park Hill Elementary School through the Read Aloud Program. This was on Thursdays with ECE and each of the two kindergartens. This gave me a full schedule – four groups on Tuesday and the three groups on Thursday.

My stories are carefully prepared ahead of time. I select stories to fit each group, and present them in a manner to hold the children at their maturity level. I discovered the series of stories about *Clifford the*

Big Red Dog, so all of my reading sessions ended with a story about Clifford.

Several times I was asked to read in first and second grades at Park Hill, but after accepting a few times, I had to refuse because my time was full with my regular schedule. I was happy reaching as many children as possible.

I had a short assignment to read to kindergarten at Barrett Elementary School. I was surprised to find the principal was one of my former first graders, Maceo Broadnax! We had a joyful reunion. The kindergarten teacher was so impressed with my reading that he gave me a Clifford hand puppet. From then on, I had an "animated" Clifford who helped me with his stories wherever I was reading. At Park Hill I became known as "Clifford's Mother." The children of all ages loved Clifford!

I felt honored when I was asked to demonstrate my reading techniques to other volunteers at a Read Aloud meeting. The Read Aloud program was designed to expose young children to books early and to stimulate interest in reading before entering school. Once a week for ½ hour a variety of stories were read to each group. The children were encouraged to react and enjoy the wonders found in books. At the end of each ten week's session, each child was given a book to take home and a library card application to encourage the children and parents to use the library.

Since I am so dedicated to believing in the importance of teaching a child to read, this Read Aloud Program, exposing children early to stories, was exactly what I needed. I enjoyed reading to every group, but Sarah Allen Pre-school was special.

There was no summer Read Aloud, but one summer I consented to read at Sarah Allen, which had school aged children in their care along with the pre-school. I did not know what to do with these older children, but I wanted to help them maintain their interest and ability in reading.

I arranged my schedule for every Tuesday to run for approximately an hour and a half. I would read to the two pre-school groups for twenty minutes each, leaving forty-five minutes, or more, for the six to ten year olds.

These school aged children were my challenge! At the library I checked out books of stories about adventure, mystery, comedy, Dr. Seuss and anything else that might be appealing. I involved them in interaction with stories as much as possible. I found an easy reading story that I passed around one day and had them take turns reading a page out loud. I was pleased at how these older children responded. I was amazed when some of the six and seven year olds asked me about Clifford. They remembered from pre-school. To my surprise, this older group enjoyed having me end my reading session with a Clifford story and my hand puppet!

I spent twelve years enjoying my volunteering through the Read Aloud Program. I stayed with Sarah Allen Pre-school until it closed.

In 1994, I received the Denver Public Library Volunteer of the Year Award, with a Resolution from City and County of Denver at a City Council meeting. I received the Dr. Juanita Gray Community Service Award in 1995.

One year the ECE and kindergarten teachers at Park Hill submitted my name to Channel 9 Who Care in appreciation for my years of reading to their classes.

In 2000, Omar and Jeweldine Blair nominated me for KMGH Denver's 7 Everyday Hero in recognition of my years spent serving Sarah Allen Pre-school. I treasure these surprising recognitions!

In February, 1999, I was interested in reading the revealing columns about outstanding Denverites during Black History Month, when I received a call telling me that a reporter and photographer from the *Rocky Mountain News* would be at Park Hill Elementary School to observe me reading to the children in ECE. What a surprise!

When I arrived, the reporter and photographer were already there. They stayed through the entire half hour, taking pictures and watching me read. After I finished, the reporter asked me if he could interview me. Since we could not think of a quiet place to talk, he asked if he could interview me at home. I had read to the two kindergartens before ECE, so I was planning to go home. Being comfortable at home was fine with me, so he followed me to my apartment.

After nearly an hour of interesting, relaxed visiting, he told me that he was amazed at how I kept the fascinated attention of those young children. He had expected to spend a short time in a squirming, fidgety class of pre-schoolers, but he stayed to watch me. He said he would let me know when the article would appear in the paper; then he said goodbye and left. This was Alan Dumas, a feature writer for the *Denver Rocky Mountain News.*_

Days went by and I heard nothing. Finally, I got a call from Alan, telling me that he presented my story to his editor, who was so impressed that he decided to run it as a <u>feature article!</u> A few days before Valentine's Day, they came to take more pictures. My grandson, Billy, came just as Alan and the photographer were leaving, so they took a picture of my grandson giving me a box of chocolates as a Valentine's present!

On February 21, 1999, to my amazement, there was a huge picture of me titled "A Class Act" on the cover of the *Rocky Mountain News Sunday Spotlight*!!! Inside there were 2 ½ pages of my story with pictures titled "Public-school Pioneer." I had no idea that this publicity would be a "springboard" to more honors and recognition!

We are a music-loving family – dancer, Louise; saxophone player, Bill, Jr.; drummer, Jim. However, the love of music was Richard's passion. He lived and breathed delivering messages through his amazing mastering of playing the violin with soulful feeling. He could play classical, jazz, and religious. You name it and he could play it. Richard's experiences and performances were so widely varied that I can write about only a few highlights that I remember.

During the 1980's Richard was the violinist at *Cliff Young's*, one of Denver's exclusive restaurants. He would wander among the diners, serenading with his violin. They could choose from a list of over 200 songs and Richard would play especially for them. One night, he invited Margaret and me to Cliff's as his guests. I was amazed at his relaxed performance, and the quiet, responsive enjoyment of the diners. When Cliff Young opened his jazz club, *Ruby*, next door, Richard was in charge. He put together the Richard Greenwood Quartet (keyboard, horns and his electric violin) to play "danceable" jazz six nights a week. Richard was with Cliff Young for five years.

He was an educator who taught in Denver, Jefferson County and Adams County, bringing to children the wonders of music through which they could learn, appreciate and enjoy its effects. He used music video that helped some "at risk" students in Jefferson County. He also taught guitar using his own special method. (He had taught classical guitar at Oxford University in England.) Richard developed a caring, understanding relationship with his autistic stepson, Jay.

Richard playing at one of his concerts

Richard used the stage name "Professor G" in his entertainment performances. He played for dances, private parties, weddings, conventions, luncheons, meetings, banquets and cocktail parties. With his beautiful voice, he sang and played the guitar. He tailored his music to fit the occasion using violin or guitar and the most effective type of music for the event. He played classical music, jazz dinner music, or rock and roll, and he would sing in his rich mellow voice.

Richard set up his own recording studio in his home in the mountains. He composed and recorded love songs, rock songs and several albums, but he never produced them commercially. He would perform the music in his programs and concerts to express the feeling and deliver the message. When needed, he played soulful religious music.

Skiing was Richard's second love. He was constantly on the slopes in winter where he found joy, relaxation and complete freedom! He was well known in several ski areas. He would often teach classes in Breckenridge, Eldora or Winter Park to compensate for his skiing.

In the winter of 1994 while skiing constantly at Breckenridge, he

366

felt his life-long love of those mountains and the important role they had played in his personal development as a spiritual being. Having been brought up in the church, his roots were firmly grounded, and in St. Laurence's Episcopal Church in Conifer he found a profound satisfying belief in God. These experiences set the beginning of Richard's writing a beautiful liturgical mass to be performed as a feature of BMI's "Music from Around the World" program at the 1995 Breckenridge Music Festival.

For his *Rocky Mountain Mass*, Richard composed the complete instrumental orchestration. He wrote music and lyrics to a five section choral mass for first and second soprano, alto, tenor and bass singers. He put together a wonderful mix of talented singers in his *Rocky Mountain Chorus*, from St. Laurence Episcopal Church Choir, Shorter A.M.E. Church choir (Margaret, Vernease and I sang soprano), Evergreen Chorale, Summit County Choral Society, *Ars Nova* Singers in Boulder, Arvada Center Chorale and others. It was interracial. In his professional, perfectionist way, Richard scheduled sectional rehearsals meeting in various areas, late May through mid-June in 1995. The last three rehearsals, in June and early July, were full chorus at Shorter A.M.E. church, since we had the only place with large enough space to accommodate the entire choir. With Richard's expressive direction and persistence of lyrical perfection, we became immersed in the beauty and sanctity of this music!

The concert was scheduled for Sunday, July 16, 1995, at 3:00pm at the *Riverwalk Center* in Breckenridge. Richard gave us a packet with all the information we needed: how to get to Breckenridge, what to wear, discount lodging for singers the weekend of July 15 and 16, schedule of full chorus and orchestra rehearsals that Saturday afternoon and Sunday morning at the *Riverwalk Center*.

I wanted to be relaxed for those rehearsals, so Jim drove Margaret and me to Breckenridge on the afternoon of Friday, July 14th. We had a restful night and Saturday morning we leisurely explored the town and found where the *Riverwalk Center* was for our rehearsals and performances. It was a beautiful outdoor theater.

Sunday afternoon the weather was perfect. The theater was full with standing room only. Many family members and friends were there from Denver.

It was amazing to see Richard's performance as he conducted his *Rocky Mountain Mass* with the Breckenridge Music Institute Orchestra and the Rocky Mountain Chorus simultaneously! The five sections of this inspirational composition are: *Kyrie*, (Lord, have mercy); *Sanctus* (Holy, holy, holy Lord); *Agnus Dei* (Lamb of God); *Lord's Prayer*, (Our Father in Heaven) set to Richard's beautiful arrangement; and *Gloria in Excelsis*, (Glory to God). It was such an inspirational performance. We sang our hearts out! My teenage grandson, Ricky, was the youngest member of the Chorus. My final surprise and joy was Richard's announcement that the last two parts of his *Rocky Mountain Mass* were dedicated to his father, William Rivers Greenwood!!!

As the concert ended, the entire audience stood and applauded for so long that Richard had to return for three bows! A videotape was made of the melodious, inspirational presentation. However, I am the only member of the chorus missing!! I was standing in the front row next to my friend Vernease singing with all my being. I was the shortest member of the group (as usual), so from the angle at which the video was made, I am in total eclipse behind a violinist!!! It was a weird feeling to watch the chorus singing, knowing that I was there, but I was completely invisible! Strange things do happen.

Early in 1999, Richard called me to tell me some shocking news. For many months he had been having pain which his doctor in Conifer had been treating him for an infection. Finally, the pain became so intense that the doctor told him he could do no more, and referred him to a specialist. Tests and x-ray proved that he had prostate cancer in an advanced stage from all the months of mistreatment. Had it been caught in the early stage, it could have been cured. Now, he had to go through radiation or chemotherapy. He told me where he would be for his first exposure, and I was there.

Since Richard needed regular treatments, driving the long distance from the mountains became difficult. Richard and his wife, Judy, decided to sell their house and move to Denver. Judy's parents owned a vacant house next door to them in Northwest Denver at 26th and Irving St.

After weeks of therapy, the cancer was getting no better, so the doctor said the final option was an operation. He gave Richard six months to a year to live!

The operation was scheduled for April, 1999 (just before his 51st birthday), at Porter Adventist Hospital on South Downing St., a long drive for me. I was there by mid-morning. Judy was already there, so we kept each other company and consoled each other. It was past mid-afternoon when the doctor finally appeared to tell us that the operation was successful. We could see Richard for a few minutes in Recovery. He was coming out of sedation, so we let him know we were there and we loved him; then we left. His sister and brothers were anxious to know how he was, so I called them immediately.

I sent up my prayers constantly for my son, and had church members, friends and everyone I knew praying for him. Richard regained his strength and resumed his activities on a limited basis. He even continued his beloved skiing!

After a year, the doctor told him that he was amazed that he was still alive. Whatever was keeping him going was beyond his power. We believed it was our concentrated prayers!

Eventually, Richard began to have pain again. Apparently, a tiny cancer spore had been left undetected from the (first) operation and began to develop in his abdomen. This time the (second) operation proved that the cancer could not be removed since it was too enmeshed in his intestines. This was at St. Anthony Hospital, so I could get to see him easily

He was placed on regular chemotherapy and constant pain killers. Judy was training to be a nurse, but she stayed home and took care of Richard until he was strong enough to be up and around. Then she resumed her nursing classes.

Richard was alone on the days that Judy was in class. Even with his limited activity, he seemed to keep busy. One day when I called, he said he drove to a movie occasionally. I love movies, so I told him I would like to go with him sometime. This worked out fine. I would drive over to his house, leave my car and away we would go!

One day when we were on our way, Richard said, "Mom, I've

wanted to tell you for some time; I am dying."

My quiet answer was, "Yes, I know."

He continued, "I want you to know what plans I have made. I am donating my body to medical science, and I have a close friend who will take care of all the arrangements for my memorial service at church."

When he and Judy moved back to Denver, Richard did not want to attend a big edifice like St. John's Episcopal Church. They found Saint Andrew's Episcopal Church at 20th and Glenarm Place, a small chapel where Richard became their choir director.

He was getting weaker, so the last time that we went to a movie, I drove. His feet had swollen. He apologized for wearing a pair of old slippers. I was happy to see that he could still walk! During the movie he showed the first outward signs of intense pain, an occasional flinch and an almost inaudible quick moan. This time he forgot to validate our parking ticket, so I left him in the car, went back in the theater and took care of it myself. <u>By the Grace of God</u>, I had these wonderful final times with him!

Not long after this outing, Judy called to tell me to come over; Richard was not doing well. I called Jim and he took me to their house. Richard was bedridden. As I sat and talked with him, he occasionally made some strange remarks, and then he would smile and say, "I was hallucinating." Jim and I visited with him separately, each for a short time only, since he was so weak.

Richard had a philosophical attitude toward life. He never complained about his cancer and pain. He even skied until he became bedridden!

Shortly after this visit, Judy called to let me know that Richard had been admitted to St. John's Hospice in far west Lakewood. Jim was out of town, so I called Judge Wiley Daniel (an extended family member). He said he had wanted to see Richard for some time, so he took me to the hospice. Richard was coherent, but so weak he could hardly move his head. We spent about twenty minutes with him. This was on Monday, January 13, 2003.

I was awakened by my phone ringing at 3:15 a.m. on Wednesday, January 15th, Martin Luther King's birthday! It was a call from St. John's Hospice informing me that my son had died at 3:00 a.m. Jim was out of town. I called Jo to let her know. She asked if I needed her to take me to the hospice. I thanked her and told her I would drive over since I had no idea how long I would be there. It is a long drive from far east Denver to far west Lakewood, but I drove so fast that I was walking into St. John's at 3:50a.m.! When I was asked how on earth I got there so quickly, I just said, "I was flying low."

Judy and her parents were there. Richard looked so peaceful. Judy told me she was with Richard until nearly midnight, before he insisted that she go home. She said he had been very quiet, but about 10:30 his face lit up and he suddenly exclaimed, "Oh, it is so beautiful!" He must have seen Heaven!

Personnel at St. John's Hospice took care of seeing that his body was turned over to proper authorities for medical science. A few weeks later, Judy received a letter informing her that Richard's corneas had given sight to two men.

Richard's memorial service was scheduled for 11:00 a.m. at St. Andrew's Episcopal Church on Monday, January 20, 2003, Martin Luther King's Holiday! The choir sang much of Richard's hymnal music. The little chapel was crowded to standing room. Outside a group of young musicians, who had known Richard, were standing by the door listening to his service. A small reception followed at the church.

I am proud of all my children and their individual achievements, but we all knew that Richard was a very unusual individual in our family! He was not perfect, but he expected perfection in all that he did.

This thoughtful, philosophical list that Richard gave me many years ago says it all:

"Food for Thought" **

The greatest sin...*Fear*

The best day..*Today*

The biggest Fool ....*The boy who will not go to school*

The best town..*Where you succeed*

The most agreeable companion.........*One who would not have you any different from what you are*

The great bore...........................*One who will not come to the point*

A still greater bore....................*One who keeps on talking after he has made his point*

The greatest deceiver..........................*One who deceives himself*

The greatest invention of the devil ....*War*

The greatest secret of production...........................*Saving waste*

The best work...*What you like*

The best play..*Work*

The cheapest, stupidest and easiest thing to do............*Finding fault*

The greatest comfort....................*The knowledge that you have done your work well*

The greatest mistake...*Giving up*

The most expensive indulgence.....................................*Hate*

The greatest trouble maker...................*One who talks too much*

The greatest stumbling block...............................*Egotism*

The most ridiculous asset...*Pride*

The bankrupt.....................The soul that has lost its enthusiasm

The most dangerous person.................................The liar

The most disagreeable person........................The complainer

The meanest feeling of which any human being is capable....Feeling bad at another's success

The cleverest man...............One who always does what he thinks is right

The greatest need..Common sense

The greatest puzzle...Life

The greatest mystery...Death

The greatest thought...God

The greatest thing, bar none, in all the world.................Love

**SOURCE UNKNOWN

CHAPTER 20

Blessings, Activities, Honors and Awards

I am blessed to have my children and grandchildren who keep in close touch with me.

Louise is a college professor and a choreographer in California, who calls regularly to check on me and would come immediately if I needed her.

Bill still lives in the family home and is surviving with his business, Greenwood and Associates. He calls me every day to make sure I am all right.

Jim is a busy recruiter for the *University of Northern Colorado* and other activities. He has been my salvation in emergencies and getting me to various functions. Jo was my help when Jim was not around.

My grandson, Billy, calls me every Sunday from North Carolina to see how I am and tell me he loves me.

I hear from my granddaughters, Chrissy and Lori, as often as possible, to tell me I am their role model and they love me. Chrissy sends me precious cards with loving messages that I cherish.

Dr. Joyce Washington was my Soror, friend and a professor at University of Northern Colorado. At a Coterie meeting in 1997, she surprised me by asking me to permit her to submit my name for the *UNC Honorary Alumni Award*. I was so startled, as I thought of all the graduates who had done so much more than I, that I told her I would have to think about it and let her know. It took me a while to realize that "win, lose or draw," it would be an honor just to have my name submitted! I told Joyce of my conclusion, gave her the needed information and gave her

Joyce Washington, Louise and Honoree Marie, at the 1997 UNC Homecoming, UNC Honorary Alumni Trailblazer Award ceremony

permission to send in my name.

To my amazement, I received word from the UNC Alumni Association that I had been selected as one of the honorees of 1997 to receive the *Trail Blazer Award*!!! I was being recognized for my pioneering and trail blazing in the Denver Public Schools.

It was an exciting three-day UNC homecoming celebration in October, a month before my 85th birthday. Louise was with me and the University provided our hotel accommodation. Joyce guided us through all the activities. There was the dedication of the big, beautiful new library. Members of my family and extended families were at the banquet when I received my *Trail Blazer Award.* The following morning we were transported to the football game on a big fire truck. Since I was the oldest, I had the privilege of sitting up front with the driver, who let me ring the bell as we drove to the stadium. After the game, Joyce took Louise and me to the *Marcus Garvey Center for Black Culture Education,* where we had a soul food lunch with the students, and I was honored with an award for outstanding achievement in the field of education. We thanked Joyce for being our wonderful hostess.

Louise had a wonderful time at all the activities. Several graduates from her class of 1967 were there, and they had fun catching up on their varied experiences over the years. We returned to Denver tired, excited and happy!

The greatest surprise of my life happened when John Smith called me in 2001 to tell me that he wanted to submit my name for a new school that was being built. He had been instrumental in getting the first African-American recognition in the Denver Public Schools by the naming of

Jessie Whaley Maxwell Elementary School. Then there was the *Rachel B. Noel Middle School* for the first African-American D.P.S. school board member. I attended that dedication. Now, for me, a first grade teacher, it was hard to believe that naming a school could happen to me! He had researched and found that I was the African-American pioneer and trailblazer in the Denver Public Schools. Again, I did not feel qualified, but I accepted the <u>honor</u> of having my name added to the list of ten names.

John Smith was a persistent go-getter and kept the pressure on, until there were only two names left for the DPS School Board to vote on – Marie L. Greenwood and Lena Archuleta, the first woman Latina principal. Imagine my amazement when it was announced that the new school being built at East 51st Avenue and Durham Court would be named *Marie L. Greenwood Elementary School*!!!

One day, John called to ask me if I would like to see my school. Of course, I was thrilled! As we drove out to Montbello, I could visualize a small school about the size of Newlon. I asked John, "How will I know this school?"

He laughed and said, "Oh, you will know it all right."

Soon, we came to a corner where there was a large building, to which John pointed. It was almost half a block long!

"That's my school?" I gasped. "It's so big!"

"Yes, that is your school," John answered. "The outside is almost finished, so they are starting to work on the inside."

As we drove around the building, I was awed at the prospect of this big, beautiful school having the name of Marie L. Greenwood!!!

My school opened in August 2001. The dedication was scheduled for October 11, 2001.

Jo's parents, Winifred and Lolita Seymour, Margaret and I were driven to the *Marie L. Greenwood Elementary School* in a limousine. This limo broke down on Peoria Street. We had to wait for another. When we finally arrived at the school there was a crowd awaiting us. Just as I stepped out of the limo, I heard loud and clear above all the other voices,

"That's my grandma!" I was thrilled to hear this exciting greeting from my grandson, Billy!

People greeted me with applause. The Prince Hall Masons performed their Cornerstone Laying ceremony. I cut the ribbon to the opening of my school, and we all entered the building for the program in the auditorium. My children, grandchildren, many friends and several of my former students were there.

Marie L. Greenwood
School opening
ceremony, 2001

Principal of Greenwood School, Shurwood Stan Reynolds, was Master of Ceremonies. Rev. J. Langston Boyd, Pastor of Shorter A.M.E. Church, gave the invocation. Elaine Berman, President of DPS Board of Education, gave the "Presentation of the Building." DPS Superintendent Dr. Jerome Wartgow's representative responded. To my surprise, there was also a response from Donald Wilson, a retired school principal, who was one of my first grade students! John Smith introduced me, and I gave my sincere thanks of awesome appreciation to all who had made this miracle happen. Cleo Parker Robinson danced and had me dance a bit with her. Betty Edwards, Alpha Kappa Alpha president of my chapter, presented a portrait of me from my sorority that now hangs in the entrance to my school. James Greenwood expressed gratitude from the family. Fourth and fifth grade students provided musical selections during the program.

There was a reception following the program and a tour of the building.

I was surprised, when after meeting me at the dedication of my school, DPS Board President Elaine Berman invited me to be her guest at the 2002 *DPS Annual Spring Gala Banquet* held at the Marriott City Center Hotel. Channel 4 News broadcaster, Anna Alejo, who lives near me, and is a friend of the Bermans, was assigned to pick me up. It was an awesome experience! In the past ten years this has become an annual honor for me to attend the *Denver Public School Spring Banquet* as their guest. I sit at Stephen and Elaine Berman's reserved table. Anna Alejo and her husband, Shepard Nevel, have become my good friends as they escort me to this affair each year. <u>By the Grace of God</u>, this is another blessing that I enjoy!

Marie L. Greenwood Academy, 2013

In September 2005, my husband was recognized (posthumously) at the United States Air Force Academy as the first African-American and the first civilian to hold the title of *Air Force Budget Officer*.

Maurice Ecung, AFA graduate of 1968, knew Bill and what he had done for the Air Force Academy. As a member of *Way of Life Alumni Group,* the African-American affiliate of the *USAF Academy Association of Graduates,* Maurice submitted the name of William R. Greenwood, Sr. for the *Pathfinder Award*. I was thrilled that after all these years, Bill was finally being recognized. I sent documents and pictures of his achievements as Air Force Budget Director. (Details that I wrote in Chapter 12). Recognition was set for Saturday, Sept. 17, 2005, at the Air Force Academy.

My grandson, Ray Weathersby, AFA graduate in 1998, arranged for our housing on the Academy base. We shopped for food and any other needs before leaving Denver. We drove to the Air Force Academy late afternoon on Thursday, September 15. We were assigned two comfortable, two-bedroom apartments. Billy, his wife Tracee, and Louise had the larger one. Our food for meals was left there. Chrissy, Lori and I shared the other one. (We ate and relaxed in our apartments in between activities).

On Friday morning a meeting was scheduled with officers and special cadets. I was amazed when we arrived at the area outside the Academy Chapel to find hundreds of people observing the activities. (A big football game was scheduled for Saturday, and this was the huge weekend crowd of visitors). I met the AFA Commander and other officials. Special Black cadets were to be our guides on a tour of the Air Force Academy.

We were taken on a fascinating walking tour of the Academy buildings and grounds that ended late afternoon.

Saturday morning we were on the patio outside Doolittle Hall at 8:00am, where the *USAF Academy Association of Graduates Way of Life Alumni Group* (WOL) Pathfinder program was held honoring the contributions of Mr. William R. Greenwood, Sr. WOL Board of Director, Mr. Maurice Ecung, was program chairman. Grandson, Ray Weathersby gave a spiritual opening. USAFA Vice Superintendent, Major General Irving L. Halter, class of 1977, and others spoke. Bill's outstanding biography was read, and then his "Official Pathfinder Portrait" was unveiled.

We were standing by a patio of bricks on which some had names of outstanding Air Force Academy families. One row was covered. To my complete, unbelieving amazement, there was a ceremony for the unveiling of the "Pathfinder Paver Brick": The cover was removed and revealed these names: Wm. R. Greenwood, AFA Budget Dir. Pathfinder 54-58; Ray R. Weathersby, USAFA 1998 Football WR #84; L.Y. Greenwood, Epitome of Mother Love; M.L. Greenwood, Pioneering Teacher/Mother.

"Pathfinder Award" recognition ceremony

I can only believe this permanent family endowment is there, because I saw it!!!

ell 1999 mory of Mizell II	Capt Bert Weinstein MD Class of 1953	Robert Dierker Lt Gen (Ret) Class of 1972	Curt USAFA '99 & Lynn Hayes August 5, 2000	Kathy & K Boone Cl. Aug. 24,
Wm R Greenwood AFA Budget Dir Pathfinder 54-58	Ray R Weathersby USAFA 1998 Football WR #84	L.Y. Greenwood Epitome of Motherly Love	M.L. Greenwood Pioneering Teacher/Mother	

The "Pathfinder Paver Brick"

There was a reception in the Atrium of Doolittle Hall. This program had been scheduled early to clear for the football game, so we were through by 10:00 a.m.

By this time, at 92 years old, I was happy, but exhausted, so I was taken back to the apartment to rest, and everyone else went to the football game. An announcement was made at the game in recognition of Bill!

The picture of William R. Greenwood, AFA first Budget Director, now hangs in Arnold hall with others in the *United States Air Force Academy Hall of Fame*!!!

Our celebration ended with a delightful dinner Saturday evening at the Officer's Club with family, friends and some official guests, hosted by my daughter Louise.

William R. Greenwood, first AFA Budget Director

Sunday we returned home elated with wonderful memories of a once-in-a-lifetime experience!

For years, when I would talk about my experiences and adventures, people would tell me I should write a book about my life. Finally, in

2007, when my son Bill kept insisting that I write about my interesting activities, I decided to document some of the various children whom I taught during my thirty years as a dedicated first grade teacher. The title of my book is *Every Child Can Learn*, in which I tried to show how every child can learn <u>something</u>, no matter what the native ability might be. Lay a sound foundation <u>early</u>. Teach a child to <u>read </u>and you can teach that child anything. These are just bits of my basic philosophy of education that work no matter how methods and systems of instruction change. To my surprise, my book is still being requested by educators and parents. My son Bill is my business manager and Valerie Thomas is my author's assistant.

After the president of UNC, Dr. Kay Norton, read my book, I was invited to be the University of Northern Colorado undergraduate commencement speaker, Saturday morning, December 15, 2007. Since Louise had missed marching with her class to receive her Master's Degree in 2000, (we were in Michigan with Chrissy), she was invited to march with the graduates at 7:00 p.m. on Friday night, December 14th.

Jim was taking us to Greeley on Friday. The weather was terrible – torrential rain, heavy slow traffic. It took us forever to get to Greeley. Louise had been told to be at the University at 5:30 p.m. It was after 6:00 p.m. when we finally arrived at the beautiful motel where the University had provided separate room reservations for us. I was exhausted. Louise was disappointed and completely upset at missing her opportunity to finally march with the December graduates. They got me settled in my room and disappeared.

Eventually, Jim returned and brought me something to eat. When I asked where Louise was, Jim grinned and said, "Oh, she's at the University. Everything turned out fine." He had told her to call her UNC contact to explain why she was late. She called and was told that they were waiting for her with a cap and gown. Her brother got his sister there safe and happy. <u>By the Grace of God</u>, my daughter was able to fulfill her dream!

A "serve yourself" breakfast was provided at the motel, so we had a "quickie" before heading for the campus. When we arrived at UNC Saturday morning, we were ushered into a room where officials were donning their caps and gowns. I was given a cap and a gown short enough for me! I met Dr. Kay Norton, a pleasant, friendly, "down to earth" president. I felt so special marching into that big auditorium with her and the other honored officials. We were seated on the dais, and I was faced with hundreds of new graduates, their parents and friends. Jim and Louise had reserved seats on the front row.

I spoke for approximately forty minutes, passing on a bit of my experiences and some of my basic philosophy of life. I told them the world would not be waiting with open arms to offer jobs, just because they had earned degrees. Those degrees are only tools to be used in working toward achieving life's goals. All the knowledge acquired during the years in college is just a drop in the ocean of what there is yet to learn out in the world. All through my speech, I continued to stress <u>Never Stop Learning</u>. When I announced that at 95 years old, I was still learning, there were audible "Ohs" and "Ahs"! I was glad to see that some of them appeared to actually be listening.

As I returned to my seat, my greatest compliment was from President Kay Norton when she whispered to me, "That was perfect!"

I was surprised and honored when she invited us over to her home for lunch. We had time to check out of the motel before arriving at the home of the UNC President. There was a small gathering of a few University officials with whom Jim, Louise and I had a most enjoyable informative, informal, relaxing visit.

On the way back to Denver, all we talked about was how special we had been treated, the delightful UNC people we met and the special welcome we had received from University of Northern Colorado President Dr. Kay Norton. <u>By the Grace of God</u>, this introduction to UNC personnel opened many future doors for us!

2009 was a very busy, active and interesting year. These are some of my memorable experiences.

On January 9th I was the key speaker at the Greeley – UNC Martin Luther King, Jr. Day Celebration. Jim and Jo drove me there. The Master of Ceremonies told me he was surprised that I was 94. When I told him that was two years ago, he was really amazed that I was 96. During my speech I had the audience sing with me "Let There Be Peace." After my presentation, I received many compliments. I was told that even the children were listening to me!

On March 31st, I was honored as key speaker for the *College of Education and Behavioral Sciences Honors Convocation* at UNC. I was tired, but Jim took me to Greeley for the banquet and the program.

I told of my college experiences in the 1930's (so different from today); my pioneering, trailblazing and thirty years of teaching in the Denver Public Schools that led to a school being named in my honor. This was an example of what can be achieved with hard work and dedication in the field of education. I was proud of those who were receiving these special honors.

I answered questions and was complimented on the revealing information given. Michael Muskin, the Associate Director of Development in the College of Education, said it was hard to believe that I arrived so tired, but how I came to life while speaking!

Jim and I were housed at the usual motel. The next morning we met Michael Muskin at the Marcus Garvey Center, where we visited with a group of interactive people. They bought copies of my book, *Every Child Can Learn,* (which we had brought with us).

Jim had been to UNC with me so often that he was becoming well known on campus. He is now the Denver area Admissions Counselor for the University of Northern Colorado.

One day, I received a call from Anna Alejo telling me that she had a friend whose son wanted to represent me at his school. Every year some of the students of this school research information about outstanding, interesting people and represent them in a program. In 2008, the boy had represented her. Anna said, if it was all right with me, she would have his mother call me. I was a bit bewildered, but I said, "O.K., have her call me."

I received a call from Margot Pinto, who explained about the program that helped children to learn about people who were famous and those who had achieved. She said they had heard so much about me that her son would like to be me in the presentation that year. I was flabbergasted! We set a time for an interview. Marc Pinto brought his eleven-year-old son, William, to meet me. As his dad and I talked, this handsome little brown boy took notes. They would let me know the date of the presentation at his school.

Anna Alejo called me again to tell me that the Pintos were having a welcoming party for the new DPS Superintendent Tom Boasberg. He was taking the place of Michael Bennett, who had just become a United States Senator. Anna and Shepard drove me out to their beautiful home in Englewood where I met our energetic, bubbly, delightful hostess, Margo Pinto. She is an active member of the *Denver Public Schools Foundation.*

When I met Superintendent Boasberg, I was surprised that he already knew about me and my school. After a round of introductions, we were served a catered buffet of delicious food. For the first time I had some sushi that I liked. As usual, I was the senior member of the group, but I thoroughly enjoyed the evening.

The date for William's school presentation was set for April 16th. Marc Pinto came for me and we had a delightful visit telling about our families as we drove to St. Anne Episcopal School. They have two older children, a daughter and son.

The children presenters were dressed to represent the person they were telling about. William was wearing a gray wig and a Marie L. Greenwood K-8 School shirt as he gave his informative speech. These children gave lively presentations of people about whom they had researched. I was

William Pinto as Mrs. Greenwood. Marc & Margot Pinto, William's parents on left

honored to be asked to give a few remarks. Before we left the school, I hugged William and complimented him on his excellent speech about me.

On April 22ⁿᵈ, the annual DPS Banquet sponsored by the *Denver Public Schools Foundation* had their greatest attendance, 1300! As usual, the students presented a fascinating program. Superintendent Boasberg was recognizing outstanding people and having them stand. I was so completely amazed when I heard him honoring *Marie Greenwood*, that Shepard had to tell me to stand up! Soon after I sat down, I heard a voice behind me saying, "I want to have a picture taken with you." To my utter surprise, it was Mayor John Hickenlooper with his broad grin!!! Shepard Nevel took the picture and sent me a framed copy, which I have on display among my honored souvenirs.

Michael Muskin ordered many of my books, *Every Child Can Learn* to distribute in the College of Education. He told me that a meeting was being planned at the UNC branch campus in Loveland, and he wanted me to speak to some of the educators.

I received a call from one of my first graders, who is a graduate of UNC and a teacher. She wanted me to know that she would be at the Loveland campus meeting on September 15ᵗʰ, and was anxious to see me. When Jim, Valerie and I arrived, she was the first person we saw. She brought her mother and dad. I also had their son in my first grade at Newlon Elementary School. We were West Denver neighbors, and our children were in school together. For Jim and me it was like "old home week" meeting these friends from long ago!

I gave a short speech and answered many questions. In answering a question from one lovely, white-haired teacher, she said I was her first grade teacher, and thanked me for giving her such a good start. What a compliment! I was pleasantly surprised to have two of my former students present, of whom I could be proud.

All of the books that the University had bought were sold out before the meeting. Valerie took charge of selling the books that we brought. After my speech, I autographed them and all of them were sold.

Early November, my grandson Billy called to tell me to keep my November 24th birthday date clear. They had some special plans and would be here to celebrate my 97th year. When I received a call from my school about honoring my birthday, I told them I had reserved the date for my family. Then I was assured that Greenwood School would set another date.

When my grandchildren picked me up on my birthday, Billy asked how to get to my school. Some of them had not seen my beautiful school, so I thought he wanted to show it to them before our celebration. I asked where Louise was. Billy said his mother had just flown in and called from the airport. He told her to meet us at my school, since it was closer to the airport. Louise was there when we arrived.

As we entered the building, two dressed-up eighth grade boys met us, greeted us and proceeded to escort me to the auditorium, which was decorated with balloons and flowers. Some children, teachers and the principal were waiting for us. This was my big surprise 97th birthday celebration!!! Billy had arranged with the Principal, Mrs. Devin Dillon, to have the party at school. With my inquisitive curiosity it is hard to really surprise me. The call from school had thrown me off, so I did not relate visiting my school with celebrating my birthday. This was the most complete surprise of my life, and I loved every minute of it!!!

Children from kindergarten through eighth grade participated in the program. The eighth grade art class presented me with a huge collage portrait of me which they had made. My grandchildren gave me a beautiful unique quilt with a picture of my book, *Every Child Can Learn* in the center, surrounded by memorable family pictures – even my school and the Mountain House. I have it on my bed where I can relive the memories every day.

We ended the program with punch and a "Happy 97th Birthday Mrs. Greenwood" cake with a picture of Clifford (the Big Red Dog) on it.

97th Birthday cake

My party ended with a student escorting me to his eighth grade class to greet the class and meet the teacher. Some of these children had been at Greenwood School since kindergarten. I had hugs from students and teacher. I told them how proud I was of the good work they were doing.

When we finally left my school, I was treated to lunch at my favorite restaurant, *The Red Lobster*. Thus ended a most exciting birthday of my life!!! Everyone stayed in Denver long enough to enjoy our annual big family, extended family and friends Thanksgiving celebration.

I received two very special 97th birthday greetings: one from President Barack Obama and First Lady Michelle Obama; and one from Congressional Representative Diana DeGette.

The following Sunday I received the warm recognition of my birthday with a beautiful box full of cards, balloons and a huge plant from the members of my church. I am so truly blessed!

January 15, 2010, I received the "Martin Luther King, Jr. Trailblazer Award" at the 25th anniversary celebration of the *Denver Business Community*. Senator Michael Bennett came over to greet me. He remembered me from the days when he was DPS Superintendent. I was honorably surprised when he escorted me to receive my award from Wilma Webb.

On Friday, February 12, 2010, US Representative Diana DeGette hosted a luncheon with leaders and interested citizens of Denver's African-American community to discuss topics of vital importance. I was invited as a Very Special Guest!

I am still awed at receiving a biographic achievement, "Tribute to Marie Louise Anderson Greenwood," written on emblem stationery and encased in an official U.S. House of Representative folder! I thanked Rep. Diana DeGette warmly and gave her an autographed copy of *Every Child Can Learn*, as a small token of sincere appreciation.

May 7, 2010 was a very full day. After attending Josh's graduation in Boulder, we had several automobile loads of family and extended family headed for Greeley, where I was to be honored in receiving a Doctorate Degree (from UNC). We stopped at a restaurant along the way and had lunch, then arrived at UNC in time for the reception at five o'clock.

President Kay Norton introduced me, and I gave my little speech of appreciation for being selected for this honor. Jenna and Josh had to get back to Boulder, so they left after the reception.

It was great having Louise and grandson Billy here for Josh's graduation and my celebration. Bill and Valerie came up to take pictures. Jim and Jo, Wiley and Ida, and Lolita were there – most of my family!

This time I was thrilled when I was fitted with a doctorate robe and cap. As I marched in with the honored doctorates, I was proud to see my family and two AKA Sorors seated in a section near the front to observe the 7:00 p.m. graduate ceremony.

My real excitement happened when UNC President Kay Norton presented me with the *Honorary Doctor of Humane Letters Degree* and placed upon me my doctorate hood!

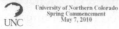

Receiving the Honorary
Doctor of Humane Letters
Degree from U.N.C.

Marie stands next to her life-
sized effigy.

I was a *Denver Urban Spectrum* honoree on June 19, 2010. To my amazement, on stage there was a life-sized effigy of me in my cap and gown holding my UNC Doctorate Degree which was presented to me by Ms. Rosalind J. Harris and her staff!

Weogia & H. Malcolm Newton with
Marie

After my introduction and receiving my *Urban Spectrum Award*, I was honored with the surprise of the evening. I was presented a framed diploma from Dr. H. Malcolm Newton granting me an *Honorary Degree of Doctor of Philosophy* from *Denver Institute of Urban Studies and Adult College* - a second doctorate!!! All by the Grace of God!

I was informed that the University of Northern Colorado was planning to establish a scholarship in my name. A meeting was arranged at my Greenwood School for the initial public announcement of the *UNC Marie L. Greenwood Teacher Education Scholarship* on November 4, 2010. It is for Denver Public School graduates who enroll in the UNC College of Education in preparation for becoming teachers. With my life-time dedication to teaching, I am honored to have this scholarship in my name to help others become teachers.

A proclamation was presented from Mayor John Hickenlooper (now Governor), officially proclaiming November 4, 2010 to be known as "Marie L. Greenwood Day." This was another surprise!

In 2011, our first $1,000 scholarship was presented to a young freshman who is majoring in Early Childhood Education. We had lunch with this delightful young woman, who is the first in her family to go to college. I was elated by her enthusiasm with the experience she was already having in working with young children.

I am proud of my school. I believe it is one of the most progressive in the Denver Public School system. We are blessed by having the best principals, faculty and staff.

The first principal, Stan Reynolds organized *Marie L. Greenwood Elementary School* into an orderly disciplined and respected institution. It was a joy to visit there with the faculty and children. When he left, there was a substitute principal for a year, and control began to weaken.

A new principal, Ruth Frasier, was assigned to Greenwood School. Order and respect were returned. Again, you would feel the relaxed, orderly atmosphere when entering the building, and see the happy expressions on the faces of the children. Mrs. Frasier introduced uniforms, monogrammed t-shirts for students to wear. Most teachers chose to wear them, also. I was given three in different colors.

In the fourth and fifth grade wings, there were several vacant rooms, so our principal visualized those rooms being converted to sixth, seventh and eighth grades, adding a middle school. After much deliberation, the DPS School Board accepted the plan and my school became *Marie L. Greenwood K-8 School*! Mrs. Frasier had a meeting with parents to explain about the expansion of our school. She passed out papers that they could sign, indicating whether they wanted their fifth grade child to remain at Greenwood for the new sixth grade the following year, or be transferred to a Middle School. Most parents chose to leave their children at Greenwood, so that was the beginning of our Middle School. It continued to progress to eighth grade over the next two years. Now, almost 100% of the children remain at our school until high school.

I was no longer actively participating in the *Denver Public Library Read Aloud Program* when my school opened in 2001, so I asked if I could read to the primary grades at Greenwood School. Principal Reynolds and the teachers were delighted.

I began reading at 10:00 a.m. to kindergarten through third grade once a month. My name was still in the computer at the library to check out books for six weeks, so I would stockpile enough for the various grades. As limited time, less energy and other activities developed, I had to eventually cut my reading to every two months – usually October, December, February and April or May. Those months I would read about holidays and special occasions. Clifford was always with me.

After Ruth Frasier came as principal, some of the fourth and fifth grades remembered me reading to them earlier, and asked if I could read to them, too. This was a real challenge for me to read to older children, but I said I would do it.

The primary children went to lunch when I finished reading to the third grades. I would go to the fourth grades to read. I was amazed when these older children asked for Clifford! At the upper grades lunch time, I would have lunch with the students, then return to read to the fifth grades. I would end my day about 2:00 p.m.

I was well into my 90's when I began to get tired carrying my books from room to room, during this extended time with the older children. When I told the principal how I was feeling, she suggested having me seated in one place and the teachers could bring the classes to me. A comfortable chair was placed for me in an area of the library where there was room for the children to sit on the floor. What a wonderful, relaxing environment for me to continue my reading!

When my school opened in 2001, I was delighted to see the pleasant, efficient secretary was one of myfirst grade students, Marilyn Norman. She remained at Greenwood School until she retired. On January 21, 2005 I had the pleasure of attending the third retirement party for one of my first graders, Marilyn Norman! A few years before I was honored to be present at the retirement celebrations of two of my other first grade students, Lorene Peters and Gloria Olivier. What a blessing and a joy!

We lost another efficient, dedicated principal when Ruth Frasier left. She was replaced by Mrs. Devin Dillon, who continued to carry on the good work that Mrs. Frasier had going at *Marie L. Greenwood K-8 School*.

During Mrs. Dillon's tenure as principal, Greenwood School received the *Colorado Title I Distinguished School Award* for Exceptional Student Performance having the greatest percentage of students above the proficient level for Adequate yearly Progress in reading, language arts and mathematics for two years, 2006-2008: 93% in reading and 93.43% in math!

In 2010, a few fourth and fifth grade students were organized into an *Each One Teach One* (EOTO) group. They were achieving students who worked with classmates who needed some academic help. These students, who are being helped, are growing in vocabulary, conversational and writing skills. They are also members of EOTO. I have attended their luncheons, and I can see in some of the older children, a developing interest in becoming teachers. I treasure an autographed picture of me with these EOTO students. What a great way to develop an interest in education, early!

At the last luncheon I attended, a seventh grade student who has been with EOTO since the beginning, handed me a colorful note with the word, "Grateful." Inside she wrote this message to me:

"Dear Mrs. Greenwood,

Thank you for coming to each of our recognition luncheon and supporting Each One Teach One. I love your story of your life and your love for kids. My favorite story of your life is the one that you taught 1ˢᵗ grade and they wanted you to move to a different grade but you said no. Thank you for teaching us to take good care of our self, so that we can live a long time.

Sincerely,

G.A.

What a great compliment! The group is growing and now includes primary grade students.

Mrs. Dillon was instrumental in having my school renamed *Marie L. Greenwood Academy*, so appropriate for the diversity of activity in Greenwood School. The middle school students are being inspired to "Think College."

In the spring of 2011, the eighth graders were taken on a visit to University of Northern Colorado. My son, Jim, who is a UNC admissions counselor led them through the campus, and said they were one of the most interesting, enthusiastic and well-behaved classes that UNC had hosted.

Mrs. Dillon resigned in 2012. She spent the last few months, before the end of the school year, orienting the new principal into the Greenwood School program and activities. At the EOTO luncheon on September 27ᵗʰ, I met the pleasant, personable, conscientious principal Rachel Payne. It appears that we have another dedicated administrator to carry on the_Greenwood Academy_ traditions.

Shorter A.M.E. church has been the center of my life for 85 years. As I have grown older, I have had to cut back on activities. However, there are some impressive highlights to remember in which I was able to participate in my senior years.

In 2002, I was active with all the planning committees when we celebrated our 134th Anniversary. We made it very special by sponsoring a significant activity once each month from March until July – fireworks in July and the release of doves on our final Sunday celebration!

I was privileged to be a speaker on Adam Dempsey's video documentary of Denver history and Shorter A.M.E. Church activitiesduring its 134 years, "Spirit at the Mountaintop."

I danced with *Spirit of Grace*liturgical dance group for several years. My last performance was when I was 97 years old. I can still feel the interpretive spirit of those performances.

When Rev. Dr. Timothy E. Tyler was assigned to Shorter in 2008, he was faced with many disastrous problems. Rev. Boyd, with the help of dedicated assistant ministers, had kept our church going for 26 years. Oh his death in 2004, our new leadership did not follow the

Dancing at church

pattern of success that Rev. Boyd had established. Our membership dwindled down to a faithful few; income did not cover bills; and we had a huge mortgage that threatened the existence of our church.

Under four years of the dedicated guidance of young Rev. Tyler, shorter Church is now financially sound; returning membership and attendance at services fill our sanctuary. There are constant activities for young and old, and our church contributes to community needs. The greatest achievement was paying off the huge mortgage in three years!!!

Since I am the oldest active member in Shorter, I had the privilege of helping to burn the mortgage at my church during Annual Conference in August 2011! I am blessed to have lived long enough to participate in the clearing of <u>two</u> Shorter A.M.E. Church mortgages – 1938 and 2011. What an honor, all <u>by the Grace of God</u>!!!

Another of Rev. Tyler's accomplishments was successfully convincing Denver City Council to rename our little park *J. Langston Boyd Park*, in honor of our former great leader.

In 2008, I attended Alpha Kappa Alpha Boulé in Washington, D.C., to attend the 100 years of celebration. I was honored as one of the Diamond Sorors (75 years). In 2012, I am now in my 80th year as an AKA.

I am the oldest member still attending Coterie and enjoying learning from the fascinating presentations. I joined this study club in 1937, resigned in 1949 to rear my family. On the death of my life-long friend, Mrs. Josephine Price, I had the joy of resuming membership in Coterie in her honor in 1969. Because of my longevity I am now an Emerita member.

2012 was another busy year! On January 13th I was one of several who were awarded the *Martin Luther King Peace Award* at Metro State College breakfast.

On January 17th, I was the honored speaker at Colorado College of Denver. I received the *Living Legend Award*, honoring the "Spirit of Martin Luther King, Jr."

I was the 99 year old moderator at the Prince Hall Centenarians Tea on March 31st. Since I wasn't sure of being a moderator, I just used my own cheerful way of introducing honorees and making comments. I was surprised to receive many complimentary comments!

The *Denver Urban Spectrum* newspaper honored 25 women as "Timeless Legends" in Denver on April 28th. To my amazement, I was selected as one of the honorees! The fabulous affair at the Renaissance Hotel was most impressive. I cherish the beautiful award designed and produced by the artist, Ed Dwight.

"Timeless Legends" and "Martin Luther King, Jr." Awards

I was asked to speak to the minority graduates at Metropolitan State College (now University) on May 8th, I did my best to prepare them for some of the experiences they will face in life after college, and passed on a few of my basic philosophies of success.

When the new *History Colorado Museum* opened in April, I was interviewed by Channel 9 in the permanent display area of Lincoln Hills and Camp Nizhoni. I am the oldest living member who was active from the 1920's on, in this African-American retreat in the mountains. The love of my life was the many summers I spent at the Phyllis Wheatley Branch Y.W.C.A. Camp Nizhoni.

By the Grace of God, I have received innumerable other memorable awards from churches, schools, community organizations, Masonic chapters and colleges. I am proud of this display which I have on the walls and counter in my apartment living room.

Wherever, I go I wear a gold chain on which I have placed Bill's wedding ring and the lovely gold cross which my parents gave me when I finished junior high school and would enter high school. This necklace is symbolic of the spirits of my loving husband and devoted parents that I know are always with me.

Now, <u>by the Grace of God</u>, I am anticipating the celebration of my 100th birthday on November 24, 2012!!!

Wall full of certificates and awards

CHAPTER 21

100 Years Old!!!

In late 2011, my children and grandchildren began talking about a big celebration for my 100th birthday on November 24, 2012.

I was informed that the *Black American West Museum* (BAWM) had made reservations for their "Annual Fund Raising Gala" at the *Museum of Nature and Science* to be held on Saturday after Thanksgiving, my birth date. Both events would involve many of the same people as guests. This presented a problem.

I spent several days thinking of a possible solution.

Earlier, Louise had called and made reservations for dinner at *The Cork House Broker Restaurant* for Friday, November 23rd. This was to be a family get-together, so our young grandchildren and great-grandchildren could be a part of my 100th birthday celebration. We had not yet made a definite decision about a meeting place for Saturday, November 24th, a big community celebration.

Our family is a part of the BAWM and Jim is a member of one of the committees. Why not combine the two by honoring me at their Gala? I called Jim to get his opinion. He thought it was a great idea. He presented it to a board member. As a result, the BAWM Board was delighted to have me as an honoree, and invited me to attend a board meeting so they could meet me. It was decided that the funds raised could be split between the Museum and my UNC Scholarship. Jim attended the BAWM Board planning meetings, and Louise kept in touch from California by conference calls.

It is amazing how much my daughter can accomplish from miles away in California. She checked military accommodations in our area, and was told that a new rental facility was being built at Buckley Air Base. When she called to check, she learned that reservations would be taken in January 2012. On January 2nd, Louise made reservations in

Rocky Mountain Lodge at Buckley Air Force.

When Louise was here for Aunt Esther Nelson's funeral in February, she stayed at the new rental accommodations at Buckley – lovely one and two bedroom apartments. She made reservations for relatives and friends from out of town who would be coming to celebrate my birthday. They would all be together in this beautiful setting.

On Sunday, November 4, 2012, President Barack Obama was scheduled to speak in Denver before election. I had been asked to do the Pledge of Allegiance. Because of an emergency, his schedule was changed from morning to night. I had originally said, "No" for the morning, but Rev. Tyler called to tell me that I was still expected to be on the evening program. He was to give the Invocation, and a church member and his family would drive us to the program. They picked me up about 7:00 p.m. for a 9:00 pm scheduled program at Aurora Community College.

We were amazed at the many cars and the hundreds of people arriving. Fortunately, our driver had a reserved parking space within a reasonable walking distance to the program.

At the entrance, everyone was carefully checked, then Rev. Tyler and I were escorted to a small V.I.P. section near the platform, since we were a part of the program. We were seated on the front row, where we had a broad view of everything.

Nine o'clock came and it was announced that President Obama was on his way from Ohio. Rev. Tyler gave his invocation. I spoke the Pledge of Allegiance in my own precise way, and was amazed at the many compliments I received.

I had not been told it would be an outdoor program, so I had dressed for indoors. It was a chilly evening, so Rev. Tyler would ask me, occasionally, if I was all right. I was comfortable in the still air, until a light breeze began to blow. When he asked me again, I admitted I was beginning to feel the cold. To my surprise, Rev. Tyler took off his overcoat and wrapped it around me. That warmth felt good! I appreciated his thoughtfulness, but I was concerned about his getting cold. He assured me that he was fine.

There were speakers and musicians filling the time as we waited for the President. Finally it was announced that President Barack Obama's plane had landed and he was on his way. At eleven o'clock, he finally appeared to a standing ovation from a crowd of over 13,000 people! With him were several Secret Service protectors. Only a few professional cameramen were permitted within the clear area near the platform.

After his inspirational speech, President Obama left the platform and began greeting and shaking hands of people waiting behind the low fenced barricade. Of course, the Secret Service was spread out, observing the crowd as he moved along, one of which was a woman who preceded him making sure that all was well, and that no pictures were permitted to be taken.

Our V.I.P. section was the last to be reached. When President Obama spoke to us and shook our hands, Rev. Tyler told him that I was about to turn 100years old. He looked at me with an amazed expression on his face and said, "I don't believe it; I need to see your birth certificate!"

Marie getting a hug from President Obama

"I have my driver's license," I replied.

"I have to hug you," he said, as he wrapped his arms around me in Rev. Tyler's overcoat.

President Obama beckoned to a nearby photographer and exclaimed, "I want a picture taken with her!"

The picture was taken. I thanked him as he moved on. That was the special thrill of my 100 years of life!!!

On the Sunday before my birthday, I was honored at my church. I received a beautiful box of birthday cards and many balloons. Rev. Tyler

401

and I told about our once-in-a-lifetime experience with President Obama hugging me and his overcoat.

100th birthday greetings

A framed "Happy Birthday 100 Years" greeting, signed by Shorter Community Church Officers and Reverend Tyler, now hangs on my wall with other honors and awards.

My daughter arrived on Tuesday before Thanksgiving. She wanted to have time to make sure that everything was taken care of properly to make my birthday celebration the very best.

Thanksgiving Day was a joyful get-together at Ida and Wiley Daniel's home with the usual family members and out of town guests, grandchildren, little great grands, cousins and friends who were here for my birthday.

The Friday dinner at *The Cork House Broker Restaurant* was scheduled for six o'clock. I was ready at five o'clock. Jim was to pick me up soon thereafter. I heard a knock on the door and when I opened it, to my surprise there stood Michael Muskin and his wife.

"We've come to get you," said Michael with a big grin.

"Does Jim know?" I asked. "He was supposed to pick me up."

"Oh, we saw Jim at the restaurant and told him that we would like to come and get you," was Michael's reply.

At the restaurant, Michael let his wife and me off, while he went to park the car. Winnie Johnson and her little granddaughter were arriving at the same time. I was so glad that the children could attend this dinner. There was a special children's menu.

My birthday party was very special with family and a few close friends. Jenna and Josh had set up the sound system for the program.

The food was delicious. My little five-year-old great grandson, Michael,, sang "Happy Birthday" to me.

Our dessert was the beautiful birthday cake which my six-year-old great granddaughter, Lauren, had chosen.

Birthday cake

I cherish two of my greatest surprises! Daryl Walker was here to spend thanksgiving with his father, Jerome Walker (who was one of my first graders). Daryl is a fabulous spiritual musician whom I have known since he was ten years old. He is now the "Minister of Worship and Arts" at *Trinity United Church of Christ* in Chicago. I was honored to have him at my party, as he played the piano and sang special songs for me.

My other tremendous surprise was "A Musical Video Tribute to Marie Louise Anderson Greenwood – 100th Birthday Celebration" by Maurice Ecung. We have known Maurice for over forty years, ever since he was a cadet at the Air Force Academy. This talented family friend composed and recorded a most beautiful and appropriate song as background music for their memorable pictures, "After All this Time." The pictures in the video and the words in the song brought back many wonderful memories. Thanks also go to Will Lloyd for editing the DVD.

Daryl sings to Marie

A representative from the office of Denver Mayor Michael B. Hancock presented me with a Proclamation proclaiming November 24, 2012, to be known as "Marie L. Greenwood Day – in Honor of Her 100th Birthday" !

Maurice Ecung

403

The Events Coordinator at *The Broker Restaurant* did everything possible to make our party the very best. It was a most enjoyable, relaxing evening with loving family, friends and children.

100th birthday celebration at the Museum of Nature and Science

On Saturday, November 24th, Jim came for me before six o'clock to take me to my big 100th celebration at the BAWM Fourth Annual Pride and Progress Gala. As we drove up to *Denver Museum of Nature and Science* and parked, I was greeted by Wilma Webb, who was just arriving. My first happy surprise was seeing one of my brilliant former first grade students, Bob Tweedell, (an attorney from Delta, Colorado, on the Western Slope), and his mother Dorothy. We have kept in contact over the years.

My family and extended family were already there. The evening progressed with community friends and members from my church stopping to congratulate me and wish me well. Maurice Ecung's "Musical Tribute" was shown, and my "Mayor's Proclamation" was read. There were other community leaders honored, but my 100th birthday celebration was the highlight of the evening. There were approximately 250 people at this Gala!

The family at the 100th birthday celebration

404

On December 7th, my school planned to have my usual birthday party. When Valerie and I arrived at *Marie L. Greenwood Academy*, I learned that a special celebration was in order. I was immediately presented with beautiful hand-woven crown, bracelet and shell necklace from the parents of children who attend my school.

I was truly surprised when I was told there would be a parade around the school! The principal and I rode in a horse drawn carriage. There was also a decorated float with a fifth grade student dressed to represent me. I could hear my school band playing ahead of the parade. The entire student body was standing on the sidewalks around the school. I waved to them as we passed by.

The horse-drawn carriage

Children encircled the school for the parade

When the parade was over, we had light refreshments in the library, prepared by the mothers. Students from various grades spoke of Greenwood School achievements and how I had influenced and inspired them. I felt so honored! I thanked them for the gifts and the wonderful surprise they had planned for me. Later, in my bag of gifts, I found a beautiful crystal apple engraved "Happy 100th Birthday Dr. Greenwood." I have it where I can see it all the time.

I know eight members of *Shorter Community A.M.E. Church* who were in my first grade class at Whittier School. As I watch these active members of my church, I feel so proud of the fact that I had a hand in helping them to get started to achieve; and they still recognize me as their first grade teacher! On Sunday, December 27, 2012, I had the thrill of having my picture taken with five of them for the church record – Marlene Brown, Gloria Olivier, Jolianne Jones, Jan Holloway and Vince Hardiman. I missed Idella Hardiman, Mary Louise Harris and Jerome Walker who were ill and could not attend church. I have many other former students scattered throughout the city and state.

L-R, Jolianne Jones, Vince Hardiman, Jan Holloway, Gloria Olivier, Marlene Brown - Whittier "first graders" with Marie

Mary Louise Harris (Whittier "first grader") with Marie

Idella Hardiman, Whittier "first grader"

Jerome Walker, Whittier "first grader"

Now that I have passed the century mark in my life, I look back and give thanks to the Good Lord for being with me in life saving situations; through trials and tribulations; providing me with devoted parents who helped me develop a sound, solid, Christian basis of life; guiding me through a successful career in education; and forty years of a wonderful marriage with a loving husband and family.

All the experiences I have written about in this autobiography have been possible only <u>By the Grace of God</u>!!!

BY THE GRACE OF GOD

SUMMARY

A Few of My Basic Philosophies of Life

Nothing is so bad that it couldn't be worse. Be thankful for what you have and make the <u>most</u> of it. Be an <u>optimist.</u>

Listen to advice and opinions of others, but make your <u>own</u> decisions.

<u>Learn</u> from your mistakes and bad decisions. They can be some of your best lessons; then "Heaven help you" if you make the same mistakes again!

Set <u>goals</u> to achieve. You may have to take detours along the way, but never give up on achieving your goals.

No matter how menial a task may be, make it the <u>very best</u>.

Have a <u>sense of humor</u>. It can lighten many a load.

<u>Remember</u> those who helped you along the way. Reach back and give a helping hand.

Do the very best at what you enjoy doing and what you are most capable of doing. You are a <u>success</u> if you do what makes you happy.

Accept the <u>differences</u> in each of us, as in this quotation:

"There's so much <u>Good</u> in

The <u>Worst</u> of us,

And so much <u>Bad</u> in

The <u>Best</u> of us,

It hardly behooves

<u>Any</u> of us

To talk about

The <u>Rest</u> of us!" * [1]

Be willing to go the "<u>second mile</u>," whenever and wherever needed.

Be <u>adaptable</u> to changes in this world…Most of all, **<u>Never Stop Learning</u>** !!!

---

[1] attributed it to Edward Wallis Hoch (1849-1925)